Cousin Marriages

Fertility, Reproduction and Sexuality

GENERAL EDITORS:
Soraya Tremayne, Founding Director, Fertility and Reproduction Studies Group and Research Associate, Institute of Social and Cultural Anthropology, University of Oxford.
Marcia C. Inhorn, William K. Lanman, Jr. Professor of Anthropology and International Affairs, Yale University.
Philip Kreager, Director, Fertility and Reproduction Studies Group, and Research Associate, Institute of Social and Cultural Anthropology and Institute of Human Sciences, University of Oxford.

Volume 1
Managing Reproductive Life: Cross-Cultural Themes in Fertility and Sexuality
Edited by Soraya Tremayne

Volume 2
Modern Babylon? Prostituting Children in Thailand
Heather Montgomery

Volume 3
Reproductive Agency, Medicine and the State: Cultural Transformations in Childbearing
Edited by Maya Unnithan-Kumar

Volume 4
A New Look at Thai AIDS: Perspectives from the Margin
Graham Fordham

Volume 5
Breast Feeding and Sexuality: Behaviour, Beliefs and Taboos among the Gogo Mothers in Tanzania
Mara Mabilia

Volume 6
Ageing without Children: European and Asian Perspectives on Elderly Access to Support Networks
Edited by Philip Kreager and Elisabeth Schröder-Butterfill

Volume 7
Nameless Relations: Anonymity, Melanesia and Reproductive Gift Exchange between British Ova Donors and Recipients
Monica Konrad

Volume 8
Population, Reproduction and Fertility in Melanesia
Edited by Stanley J. Ulijaszek

Volume 9
Conceiving Kinship: Assisted Conception, Procreation and Family in Southern Europe
Monica M. E. Bonaccorso

Volume 10
Where There is No Midwife: Birth and Loss in Rural India
Sarah Pinto

Volume 11
Reproductive Disruptions: Gender, Technology, and Biopolitics in the New Millennium
Edited by Marcia C. Inhorn

Volume 12
Reconceiving the Second Sex: Men, Masculinity, and Reproduction
Edited by Marcia C. Inhorn, Tine Tjørnhøj-Thomsen, Helene Goldberg, and Maruska la Cour Mosegaard

Volume 13
Transgressive Sex: Subversion and Control in Erotic Encounters
Edited by Hastings Donnan and Fiona Magowan

Volume 14
European Kinship in the Age of Biotechnology
Edited by Jeanette Edwards and Carles Salazar

Volume 15
Kinship and Beyond: The Genealogical Model Reconsidered
Edited by Sandra Bamford and James Leach

Volume 16
Islam and New Kinship: Reproductive Technology and the Shariah in Lebanon
Morgan Clarke

Volume 17
Childbirth, Midwifery and Concepts of Time
Edited by Christine McCourt

Volume 18
Assisting Reproduction, Testing Genes: Global Encounters with the New Biotechnologies
Edited by Daphna Birenbaum-Carmeli and Marcia C. Inhorn

Volume 19
Kin, Gene, Community: Reproductive Technologies among Jewish Israelis
Edited by Daphna Birenbaum-Carmeli and Yoram S. Carmeli

Volume 20
Abortion in Asia: Local Dilemmas, Global Politics
Edited by Andrea Whittaker

Volume 21
Unsafe Motherhood: Mayan Maternal Mortality and Subjectivity in Post-War Gautemala
Nicole S. Berry

Volume 22
Fatness and the Maternal Body: Women's Experiences of Corporeality and the Shaping of Social Policy
Edited by Maya Unnithan-Kumar and Soraya Tremayne

Volume 23
Islam and Assisted Reproductive Technologies: Sunni and Shia Perspectives
Edited by Marcia C. Inhorn and Soraya Tremayne

Volume 24
Militant Lactivism? Attachment Parenting and Intensive Motherhood in the UK and France
Charlotte Faircloth

Volume 25
Pregnancy in Practice: Expectation and Experience in the Contemporary US
Sallie Han

Volume 26
Nighttime Breastfeeding: An American Cultural Dilemma
Cecília Tomori

Volume 27
Globalized Fatherhood
Edited by Marcia C. Inhorn, Wendy Chavkin, and José-Alberto Navarro

Volume 28
Cousin Marriages: Between Tradition, Genetic Risk and Cultural Change
Edited by Alison Shaw and Aviad Raz

COUSIN MARRIAGES
Between Tradition, Genetic Risk and Cultural Change

Edited by Alison Shaw and Aviad Raz

berghahn
NEW YORK · OXFORD
www.berghahnbooks.com

First published in 2015 by
Berghahn Books
www.BerghahnBooks.com

© 2015, 2020 Alison Shaw and Aviad Raz
First paperback edition published in 2020

All rights reserved. Except for the quotation of short passages for the purposes of criticism and review, no part of this book may be reproduced in any form or by any means, electronic or mechanical, including photocopying, recording, or any information storage and retrieval system now known or to be invented, without written permission of the publisher.

Library of Congress Cataloging-in-Publication Data
Cousin marriages: between tradition, genetic risk and cultural change / edited by Alison Shaw and Aviad Raz.
   pages cm. -- (Fertility, reproduction and sexuality; volume 28)
Includes index.
ISBN 978-1-78238-492-2 (hardback: alk. paper) --
ISBN 978-1-78238-493-9 (ebook)
 1. Cross-cousin marriage. 2. Genetic disorders. I. Shaw, Alison, 1957- II. Raz, Aviad E., 1968-
GN480.4.C68 2014
306.84--dc23
                                                            2014029066

British Library Cataloguing in Publication Data
A catalogue record for this book is available
from the British Library.

ISBN 978-1-78238-492-2 hardback
ISBN 978-1-78920-800-9 paperback
ISBN 978-1-78238-493-9 ebook

Contents

List of Figures and Tables   vii
Preface and Acknowledgements   ix

Introduction   1
Alison Shaw and Aviad Raz

Chapter One. The Prevalence and Outcomes of Consanguineous
    Marriage in Contemporary Societies   33
    Alan H. Bittles

Chapter Two. Risk Calculations in Consanguinity   46
    Leo P. ten Kate, Marieke E. Teeuw, Lidewij Henneman and
    Martina C. Cornel

Part I: Continuity and Change in Traditional Consanguineous Marriage

Chapter Three. Cousin Marriages and Inherited Blood Disorders
    in the Sultanate of Oman   65
    Claire Beaudevin

Chapter Four. 'Dangerous Liaisons': Modern Biomedical
    Discourses and Changing Practices of Cousin Marriage in
    Southeastern Turkey   88
    Laila Prager

Part II: Cousin Marriages within Migrant Populations in Europe

Chapter Five. British Pakistani Cousin Marriages and the
    Negotiation of Reproductive Risk   113
    Alison Shaw

Chapter Six. A Cousin Marriage Equals a Forced Marriage: Transnational Marriages between Closely Related Spouses in Denmark 130
Anika Liversage and Mikkel Rytter

Chapter Seven. Changing Patterns of Partner Choice? Cousin Marriages among Turks and Moroccans in the Netherlands 154
Oka Storms and Edien Bartels

Part III: Consanguinity and Managing Genetic Risk

Chapter Eight. Using Community Genetics for Healthy Consanguinity 175
Joël Zlotogora

Chapter Nine. Premarital Carrier Testing and Matching in Jewish Communities 185
Aviad E. Raz

Chapter Ten. Preconception Care for Consanguineous Couples in the Netherlands 202
Marieke E. Teeuw, Pascal Borry and Leo P. ten Kate

Afterword The Marriage of Cousins in Victorian England 218
Adam Kuper

Notes on Contributors 229
Index 235

Figures and Tables

Figures

Figure 1.1	Global Distribution of Marriages Between Couples Related as Second Cousins or Closer	35
Figure 2.1	Pedigree of Family with One Patient with CF (H) whose Brother (G) Wants to Marry his First Cousin (F)	51
Figure 2.2	First-Cousin Marriage in a Family with No Known Patients with Autosomal Recessive Disorders	53
Figure 4.1	Two Thirds-One Third Differentiation of Male and Female Blood	97
Figure 4.2	The Decrease of Patrilineal Relatedness in Consecutive Ascending Generations (in percentages)	98
Figure 4.3	Relative Closeness among First Cousins According to Alawi 'Genetics'	102
Figure 6.1	Categories of Kin with whom Marriage is Considered Forced by the Danish Immigration Authorities	139
Figure 8.1	Origin of Two of the Mutations in a Single Village	182
Figure 11.1	Darwin's Marriage	219

Tables

Table 1.1 Religious Attitudes to Consanguineous Marriage 36

Table 2.1 Autosomal Recessive Inheritance when Both Parents are Carriers 48

Table 2.2 Inbreeding Coefficients for Some Different Types of Consanguineous Marriages 52

Table 2.3 Comparison of Expected Frequencies of Some Selected Autosomal Recessive Diseases in the General Population and in Offspring of First and Second Cousins, with Fractions Attributable to the Consanguinity of the Parents 55

Table 4.1 Marriage Partner Choices among First Cousins (according to different age groups) Based on Data Collected in Three Villages in Hatay from 2006 to 2008 100

Table 8.1 Autosomal Recessive Diseases Diagnosed in a Single Village among Descendants of the Founders 181

Preface and Acknowledgements

Cousin marriages are marriages between people considered to be relatives, and who are usually, but not necessarily, biological kin. Increasingly, in recent years, cousin marriages have come to be regarded as genetically risky. A discourse of genetic risk in marriages between consanguineous kin – defined by geneticists as second cousins or closer – has been promulgated in media and public health debate in many countries where cousin marriage is practiced. There has, however, to date been little systematic comparative analysis of how these understandings of genetic risk are being incorporated within state health policies and how they may be influencing traditional forms of spouse selection. This book attempts such an analysis. It is an interdisciplinary volume presenting the work of anthropologists and geneticists from the Netherlands, Denmark, Germany, France, Israel and the UK. The case studies in this collection represent a range of societies in the Middle East, the Mediterranean and Europe, and minority populations of Middle Eastern and South Asian origin in Europe.

Alison Shaw wishes to thank Hanan Hamamy for encouraging comparative thinking about the social aspects of consanguinity. Aviad Raz wishes to acknowledge his debt to Gideon Kressel, who many years ago introduced him to the value inherent in the anthropological study of cousin marriage. We thank Joel Zlotogora for putting us in contact with one another, and all the contributors to this volume for their enthusiasm, hard work and patience. Special thanks to Philip Kreager, Director of the Fertility and Reproduction Studies group (FRSG) at the Institute of Social and Cultural Anthropology (ISCA) at the University of Oxford. For funds for seminars at Oxford in 2011 on the theme of 'Cousin Marriages and the Medicalisation of Spouse Selection' we thank the Galton Institute, FRSG and ISCA. We are grateful to two reviewers for suggestions for revising the manuscript for publication.

Alison Shaw and Aviad Raz
December 2013

INTRODUCTION

Alison Shaw and Aviad Raz

This book explores what is happening in different parts of the world to traditional practices of cousin marriages in the light of an increasingly global discourse of genetic risk and new and emerging technologies for managing this risk. Cousin marriages can be understood as marriages between people who are closely related, usually as biological kin and often as first cousins, but 'cousin' can also denote genealogically more distant kin or even a social category rather than a genealogical position. Cousin marriage is widely described in anthropological literature as the 'preferred' type of marriage in many populations, particularly in the Middle East, but, contrary to popular understandings, it is not enjoined by Islam, and can be found in most of the major faith groups (see chapter one, this volume). It has now also come to be widely regarded by the media and in public health discourse as genetically risky because cousin marriages are usually consanguineous to some degree.

Consanguineous literally means 'related (*con*) by blood (*sang*)'. Geneticists define marriages between people related as second cousins or closer as consanguineous. According to the principles of Mendelian genetics, consanguineous marriage confers an elevated risk that a child will have an autosomal, recessively inherited genetic disease (Modell and Darr 2002; chapter two, this volume). A recessive condition is one that is caused by inheriting two copies – one from each parent – of a gene mutation that in a single copy carries no significant health risk. If two people carry the same recessive mutation, their risk of having an affected child is 25 per cent. Two biologically unrelated people have a chance of about 2–3 per cent of both being carriers of the same gene mutation, but for first cousins this risk increases to approximately 4–6 per cent because they have a grandparent in common from whom they might inherit the same gene mutation (see chapter two, this volume, for elaboration).

Consanguineous marriages account for 20–55 per cent of marriages in the Middle East, North Africa and Central Asia today (chapter one, this volume). They are also practised by migrants from these parts of the world living in Europe, North America and Australia. In Europe in recent years, as we discuss in more detail later in this Introduction, media attention and public health debates have centred on the genetic risks and the apparently forced nature of cousin marriages among Muslim migrants, raising concerns about the potential stigmatization of consanguineous couples and migrant communities on the basis of their marriage patterns. In the ensuing policy debates, attention has been focused on connecting the social practices of these minorities with their apparent failure to integrate into contemporary European society. An important comparative question for us concerned the degree to which this discourse of genetic risk in cousin marriage is confined to Muslim migrants in Europe. Has it also gained hold in many of Europe's Muslim migrants' countries of origin, where consanguineous marriage is more widely practised, and if so, what forms does it take, and what steps are being taken to manage it?

To date, there has been little comparative analysis of the forms and impacts of this discourse of genetic risk in consanguineous marriage across diverse global settings. This book aims to provide a state-of-the-art overview of this complex new area of enquiry. It juxtaposes contributions from medical geneticists, clinical geneticists and social anthropologists who, from slightly different angles, address the key questions that motivate our project. What trends and common themes can be identified in state and local people's perceptions of cousin marriages in the light of risk discourse? Through what kinds of strategies, and with what effects, is the biomedical identification of genetic risk in consanguineous marriage being accommodated within genetic service provisions in different parts of the world? And what, more broadly, might these strategies reveal about the nature of social change, such as changing processes of spouse selection under 'modernizing' influences that include more education for women and more opportunities for young people to choose partners without deferring to parents, elders or religious orthodoxy (chapters five, seven and nine, this volume)?

In this book, we use cousin marriage as a lens through which to explore the ways in which genetic risk is being understood and put to work in different global contexts. Our focus on consanguinity enables us to locate the contribution of this volume within the burgeoning literature concerned with exploring the construction of the idea of genetic risk. The recent rapid growth in genetic research made possible by techniques of molecular analysis that date from the mid-1980s, and now also by advanced techniques of 'next generation' genomic sequencing, continues to open up new possibilities for preventing the births of children with serious genetic conditions. Alongside these technical developments there has been a parallel expansion in public and academic engagements with genetic research and its social and ethical implications. Critics have raised questions concerning the positive and negative social consequences of measures to identify genetic risk for individuals and communities (Duster 2003). There is potential for coercion in constraining reproductive choice, and for stigmatizing carriers in programmes aimed at preventing the births of babies with haemoglobin disorders in immigrant communities in Europe, even in initiatives without any particular focus on consanguinity (Giordano, Dihal and Harteveld 2005). The relative novelty of genetic – rather than, for example, infectious – illness as a disease category demanding public health provision invites further questions about how scientific and local understanding of illness causality may differ from one another (Böck and Rao 2000; Meiser et al. 2001; Richards and Ponder 1996). It also raises questions about the novel ways in which 'genetic' concepts can be accommodated within local conceptual systems concerning ancestry, the structure of kinship relations, inheritance practices, and personal and family identity (Shaw and Hurst 2008; chapters four and five, this volume).

Geneticization and Medicalization

In theorizing on these processes of societal engagement with genetics, much recent debate has centered on 'geneticization' and related terms used by sociologists to describe media and popular accounts of the achievements of genetic science. The term geneticization was first coined to refer to the prioritizing of genetic over other understandings of human behaviour (Lippman 1992, 2003). It is closely related to 'genetic essentialism', a phrase used to denote scientific discourse 'with the potential to establish social categories based on an essential truth about the body' (Franklin 1993: 43). Scholars have elaborated on the idea of the gene as a 'cultural icon', suggesting that cultural representations of genetics have a life of their own, independent of the scientific research that gives rise to them (Nelkin and Lindee 1995). The thesis of geneticization has since been challenged on grounds that include the fact that empirical evidence to support it is thin: the increasing use of genetic technologies in medical practice is not in dispute, but this does not necessarily entail a widespread acceptance of deterministic or essentialist genetics (Hedgecoe 1998).

A similar debate occurred in the 1970s over the use of 'medicalization' to denote medical, scientific understandings of human behaviours that define these behaviours as problems requiring surveillance and control, through treatment or management (Zola 1972; Illich 1975). Medicalization in this broad sense has occurred across many areas of human life, from 'deviant' behaviours such as mental illness to 'normal' life processes such as pregnancy, childbirth and even partner choice – as we discuss in this book in relation to genetic risk. Genetic research can be seen as an extension of the medicalization of human life by means of its clinical applications in reproductive medicine and genetic counselling, while, simultaneously, medicine is increasingly geneticized. It has for example been claimed of American breast cancer patients that the 'new' genetics is medicalizing kinship by promoting inter-family discussion of genetic risk information (Finkler 2001).

A key difficulty with medicalization and geneticization is that this terminology generally implies that laypeople passively accept and use biomedical knowledge and its associated technologies, and that medical and genetic models increasingly dominate our understandings of human behaviour. For all the contributors to this volume, this is something to examine rather than a premise to be taken for granted. This volume asks whether acceptance and dominance of biomedical models and technologies is uniformly and unidirectionally occurring in relation to genetic risk and cousin marriage. Modern genetic counselling, governed by principles of respect for patient autonomy and non-directiveness, itself demands a degree of reflexivity on the part of practitioners about the values and motivations underpinning the provision of genetic risk information and the offer of reproductive options to at-risk couples (see chapter ten, this volume). Alongside the study of traditional practices of cousin marriage through the medical lens of genetic risk, there are other perspectives that interrogate the discourse of risk and explore the diversity of influences on contemporary patterns of partner choice in migrant communities in European countries (chapter seven, this volume) and within families with a history of a genetic condition (chapter five, this volume).

Within genetic epidemiology and genetic medicine, the interest lies in establishing degrees of genetic (or 'blood') relatedness (i.e. consanguinity) that significantly increase a couple's risk of having a child with a genetic problem in comparison with the risk for more distantly-related or unrelated couples. On the basis of elevated risk, geneticists usually define consanguineous marriages as unions of people related as second cousins or closer. Consanguineous or 'shared blood' marriages are therefore already implicitly medicalized by their distinct biological terminology.

However, 'cousin' marriages and 'consanguineous' marriages are, as noted, analytically distinguishable. The study of 'cousin' marriage is not solely the study of consanguinity but may instead entail an exploration of the socio-economic and political forms and cultural meanings of the practice, even as concerns about consanguinity and genetic risk become increasingly global. Moreover, in the contemporary study of cousin marriage, where we locate this book, there is considerable scope for examining the synthesis of traditional social and cultural perspectives with medical representations, rather than for merely essentializing cousin marriage as consanguinity – even where consanguinity is the focus of discussion. As the chapters in this volume show, this hybridizing process is visibly at work in the strategies of health professionals themselves, where there is a concern to enable 'healthy consanguinity' (see especially Part 3 of this volume). It is also apparent in the strategies of patients and lay populations, as they negotiate the meaning of health messages that portray cousin marriages as genetically risky (see Parts 1 and 2). Our choice of subtitle, 'Between Tradition, Genetic Risk and Cultural Change', is intended to open up these themes, which run throughout this book.

To situate our contribution within the existing literature on cousin marriage and consanguinity, we turn now to distinguishing (i) traditional anthropological perspectives on cousin marriage, (ii) contemporary concerns with consanguinity and genetic risk, and (iii) a third approach, where we locate this book, that of current reflexive and synthetic responses that attempt to engage with the cultural and social meanings of cousin marriage without dismissing genetic risk. There has been, we argue, a general shift from social and cultural analysis of cousin marriage to analysis and arguments that focus on the medical representation of genetic risk in consanguinity. We describe this shift and then argue in favour of a third, synthetic perspective that looks at cousin marriage from both previous perspectives. This third space of synthesis provides elbow room for hybridity, such as in strategies to enable 'healthy consanguinity', and emphasizes reflexivity and representation, for instance in focusing on lay representations of health professionals' representations of cousin marriage.

The Tradition of Cousin Marriage

The 'tradition' of the book's title refers to anthropological and also, very often, lay descriptions of a marriage practice common in parts of North Africa, the Middle East and the Eastern Mediterranean region as well as among migrants from these parts of the world now living in Europe, North America and Australia. In anthropological analysis, traditions of cousin marriage encompass two main forms. One is the Middle Eastern pattern of preferential patrilateral parallel cousin marriage, whereby a man marries a father's brother's daughter (FBD) or a woman referred to by the genealogical kinship term for a FBD. This is the pattern of cousin marriage most commonly cited in the case studies in this volume. The other is matrilateral cross cousin marriage, as in the South Indian system, whereby a man marries his mother's brother's daughter (MBD) or a woman classified as standing in this genealogical relationship to him.

According to nineteenth-century evolutionary theories in anthropology, prohibitions against close cousin marriage were characteristic of fitter, more intelligent human groups (Lubbock 1870 Morgan 1871, 1877; Westermarck 1891), because 'marrying out' of the close kin group enabled the creation of extra-group alliances that were crucial to socio-political survival (Tylor 1889: 267). Cousin marriage, as the marriage of close kin, confused this theory. Some eminent Victorian anthropologists were married to first cousins (Kuper 2008, 2009). Conveniently, certain types of cousin marriage could be defined as forms of exogamy (marrying out). Exogamy here referred not to genetic distance, but to marriage 'outside the descent group', and a descent group did not necessarily map onto biological consanguinity or genetic relatedness (McLennan 1865;

Morgan 1877). In these analyses, the kinship categories employed referred, moreover, to genealogical classifications, not to genetic relationships, so a 'cousin' might be someone only distantly related, or someone *classified* as a particular kind of cousin (Morgan 1877). The North American Iroquois, for example, forbade marriage with the FBD but prescribed marriages with the MBD and the FZD (father's sister's daughter) because these women belonged to different descent groups (Morgan 1877). In later work, the South Indian or 'Dravidian' kinship system of prescribed MBD marriage became recognized as the exemplar of cross cousin marriage.

From this perspective, the so-called 'Arab' or Middle Eastern pattern of parallel cousin marriage challenges conventional anthropological approaches to kinship and marriage: 'It represents a striking exception to the principle of exogamy and, because it unites people who are already united and between whom there is, in a structural sense, no sociological difference, it plays precisely the opposite role from that played by marriage throughout most of the world' (Holy 1989: 1). In his review of ethnographic accounts of cousin marriage in the Middle Eastern region, Ladislav Holy notes that anthropological attempts to explain the motivations, functions, meanings and structural consequences of 'preferential patrilateral parallel cousin marriage' are beset with problems of theory, definition and representation (Holy 1989: 2–8). For one thing, there is considerable statistical variation across the region in the proportions of different types of marriages actually contracted: the most frequent cousin marriage is not always or necessarily with the FBD or someone considered to be in this genealogical category, and marriages may be with parallel and cross cousins (children of same sex and opposite sex siblings – FBD, MZD, FZD and MBD), more distant kin and even with unrelated women. In societies where cousin marriage is practised, it is unusual for more than 20–50 per cent of marriages to take place with people related as second cousins or closer (see chapter one, this volume). Thus, cousins are not prescribed but are preferred as spouses, with close agnatic and cognatic kin generally preferred over distant agnates and strangers (Holy 1989).

Analytically, the preference for marriage with cousins is distinguishable from what governs actual marriage choices. The motives underlying particular choices of spouse in practice are the result of a balance of quite varied, pragmatic, instrumental and individualistic interests, which seemingly have little direct relationship with cultural preference (Eickelman 1981; Donnan 1985; Bourdieu 1990).

As a result, largely endogamous (intermarrying) patrilineal descent groups ('tribes', in the Middle East, and *birādarīs* in Pakistan) cannot be assumed to be biologically self-contained units (see chapter three, this volume). What, then, is the justification for the preference? Is preferential FBD marriage best viewed as a rhetorical device, a metaphor for preferential endogamy (Bourdieu 1977), or is it merely a construct of the anthropological imagination (Holy 1989)?

Cousin marriage has deep historical origins: it was permitted and practised within ancient Israel, Greece and Palestine, was not prohibited in the early Hebrew or Christian religion and predates the rise of Islam (Tillion 1983). Anthropologist Germain Tillion links it with the rise of settled agriculture, with the strengthening of ties between kin who held land in common, and with the perpetuation of gender norms that promote female seclusion and dependence on men. Throughout the ancient Mediterranean world, she argues, the most desirable marriage came to be defined as 'marriage with a very close relative belonging to your own lineage' (Tillion 1983 37). Rather than exchanging women, the idea became 'to keep all the girls in the family for the boys in the family' (Tillion 1983: 74), a cultural ideal that has emotional and psychological consequences for gender roles and female dependency on men.

Holy's analysis of the cultural meaning of preferential FBD marriage takes forward Tillion's observations and raises several points that are relevant for the themes in this book. In Holy's view, preferential FBD marriage represents a desire to marry the closest kinswoman outside the category of prohibited spouses, a desire more powerful than concerns with lineage (Holy 1989: 34–35). As Tillion puts it, across the Magreb, the ideal marriage 'takes place with the female relative who, while not a sister, most resembles one' (Tillion 1983). Holy notes that this preference has various pragmatic socio-economic consequences. Such marriages are easier to arrange than those outside the kin group, they help to keep property and other assets in the family – as many other observers have noted (e.g. Westermarck 1891) – and they expresses the solidarity and honour of kin. Holy concludes by emphasizing that preferential FBD marriage should be understood as supporting the region's gender norms, which require male control of women in a kinship system that emphasizes the solidarity of agnatic kin at the expense of conjugal relationships and affinity. This point has particular salience within contemporary debates of cousin marriage. In Europe, as we discuss below (and in Part 2 of this volume) cousin marriage has been linked to forced marriage and to conservative, 'outdated' gender norms. It has also been theorized anthropologically as a mechanism for protecting cultural and religious values by ensuring their effective transmission over generations (Ottenheimer 1996).

The observation that it is the closeness of kin ties that matters most also has implications for how people who practise this form of marriage understand descent and the construction of patrilineage identity. Marriages of first cousins or their genealogical equivalents generally secure socio-economic and emotional connections between the households of siblings. These connections are usually more important than the precision of the genealogical relationships through which they are created. One means of creating interhousehold solidarity is by sibling-exchange marriages, known in the Middle East by the Arabic term *badal* (exchange) and in Pakistan as *watta satta*, whereby a pair of siblings from one household marries a pair of siblings from another household (see chapter five, this volume). These are usually (but not necessarily) first cousin marriages, and the children of such marriages will be related to each other as double first cousins, through both their fathers and their mothers. Consequently, lines of descent are frequently traceable both through men and through women and are characteristically complex and overlapping, while simultaneously preserving the identity of the patrilineage (*nasab*) across generations (Conte and Walentowitz 2009). In this process, the 'closest' ties are between male kin, following the logic that Holy identifies in demonstrating that marriage with the FBD represents a marriage with the closest kinswoman permitted by incest rules. In a similar vein, Marks (1974) explained cousin marriage among the Bedouin as a factor contributing to the clustering of men into 'co-liable groups'. The first right of a Bedouin man to marry his cousin (*awlād 'amm*) – that is, the expectation that for a man the first proposition to be considered will be a cousin marriage – is functional in sustaining clan (*khamule*) borders and implies respect for one's family. Where first cousin marriage is not feasible, alternate choices (in descending order) consist of more distant paternal kin, agnates and group members in general, and finally strangers (Kressel 1986, 1992). We see the same logic at work in two case studies in this book: in Turkish Alawi and British Pakistani constructions of 'genetic' ties in marriage. Of all first cousin marriages, the marriage of the children of brothers (i.e. of a man to his FBD) is the closest (chapters four and five, this volume).

Predictors of Change

The practice of cousin marriage depends essentially on two things. One is having cousins to marry. The other is having good reasons for arranging such marriages for one's children or desiring such a marriage for oneself. Over the centuries, high birth rates and large families, combined with socio-economic and cultural motivations, have sustained the practice across culturally and religiously diverse populations.

In industrializing Europe, close kin and first cousin marriages served to protect economic interests in land, property, businesses and to safeguard cultural and religious identities, a striking example being the Rothschild banking dynasty (Kuper 2009: 117–125). Sibling exchange marriages, such as that of a sister and brother to a brother and sister, other close kin marriages and first cousin marriages were important in such groups as Highland Scots in the first few generations of their settlement in the New World, where they were not inclined 'to mix with strangers' (Molloy 1986). They were also key to the establishment of English middle-class family businesses (Davidoff 2006; Davidoff and Hall 2002). Indeed, in a wide-ranging new analysis of first cousin and close kin marriages within prominent families during the Victorian era, Adam Kuper argues that the preference for marriages within the family was a crucial factor in the success of the leading bourgeois clans of industrial and imperial Britain. 'In short', he writes, 'the preference of the English bourgeoisie for marriage with relatives is one of the great neglected themes of nineteenth-century history' (2009: 28). And not just in England: historian David Sabean argues that close kinship networks were a crucial resource in nineteenth-century capital accumulation and business enterprise across most European countries (Sabean et al. 2007).

What brought this tradition into decline in England and beyond, across other parts of Europe and North America? The popular belief today is that people in Britain gradually came to realize that cousin marriage harms children's health. In the mid-nineteenth century, people such as Charles Darwin (himself married to his cousin) were beginning to worry that cousin marriage might have biologically harmful effects on children (see Afterword, this volume), even though the scientific evidence at the time was inconclusive. The puzzle of why only some but not all cousin marriages have deleterious effects was one that could not be settled then, because Mendel's work on the inheritance of recessive traits was not re-discovered until 1900 and modern population genetics developed even more recently, in the 1950s. Even so, in North America, legal prohibitions against cousin marriage began to be enforced in many states; rather than being grounded in scientific evidence, these prohibitions emanated from the desire to promote more rapid assimilation of cultural and religious minorities (Ottenheimer 1996). In England, popular opinion towards cousin marriage had changed by the end of the nineteenth century. However, a far more convincing explanation for the decline in cousin marriage lies in the fertility transition that occurred from about 1870 onwards, in the context of wider social change.

A falling birth rate meant smaller families, so people had fewer cousins among whom they might find a spouse. In addition, the social transformations of the late nineteenth century gave women (in Western Europe and North America) greater financial and emotional independence from their fathers and brothers, and more opportunities to meet men outside the close family circle. As a result, processes of spouse selection became more diverse (Anderson 1986). Today, around 0.6 per cent of marriages in Europe, North America and Australia are to consanguineous relatives, except among certain immigrant-origin minority populations.

A demographic transition is now occurring across many parts of the world where cousin marriages are common. Epidemiological and demographic studies from the Middle East indicate that with increasing urbanization and modernization, rates of close kin marriage can be expected to decline alongside an overall decline in total fertility rates, because there will be fewer suitable spouses among a person's diminishing circle of cousins (see chapter one, this volume). Later age at marriage, higher levels of female education and employment, contraceptive use, a larger number of people who never marry, and changes in ideas about desirable family size will all contribute. A similar change is expected among minority groups from this region now living in Europe, North America and Australia as their marriages practices diversify and shift towards those of their new societies of residence (Hamamy et al. 2011).

In practice, though, trends in close kin including cousin marriages are rather variable, especially across the Middle East, where local continuities and increases in rates of cousin marriage are inconsistent with the prediction of a decline (chapter one, this volume; Raz 2005). Fertility rates themselves vary, not just as a result of differences in such factors as the desired number of children but because of variation in people's ability to have children (Kreager 2005). A decline in the rate of cousin marriage may also be slower than expected even with low fertility, depending on sibling configurations: if half a population, sub-population or minority group has no children, but half has three children, then everyone in the next generation has two siblings. Cousin marriage may also remain important within some minority populations for socio-economic and cultural reasons, under conditions of political instability or economic insecurity (Khlat 1988; Al Gazali et al. 1997; Raz 2005; chapter five, this volume; Selby 2010; Hamamy et al. 2011). Indigenous ideas about which cousins are suitable as spouses may also be changing or widening, with the result that, despite a falling birth rate, rates of consanguineous marriage show no significant decline. In the 'ultra modern' Gulf societies of Qatar, Yemen and the UAE, a traditional preference for FBD marriage seems to be shifting towards a situation in which patrilateral and matrilateral cousins are acceptable spouses (Dresch 2005, 2006), though it should be remembered that preferential FBD has never been exclusively (patri)lineage endogamous.

Among immigrant-origin minorities in Europe, too, trends in cousin marriage have not always declined as expected (Reniers 2001; Selby 2010; chapter five, this volume; chapter seven, this volume). Frequently these are transnational marriages, in which a European citizen of minority background marries in their country of origin and their spouse joins them in Europe once entry clearance from the authorities is obtained (Beck-Gernsheim 2007). Such marriages have a number of practical and expressive aspects. Structurally, they help to maintain transnational connections, which in turn may have the effect of countering pressures that may lead towards the fragmentation of minority communities and families. In minority groups such as British Pakistanis, transnational cousin marriages are often also viewed as less risky, in socio-economic, cultural and emotional terms, than marriages outside the family (Shaw 2009; Charsley 2007).

At the same time, access to higher education and employment, motivated by the desire for socio-economic improvement, creates new opportunities for young people to meet and marry outside the family circle. In Denmark, marriage is being redefined not only by generational change within families but also by the state, through its policy of family reunification across the generations (Rytter 2013; chapter six, this volume). Future trends are difficult to predict because of the complex interplay of internal and international socio-economic and political factors (Reniers 2001). Even so, there are clear signs of heterogeneity and intergenerational change in attitudes towards arranged transnational cousin marriages within South Asian and Middle Eastern Muslim minorities in Europe; for some, cousin marriage is not the safe haven their families assumed it would be (chapters five and seven, this volume).

Consanguinity and Genetic Risk

A further and, up to now, relatively unexplored influence on the processes of spouse selection discussed above is the medical genetic evidence that parental consanguinity increases the risk of recessive genetic problems in children. A great many medical genetic and epidemiological studies have demonstrated an association between parental consanguinity and adverse birth outcomes, mainly as pregnancy loss (miscarriage and stillbirth), infant death and childhood morbidity (chapter one, this volume; see also Bittles 2012 for elaboration). This association reflects the elevated risk of recessively inherited single-gene disorders (associations between parental consanguinity and dominant, sex-linked or multifactorial conditions are poorly established). There are literally hundreds of recessive conditions, many of which are serious or fatal, and some of which are so rare that only a handful of cases have ever been reported globally. Recessive conditions can and do occur in the general population without there being a family history of the condition and in the absence of parental consanguinity, although these factors make their occurrence more likely.

Examining the actual and potential social impacts of this evidence on traditional processes of cousin marriage is complex because it requires an engagement with diverse arenas of representation. First of all, some understanding of the basic science of genetic risk in consanguinity is necessary, as well as of the kinds of calculation of risk that geneticists can make for individual couples. In their chapter in this volume, Ten Kate et al. describe how these risks are calculated, both at the population level and in the genetic counselling of patients. Risk estimates are usually given as 4–6 per cent (for couples who are cousins) or approximately 'double' the baseline risk (2–3 per cent) for an unrelated couple. However, actual risks can vary quite considerably, depending on the prevalence of carriers for particular recessive conditions in given populations, and on whether a couple has a family history of consanguineous marriage over generations, and/or of a genetic condition. In the case of a consanguineous couple with an affected child, one should not jump to the conclusion that the condition is the result of the parental consanguinity, but one must take into account the family history of the parents, 'the inbreeding coefficient, the relative frequencies of different pathogenic mutations and the total gene frequency' (chapter two, this volume).

Alarmist Statistics and Moral Panics

Yet in public health circles, the public domain, media representations and lay understandings, the risk for and cause of genetic conditions in children of consanguineous couples are frequently confused. Not surprisingly, the families and communities targeted by risk discourse and medical intervention are sometimes sceptical of the messages they receive, observing, for example, that not every child of consanguineous parents has a genetic condition and that children of non-consanguineous parents may also have health problems (see chapters three and seven, this volume).

In addition, scientific risk estimates are frequently exaggerated in media reporting through alarmist presentations of statistics. A feature of this risk discourse, particularly as it is promulgated in the media, is that the statistics documenting the risk are frequently presented in an alarming manner. Sometimes the emphasis is not on the rarity of many recessive conditions but on the fact that there are *more* recessive conditions diagnosed within consanguineous than in non-consanguineous groups. In such reporting, cousin marriage is, in effect, 'reduced' to a long list of – sometimes hundreds – severe or fatal genetic conditions, some marked by peculiar constellations of dysmorphic physical features, a list that is then compared with the smaller number of conditions diagnosed in non-consanguineous populations.

Recently, British researchers linked data for congenital anomalies and consanguinity in a multi-ethnic population as part of the 'Born in Bradford' (BiB) study (Sheridan et al. 2013). They found that the risk of having affected children was about 2 per cent greater for mothers of Pakistani origin than for those of white British origin. A similar increase in risk was found for mothers of white British origin older than thirty-four years. The researchers conclude that sensitive advice about the risks should be provided to communities at increased risk, and to couples in consanguineous unions, to assist in reproductive decision making.

While the researchers insist on 'sensitive advice', the media and public interpretation of such studies is often alarmist. Radio 4 programmes about the BiB study were quite carefully put together to try to de-sensationalize the findings; they included observations where some of the behaviours of Pakistani mothers were constructed as 'protective' against birth defects compared with white mothers (alcohol, smoking, etc.). But the headline in the Guardian story covering this study stated that 'Marriage between first cousins doubles risk of birth defects, say researchers' (Boseley 2012).

A perceived 'doubling' of a risk is much more likely to alarm rather than to inform, unless it is accompanied by the baseline disease prevalence. Doubling a low risk result is a risk that is still not high, but at most moderate. As noted, 2–3 per cent is usually quoted as the baseline risk in unrelated couples, to which another 2–3 per cent can be added for first cousin offspring, resulting in a risk of 4–6 per cent. Some of this extra risk can, moreover, be pinpointed and foretold by looking at the family history. Case-by-case genetic counselling, taking advantage of next generation sequencing, to identify carrier couples who are at 25 per cent risk is the way forward in the care for consanguineous couples, who can then be offered appropriate reproductive choices (see chapter two and all chapters in Part 3 of this volume). However, this type of case-by-case counselling, which has been advocated under the premise of 'healthy consanguinity' (see chapter eight, this volume) is frequently contradicted by the message that cousin marriage should be strongly discouraged, or stopped altogether.

In these messages, moreover, consanguineous marriage frequently acts as a vehicle through which social and political agendas concerning apparently 'non-assimilating' minority groups are played out. The assumption that marriage between cousins in Muslim communities is causing terrible disabilities in children, and/or is 'forced', is often used to stereotype and stigmatize on medical and/or political grounds (chapters five and six, this volume). Data on the linkage between cousin marriage and forced marriage is scarce and full of loopholes. In 2012, the UK Forced Marriage Unit gave advice or support related to a possible forced marriage in 1485 cases. While these cases involved 60 different countries, most were from Pakistan (47.1 per cent), Bangladesh (11 per cent), and India (8 per cent). In all of these communities, cousin marriage is prevalent; however, we do not have data on how many of these cases represent cousin marriages (Forced Marriage Unit 2012). Forced marriage evidently exists and should be determinedly discouraged; our point is that it would be wrong to label each and every cousin marriage as forced unless proven otherwise, just as it is wrong to claim that each and every cousin marriage is genetically risky. The analytically separable issues of forced marriage and of genetic risk have been connected in policy-related debate linking consanguineous marriage to the creation of 'a high degree of insularity with barriers to integration and lack of contact with the wider community' (Hasan 2009: 275). Cousin marriage is, moreover, frequently portrayed as the practice of outdated traditionalists, as 'a centuries-old Islamic custom' that is 'unacceptable in the twenty-first century' (see chapter five, this volume), with rarely any attention paid to the fact that Islam permits but does not prescribe cousin marriage, and to the diversity of Islamic opinions about its desirability, including concerning the risk of birth defects (chapter seven, this volume; Shaw 2009: 52, 55–56). Yet an earlier, wide-sweeping claim by a conservative commentator in the United States held that the 'Muslim kinship structure is an unexamined key to the war on terror'; for this commentator, the 'in-group solidarity' that results from cousin marriage produces a 'self-sealing insular world' (Kurtz 2007).

This stigmatization of cousin marriage in Europe on medical/social/political grounds prompts comparison with the situation elsewhere in the world where cousin marriage is still practised by a substantial proportion of the population. In fact, awareness of genetic risk in consanguineous marriage is now global in biomedical circles, as a result of the international training and transnational movement of medical personnel (see chapter three, this volume). As Beck has observed for modern society in general, identifying risk is accompanied by the imperative to 'manage' it (Beck 1992). Concern with managing the risks associated with consanguineous marriage is now also prominent among public health professionals across the Middle East, Central Asia, and parts of the Indian subcontinent, disseminated through government health institutions and by doctors, geneticists and the media (see, for example, chapters three and four, this volume).

In a recent public debate held in Qatar and broadcast by the BBC, the motion 'marriage between close family members should be discouraged' was overwhelmingly supported, by 81 percent (Doha Debates 2012). It is likely that such public condemnation is fuelled by both popular prejudice and powerful media constructions, in which the nature of the genetic risk, at the population level, is not sufficiently understood. The difference between one-off cousin marriage and continuous intra-family cousin marriage over generations, for example, is important and not sufficiently understood in such debates (chapter one, this volume). The concentration of genetic diseases that are the result of descent/consanguinity might well occur in a subgroup of families while other cousin marriages may not have a significantly higher risk compared to the general population. In the wider context of the Doha debate on cousin marriage one can spot powerful and rapid forces of modernization already at work. Changes in gender norms, education and employment patterns, age at marriage and patterns of spouse selection are all likely to have an impact on attitudes towards cousin marriage, and across the Gulf region there is considerable investment in new, modern medical facilities including genetic screening and counselling (chapter three, this volume).

What we witness in these processes is that cousin marriage globally is not only 'medicalized' but also represented as the unreflexive and irresponsible custom of 'backward' and 'ignorant' traditionalists. We see here an inversion of the original anthropological representations of cousin marriage: the antithesis of 'cultural continuity' (Ottenheimer 1996), security and 'solidarity' (Holy 1989) being re-cast as 'cultural stasis and isolation', 'insularity' and 'the terror wars' (Kurtz 2007). So much so that cousin marriage even features as the focus of a recent study on 'Consanguinity as a Major Predictor of Levels of Democracy' that examines the hypothesis that although the level of democracy in a society is a complex phenomenon involving many antecedents, consanguinity is 'an important though often overlooked predictor' of it. This recent study found that measures of democracy and consanguinity negatively correlate to a large extent in a sample of seventy nations, advancing the explanation that 'restricted gene flow arising from consanguineous marriage facilitates a rigid collectivism that is inimical to individualism and the recognition of individual rights, which are key elements of the democratic ethos' (Woodley and Bell 2013: 263). In addition, the authors argue that 'genetic similarity stemming from consanguinity may encourage resource predation by members of socially elite kinship networks as an inclusive fitness enhancing behavior'. In citing this study, our purpose is to highlight how it illustrates the social construction of 'consanguinity as taboo', i.e. as a source of symbolic and perceived physical danger (Douglas 1966, 1992) in which the rudiments of 'primitive society' are supposed to endure as obstacles to modernity and democracy.

Cousin Marriage and Consanguinity: Hybrid Perspectives

The case studies in this book represent a synthesis of traditional anthropological perspectives on cousin marriage and the contemporary concern with consanguinity and genetic risk. Only after appreciating the nature of this risk, and examining how it is propagated in public health circles and in the public domain, particularly in the media, can we fully understand the significance of how these risks are understood within the families and communities that are the direct and indirect 'targets' of risk discourse and medical intervention.

To establish the perspective that we wish to advocate in this book, the first two chapters provide the epidemiological and medical genetic background for the case studies presented in the book's three main sections. Bittles offers up-to-date background information on the current global prevalence of and trends in consanguineous marriages, reflecting on consanguinity as both a genetic and a legal concept. As a legal concept, consanguinity is used in laws of inheritance and in codes governing which marital unions are permitted and which are considered incestuous. As a genetic concept, it usually refers to the marriages of people related as second cousins or closer, but endogamy and population structure can also affect a couple's risk of having a child with a recessive genetic condition, and this is one reason why it is so difficult to establish the precise contribution of parental consanguinity to infant mortality and morbidity. Where the carrier frequency of particular recessive mutations is high, the prevalence of these conditions – for example, thalassemia and Tay Sachs disease – may be high without the parents being first or second cousins (see also chapters three and nine, this volume).

Ten Kate and colleagues take forward the points about genetic risk in consanguineous marriage raised by Bittles. This risk is frequently overestimated, and their chapter explains how realistic estimates can be made using mathematical calculations and observational data. It also shows how risk estimates can be made in the clinical context for individual consanguineous couples, both where there is a family history of disease and where there is none. The chapter introduces some formal genetics and population genetics concepts, in order to explain essential concepts such as gene frequency and carrier frequency. Readers unfamiliar with these concepts can refer back to this chapter as and when they need when reading the individual case studies that follow.

We have organized the rest of the book into three parts, in order to trace the routes that the discourse of risk has taken across three domains: in countries where cousin marriage is, or until very recently has been common; in countries where it is now a minority marriage pattern; and in situations detailing active attempts to manage genetic risk in cousin marriages.

Part 1, 'Continuity and change in traditional consanguineous marriage', presents case studies where the state-level genetic risk discourse focuses on the significant public health challenges caused by β-thalassaemia and sickle cell anaemia (SCA), conditions that occur at a particularly high frequency among people of Mediterranean, Middle Eastern and South Asian ancestry. β-thalassaemia is a major cause of childhood mortality in poorer parts of the world, and its treatment is expensive and entails a lifetime of regular blood transfusions and medications. In the UK, prenatal screening to identify carrier-status women is offered generically in areas of high ethnic minority concentration, and to women of Mediterranean, Middle Eastern or South Asian ancestry in other areas. Couples identified as carriers with 25 per cent risk of having an affected child are then offered prenatal diagnosis with the option of abortion for an affected foetus.

In countries with less developed screening, diagnostic and treatment services for thalassaemia, and where the condition is more prevalent, an alternative strategy is to focus on identifying at-risk couples before they marry – following the well-known example of Cyprus where this strategy has resulted in the almost complete elimination of thalassaemia. What is less well known is that the reduction of thalassemia births in Cyprus is mostly due to prenatal diagnosis and selective abortion, in a medical environment in which couples' reproductive choices are strongly influenced by health professionals (Angastiniotis et al. 1986; Hoedemaekers and ten Have 1998). Some of the rapidly modernizing Gulf countries have introduced mandatory pre-marital screening; how directive these policies are is an open question, given the uneven implementation of prenatal diagnostic facilities and the variability of laws permitting termination of pregnancy.

In Oman and Turkey, as chapters three and four show, cousin marriage has been identified as an obstacle to be overcome in reducing the incidence of haemoglobin disorders. In Oman, which currently lacks systematic prenatal diagnostic facilities, a public health discourse advocates the carrier screening of couples on the basis of their consanguinity, rates of which are believed to be especially high among people from tribal areas, since tribes are assumed to be biological units. Ironically, Beaudevin suggests, this targeting of already-stigmatized categories of people is unlikely to reduce the incidence of haemoglobin disorders because of the high proportion of unaffected carriers in the Omani population, which is in effect endogamous because Omani marriage regulations – like those of Saudi and some other Gulf states – restrict marriage with non-Omanis.

In Turkey, a recent public health campaign discourages cousin marriages. Together with premarital screening and diagnosis for consanguineous couples, it represents the government's attempt to reduce the incidence of haemoglobin disorders, which are seen as arising from consanguineous marriages. In keeping with attempts to improve the nation's health that date from the 1920s, consanguinity has been added to the list of mandatory pre-marital health checks for 'social diseases'. Prager describes a striking form of indigenous response to this situation: one of the targeted ethnic groups has adapted the biomedical discourse to their own understandings of genetic risk and reshaped the system of cousin marriage in a way that would cause Mendel 'to turn in his grave'. This neatly illustrates how biomedical risk as a scientific construct derived from a set of statistical assumptions can be re-interpreted rather than readily transferred across different contexts.

Part 2, 'Cousin marriages within migrant populations in Europe', turns to case studies from the United Kingdom (chapter five), Denmark (chapter six) and the Netherlands (chapter seven). We see here an overwhelmingly negative public perception of cousin marriage broadly embedded within debates about integration and immigration, especially with regard to Muslim minorities. Yet there are also some intriguing differences across these contexts in terms of the emphasis placed on genetic risk.

In the UK, Pakistani consanguineous marriage shows no sign of decline, contradicting conventional expectation, and despite evidence of a disproportionately high number of rare genetic conditions in Pakistani children and heated debate in public health and the media about the management of this situation. In the UK, risk of haemoglobinopathies is managed through prenatal screening for all pregnant women in high prevalence areas of the UK and by ethnicity in low prevalence areas, with no formal top-down medical management of risk associated with parental consanguinity. Shaw's discussion in chapter five of the experiences of families with genetic conditions complicates the stereotypical media and public health view that British Pakistanis are in denial about genetic risk and do not engage with clinical genetics services or techniques of risk management. She describes parents' deliberations over their children's marriages in the light of awareness of genetic risk, and details a variety of ways in which couples given an estimate of reproductive recurrence risk engage with genetic risk and its management.

In Denmark, by contrast, as Liversage and Rytter show in chapter six, cousin marriage has not been debated in terms of genetic risk. Rather, bureaucrats have reconfigured cousin marriage as 'forced' unless proven otherwise, and put this concept to work in the loaded political context of immigration policies. In Denmark, the 'family reunification' of foreign ethnic collectivities – of Turks and Pakistanis, in the examples provided – is represented as endangering the political identity of another collectivity – that of the Danes.

In the Netherlands too, Storms and Bartels note in chapter seven, politicians have also constructed cousin marriage as 'forced marriage', but a proposal to legislate against it on these grounds is in abeyance since the election of the current government. In these debates, there is an echo of the nineteenth-century concern, which was prevalent in the United States, that the marriage practices of 'non-integrating' linguistic and religious minorities would threaten social progress, concern that resulted in thirty-one states making cousin marriages illegal (Ottenheimer 1996: 113). In the Danish situation, as Liversage and Rytter show, one consequence is that some cousin marriages that the authorities would define as 'forced' take place instead in Sweden, while other couples may be separated for years while trying to prove their marriage was not forced.

The case studies in this section also remind us that any assessment of the impact of legislation or genetic risk discourse upon spouse selection must recognize that within Europe's consanguineous minority populations, marriage patterns are already undergoing change. Turkish and Moroccan women in the Netherlands are aware of the genetic risk in consanguineous marriage, but this awareness – perhaps traceable to their countries of origin – is mediated by religious, social and cultural considerations, which, among younger women, indicate that arranged cousin marriages will become less common. Trends in consanguineous marriage across Europe are likely also be influenced by internal, national and interstate diversity in the socio-economic characteristics of Europe's consanguineous minority populations. British Pakistanis, for example, are socio-economically heterogeneous, and also differ in socio-economic background, migration history and regional origin from Norwegian and Danish Pakistanis (Rytter 2013; Shaw 2014). Variations in government stances towards minorities, as already illustrated by the recent Danish policy, are also likely to influence trends in consanguineous marriage across Europe.

Part 3, 'Consanguinity and managing genetic risk', presents case studies of schemes aimed at managing the elevated genetic risk for consanguineous couples, thus promoting 'healthy consanguinity'. A number of genetic carrier testing and screening programmes aimed at particular endogamous or consanguineous communities are in place. These include premarital carrier matching for the ultra-Orthodox Jewish community (Raz and Vizner 2008; chapter nine, this volume) and for Arab-Bedouins in Israel (Raz 2005), and schemes for British Pakistani families with recessive conditions for which mutations have been identified (chapter five, this volume). Targeted ancestry-based preconception screening for carriers of cystic fibrosis and haemoglobinopathies, for which risks vary with ancestry, was piloted in the Netherlands for Dutch couples and those of immigrant-origins in Surinam, the Antilles, Turkey and Morocco (Lakeman et al. 2008, 2009). There is a diversity of opinion across these different contexts with regard to whether the increased genetic risk associated with cousin marriage is best confronted by education, counselling, prevention, or some combination of these strategies. The schemes also raise questions about the potential medicalization of partner choice and the effects on marital norms, including through health interventions that have the explicit objective of identifying carriers of particular conditions not in order to discourage consanguineous marriage but to promote 'healthy consanguinity'.

The first case study in this section is from Israel, which has an ethnically diverse population with many endogamous communities. Zlotogora describes an innovative state programme devoted to 'healthy consanguinity' via genetic counselling, in which the genetic counselling takes place not in hospital departments but alongside family doctors, nurses and counsellors working in the various, usually rural and peripheral, communities of Arab Israelis, Druze and Bedouin, all characterized by a high degree of consanguinity. Zlotogora discusses the construction of a genetic database containing information about the genetic conditions present in the community as an invaluable genetic counselling tool, enabling the medical impact of consanguineous marriage to be reduced without directly intervening in local marriage traditions. This is striking, because in places such as the UK, the creation of genetic databases – for example on consanguineous Pakistani families to enable family doctor-led genetic counselling – has generated ethical debate about patient confidentiality (see chapter five, this volume). Zlotogora comments that in Israel there has long been acceptance of the use of ethnicity/community of origin data, including for medical purposes, with the frequency of particular genetic conditions varying in different communities. Indeed, the genetic database created initially for the Arab Muslim community has since been extended nationally as an important aid to state genetic counselling provision.

We then turn, in chapter nine, from a state-administered to a community-administered programme promoting 'healthy endogamy': that of the much celebrated carrier screening programme *Dor Yesharim*, founded in 1983 to prevent suffering caused by births of children with Tay Sachs disease in a community where marriages are arranged and there is a religious ban on abortion. Marriages are advised only where both partners do not carry a mutation for the same condition, but to avoid stigma individuals are not informed if they are carriers or not. Since the programme's inception, the number of Tay Sachs births has greatly decreased, and the programme has been hailed as a triumph as a result of its sensitivity to the norms of the community.

However, Raz argues, *Dor Yesharim* has been less successful in preventing stigma. Public messages stressing the negative aspects of knowing about and being identified as a carrier constitute a powerful directive message that reproduces rather than challenges stigmatization: being a carrier is so bad that you had better not know. The stigma is such that carrier matching is often sought late in the marriage-arranging process, only after matches that might have proved 'advisable' have already been ruled out on grounds of a family history of the condition. Stigmatization is strong enough to contaminate even 'presumed carriers'. *Dor Yesharim* primarily serves an orthodox community with specific social characteristics, but may also be utilized by modern religious Jews who may also access state genetic counselling with its emphasis on non-directiveness, individual autonomy and informed consent. It is here, Raz notes, that we witness tensions between 'communitarian' approaches, which may be 'culturally appropriate' but compromise western bioethical principles, and 'liberal' approaches to genetic counselling, as he has also discussed in his ethnography of genetic counselling in a Bedouin community in Israel (Raz 2005).

In the final chapter, Teeuw and colleagues discuss a scheme for preconception genetic screening of couples that could be offered to couples on the basis of their consanguinity, or even to all couples. Significantly, the recording of ethnicity data in the Netherlands remains a topic of political debate, reflecting eugenic concerns and fear of stigmatization (Jans et al. 2011). A tool that could screen the coding sections of the genome of both partners would enable risks for recessive conditions to be identified; from this, the risks associated with consanguinity could be refined in individual cases. The key question will be whether to offer this tool, once developed, to all or only to consanguineous couples. As the companion chapter by Storms and Bartels in this volume shows (chapter seven), cousin marriage in minority communities in the Netherlands is both stigmatized and undergoing significant change. Teeuw et al.'s discussion of the conditions under which such a scheme could be implemented is exemplary in its reflexivity and awareness of the need to incorporate ethical and social perspectives in the development of reproductive genetic technologies.

In the afterword, Adam Kuper provides a discussion of the marriage of cousins in Victorian England, which is elaborated in his *Incest and Influence: The Private life of Bourgeois England* (2009). Kuper's account of cousin marriages in the Darwin-Wedgwood family reminds us that close kin marriages, including first cousin marriages, were common in upper-middle-class Victorian England; cousin couples could feel as close as siblings, already connected through family ties, without actually being siblings. This observation resonates with Tillion's that across the Maghreb the idea of marriage is 'with the female relative, who, while not a sister, most resembles one' (1983). But in Victorian England doubts were already emerging in the minds of people such as Charles Darwin concerning where to draw the line between consanguinity and incest, and about the potential biological risks of cousin marriage.

By stepping back to Victorian England, Kuper shows us that much of the contemporary discussion of genetic risk in cousin marriage has its origins in our recent past, in the intellectual and social background to the rise of modern genetics. This offers historical depth to our analysis of how the study of cousin marriage has shifted to focus on the construction of risk. In the emerging nineteenth-century research, we can already trace many contemporary themes. The issue of genetic risk was clearly a sensitive one: one attempt to establish the effects of cousin marriage on fertility and birth defects took the form of a proposal taken to parliament that the 1871 census of England should include a question on cousin marriage, but the proposition was rejected on the grounds that it would be prying. There is also a contemporary ring to the concern to establish the influence of environmental factors on birth outcomes and quantify the particular risks of close kin marriage in remote inbred populations. The historical account shows us that much of the contemporary discussion of cousin marriage is also part of our past, with the significant difference that today's discourse tends to be focused on Muslim minority populations in Europe, and on 'tribal', 'traditional', 'rural' and 'uneducated' populations in other parts of the world.

Negotiation, Reflexivity and Representation

This volume addresses leading questions for a socio-anthropological study of consanguineous marriages underpinned by the modern medical focus on managing genetic risk. As far as we know, it represents the first comparative exploration of the forms and effects of the discourse of genetic risk on contemporary practices of cousin marriage, in interaction with existing and emerging facilities for genetic counselling, screening and testing. The contributions to this book show that the concept of genetic risk in consanguineous marriage is now global, and it circulates not only where marrying cousins is a minority marriage pattern, but also in areas where cousin marriage remains common. They also show how this discourse takes diverse forms, in the views and messages of health professionals and in the views of lay populations. The scientific information is itself diverse, depending on what is included in the risk calculation, and is more or less alarmist depending on its representation. Yet the general effect of much of the reporting is to suggest that the risk is 'high', that it applies to all consanguineous marriages, and that it equates to 'cause' and 'doubling' the background risk. The risk discourse is frequently also a vehicle for social and political agendas. To demonstrate this, we invite our readers to ask themselves whether public discouragement of pregnancy in women older than thirty-four years would be socially and ethically acceptable, and then consider the fact that women over thirty-four and first cousin couples are generally considered to have a similar increase in risk.

As the case studies demonstrate, there is, nonetheless, no straightforward medicalization at work across these contexts. There is heterogeneity in formal medical provisions for managing risk and also in how consanguineous couples and intermarrying communities perceive and negotiate the implications of risk information (Shaw 2011). Sometimes people calculate risk in quite unexpected ways that do not correspond with the bilaterality of Mendelian genetics but, as in the South Asian and Turkish cases discussed here, reflect local understanding of closeness in patrilineal kinship. These accounts contribute to knowledge concerning how biology (genetics) and relatedness (kinship) are not identical (Böck and Rao 2000; Franklin 1997; Meiser et al. 2001; Richards and Ponder 1996; Shaw and Hurst 2008). It would be interesting to compare these cases with change in the quintessentially South Indian 'Dravidian' pattern of cross cousin marriage (to the MBD) under the influence of the discourse of risk in close kin marriage. In interpreting change in marriage patterns, the discourse of genetic risk is, of course, just one factor among others, such as the move toward smaller families, wider contraceptive use, and the shift away from family arranged marriages to individual choice of marriage partners.

In the rapidly modernizing economies of the Gulf States, genetics service infrastructure is being established with varying levels of integration of services, inviting further comparative research on the relationships between service provisions, and professional and lay discourses of genetic risk in consanguineous marriage. Is the misleadingly equation of risk in consanguineous marriage with risk of haemoglobinopathies noted in the Oman case made elsewhere in the Middle East? What public discourses circulate and what provisions exist for the clinical diagnosis and management of rare recessive conditions? Are minority groups always the targets of stigmatizing discourse?

In the community and public health programmes aimed at identifying carriers and promoting 'healthy consanguinity' discussed in this volume, we see that 'culturally sensitive' strategies are not entirely free of stigma, and also raise questions of coercion and consent regarding access to and the holding of genetic information. Such approaches may be appropriate at the level of 'traditional' religious/ethnic communities governed by more 'communitarian' ethics, but are less appropriate in multi-ethnic populations in Europe where genetic counselling is governed by principles of autonomy and individual informed consent (Raz 2005; Simpson 2004). Tensions between inducing change informed by individualistic western ethics and being sensitive to local cultural norms are also present within educational aids designed by health professionals to inform about genetic risk in cousin marriage or to promote 'healthy consanguinity' (Raz 2003). While top-down interventions may be too coercive, leaving the management of genetic risk entirely to the community has also proven to be problematic (Raz 2009a). The management of risk as part of 'healthy consanguinity' thus requires a careful, on-going dialogue between policy-makers, health professionals, and networks of individuals genetically at risk (Raz 2009b). In multi-ethnic populations, moreover, in order to avoid stigmatization by ethnicity, the question remains open whether a risk assessment tool for consanguinity, offered 'independently' of ethnicity, is the best means of informing couples' reproductive choices. Of note, the majority of the problems highlighted in this book are in fact manageable, but this requires moving beyond both the traditional celebration of cousin marriage as well as the modern, medically led discouragement of consanguinity. Our comparative approach thus has implications for professionals developing and providing genetic screening programmes for consanguineous couples in diverse global settings, because it underlines the importance of taking account of the far-reaching influences of the local political, social and cultural context instead of assuming that a single approach will be suitable for all. The future of 'healthy consanguinity', if this approach is indeed to gain prominence, depends on the successful balancing of the interests of health professionals and providers, as well as of individuals genetically at risk and their communities and networks.

We end with some reflections on the challenge taken up in this book. We have described an historical shift in perspectives, from a traditional anthropological approach to 'cousins' as a social category/genealogical position and 'cousin marriage' as a social phenomenon, to the contemporary focus in epidemiology, public health and media reporting on cousin marriage as (risky) 'consanguinity'. What we offer across the case studies in this book is a contemporary, hybrid perspective on cousin marriage, one that draws together the cultural representations of anthropologists (as well as laypersons) and the scientific representations of geneticists, and encourages reflexivity in both.

In the accounts presented here, cousin marriage is sometimes given alternative social and cultural representations/labels, for example in its presentation as 'forced marriage' and as being inimical to democracy. But we have also seen that in most contemporary accounts it is represented mainly through the medical lens of genetic risk, indicating a continuing strong linkage between nature and culture, between the biological and the social, to the extent that cousin marriage is frequently essentialized, reduced to the literal and ominous metonymies of congenital defects and genetic diseases. This continues despite new genetic studies showing that generalized estimates of the increased genetic risk in consanguinity are often exaggerated or otherwise presented in an alarmist manner. However, the popular medical representation of cousin marriage as risky, and the association of cousin marriage with 'non-integrating', 'conservative', 'traditional', 'undemocratic' peoples, continues to provide an important source of lingering antagonism. In a world of cultural compounds, social fragmentation and rising individualism, cultural elements that appear to resist modernity and globalizing trends are a symbolic source of danger. 'Cousin marriage' may be another case in point in the list of modern-day taboos.

Indeed, in a global world dominated by mass media and impregnated with a declared transnational desire for ubiquitous human communication, cousin marriage may be seen as evading 'the civilizing process', resisting assimilation, defying pluralism, negating the plausibility of change and blind to multi-cultural differences. However, as the collection of case studies in this anthology demonstrates, to generally denounce cousin marriage is in itself a normative act of defying pluralism and multi-cultural differences. We argue here for a renewed reflexivity that considers the complexity of cousin marriage, avoiding generalized stereotypes in favour of a hybrid approach that is sensitive to both the social and cultural importance of cousin marriage and the health issues it raises.

References

Al-Ghazali, L.I., A. Bener, Y.M. Abdulrazzaq, R. Micallef, A.I. Al-Khayat and T. Gaber. 1997. 'Consanguineous marriages in the United Arab Emirates', *Journal of Biosocial Science* 29: 491–497.
Anderson, N.F. 1986. 'Cousin marriage in Victorian England', *Journal of Family History* 11(3): 285–301.
Angastiniotis, M.A., S. Kyriakidou and M. Hadjiminas. 1986. 'How thalassaemia was controlled in Cyprus', *World Health Forum* 7: 291–297.
Beck, U. 1992. *Risk Society: Towards a New Modernity*. London: Sage.
Beck-Gernsheim, E. 2007. 'Transnational lives, transnational marriages: a review of the evidence from migrant communities in Europe', *Global Networks* 7: 271–288.
Bittles, A.H. 2012. *Consanguinity in Context*. Cambridge: Cambridge University Press.
Böck, M. and A. Rao. 2000. *Culture, Creation and Procreation: Concepts of Kinship in South Asian Practice*. Oxford and New York: Berghahn Books.
Boseley, S. 2012. 'Marriage between first cousins doubles risk of birth defects, say researchers', *The Guardian*, 4 July.
Bourdieu, P. 1977. *Outline of the Theory of Practice*. Cambridge: Cambridge University Press.
———. 1990. *The Logic of Practice*. Stanford: Stanford University Press.
Charsley, K. 2007. 'Risk, trust, gender and transnational cousin marriage among British Pakistanis', *Ethnic and Racial Studies* 30(6): 1117–1131.

Conte, E. and S. Walentowitz. 2009. 'Kinship matters: tribals, cousins, and citizens in South West Asia and beyond', *Etudes rurales* 184: 217–247.
Davidoff, L. 2006. '"Close marriage" in the nineteenth and twentieth century middle strata', in F. Ebtehaj, M. Richards and B. Lindley (eds), *Kinship Matters*. Cambridge: Hart Publishers, pp.19–45.
Davidoff, L. and C. Hall. 2002 [1987]. *Family Fortunes: Men and Women of the English Middle Class, 1780–1850*. Routledge: London and New York.
Doha Debates, 2012. 'Arabs vote to discourage close family marriage', Tuesday 20 March. http://www.thedohadebates.com/news/item/?n=14908. Last accessed 20 November 2013.
Donnan, H. 1985. 'The rules and rhetoric of marriage negotiations among the Dhund Abbasi of North East Pakistan', *Ethnology* XXIV(3): 183–196.
Douglas, M. 1966. *Purity and Danger: An Analysis of Concepts of Pollution and Taboo*. London: Routledge.
———. 1992. *Risk and Blame: Essays in Cultural Theory*. London and New York: Routledge.
Dresch, P. 2005. 'Debates on marriage and nationality in the United Arab Emirates', in P. Dresch and J. Piscatori (eds), *Monarchies and Nations: Globalization and Identity in the Arab States of the Gulf*. London: IB Tauris, pp.136–157.
———. 2006. 'Foreign matter: the place of strangers in Gulf society', in J. Fox, N. Mourtada-Sabbah and M al-Mutawa (eds), *Globalization and the Gulf*. London: Routledge, pp.200–222.
Duster, T. 2003 [1990]. *Backdoor to Eugenics*. New York: Routledge.
Eickelman, D.F. 1981. *The Middle East: An Anthropological Approach*. New Jersey: Prentice Hall.
Finkler, K. 2001. 'The kin in the gene: the medicalization of family and kinship in American society', *Current Anthropology* 42: 235–263.
Forced Marriage Unit. 2012. 'Statistics on Forced Marriage for 2012'. https://www.gov.uk/government/uploads/system/uploads/attachment_data/file/141823/Stats_2012.pdf. Accessed 25 November 2013.
Franklin, S. 1993. 'Essentialism, which essentialism? Some implications of reproductive and genetic technosciene', in J. Dececco (ed.), *Issues in Biological Essentialism versus Social Constructionism in Gay and Lesbian Identities*. London: Harrington Park Press, pp.27–39.
Franklin, S. 1997. *Embodied Progress: A Cultural Account of Assisted Conception*. London: Routledge.
Giordano, P., A. Dihal and C. Harteveld. 2005. 'Estimating the attitude of immigrants toward primary prevention of the hemoglobinopathies', *Prenatal Diagnosis* 25(10): 885–893.
Hamamy, H., et al. 2011. 'Consanguineous marriages, pearls and perils: Geneva International Consanguinity Workshop Report', *Genetics in Medicine* 13: 841–847.
Hasan, K. 2009. 'The medical and social costs of consanguineous marriage among British Mirpuris', *South Asia Research* 29(3): 275–298.

Hedgecoe, A. 1998. 'Geneticization, Medicalisation and Polemics', *Medicine, Health Care and Philosophy* 1(3): 235–243.
Hoedemaekers, R. and H. ten Have. 1998. 'Geneticization: the Cyprus case', *Journal of Medicine and Philosophy* 23(3): 274–287.
Holy, L. 1989. *Kinship, Honour and Solidarity: Cousin Marriage in the Middle East*. Manchester: Manchester University Press.
Illich, I. 1975. 'The medicalisation of life', *Journal of Medical Ethics* 1(2): 73–77.
Jans, S.M.P., C.G. van El, E.S. Houwaart, M.J. Westerman, R.J.P.A. Janssens, A.L.M. Lagro-Janssen, A.M.C. Plass and M.C. Cornel. 2011. 'A case study of haemoglobinopathy screening in the Netherlands: witnessing the past, lessons for the future', *Ethnicity and Health* 1–23, iFirst article, DOI:10.1080/13557858.2011.604126.
Khlat, M. 1988. 'Consanguineous marriage in Beirut: time trends, spatial distribution', *Social Biology* 35: 324–330.
Kreager, P. 2005. 'Where are the children?', in P. Kreager and E. Shroeder-Butterfill (eds), *Ageing without Children: European and Asian Perspectives on Elderly Access to Support Networks*. Oxford and New York: Berghahn Books, pp.1–45.
Kressel, G. 1986. 'Prescriptive patrilateral parallel cousin marriage: the perspective of the bride's father and brothers', *Ethnology* 25: 163–180.
———. 1992. *Descent through Males*. Wiesbaden: Harrassowitz.
Kuper, A. 2008. 'Changing the subject – about cousin marriage, among other things', *Journal of the Royal Anthropological Institute* 14(4): 717–735.
———. 2009. *Incest and Influence: the Private Life of Bourgeois England*. Cambridge: Harvard University Press.
Kurtz, S. 2007. 'Marriage and the terror war'. http://www.nationalreview.com/articles/219989/marriage-and-terror-war/stanley-kurtz. Last accessed 20 November 2013.
Lakeman, P., A.M.C. Plass, L. Henneman, P.D. Bezemer, M.C. Cornel and L.P. ten Kate. 2008. 'Three-month follow-up of Western and non-Western participants in a study on preconceptional ancestry-based carrier couple screening for cystic fibrosis and hemoglobinopathies in the Netherlands', *Genetics in Medicine* 10(11): 820–830.
———. 2009. 'Preconceptional ancestry-based carrier couple screening for cystic fibrosis and haemoglobinopathies: what determines the intention to participate or not and actual participation?', *European Journal of Human Genetics* 17(8): 999–1009.
Lippman, A. 1992. 'Led astray by genetic maps: the cartography of the human genome and health care', *Social Science and Medicine* 35(12):1469–1476.
———. 2003. 'Eugenics and public health', *American Journal of Public Health* 93(1): 11.
Lubbock, J. 1870. *The Origin of Civilization and the Primitive Conditions of Man*. London: Longmans.

Marks, E. 1974. *The Bedouin Society in the Negev.* Tel-Aviv, Israel: Reshafim Press (in Hebrew).
McLennan, J.F. 1865. *Primitive Marriage.* Edinburgh: A.C. Black.
Meiser, B., M. Eisenbruch, K. Barlow-Stewart, K. Tucker, Z. Steel and D. Goldstein. 2001. 'Cultural aspects of cancer genetics: setting a research agenda', *Journal of Medical Genetics* 38: 425–429.
Modell, B. and A. Darr. 2002. 'Genetic counselling and customary consanguineous marriage', *Nature Review Genetics* 3: 225–230.
Molloy, M. 1986. '"No inclination to mix with strangers": marriage patterns among Highland Scots migrants to Cape Breton and New Zealand, 1800–1916', *Journal of Family History* 11(3): 221–243.
Morgan, L.H. 1871. *Systems of Consanguinity and Affinity of the Human Family.* Washington, DC: Smithsonian Institute.
———. 1877. *Ancient Society: Researches in the Lines of Human Progress from Savagery through Barbarism to Civilization.* New York: Holt.
Nelkin, D. and S. Lindee. 1995. *The DNA Mystique: The Gene as a Cultural Icon.* New York: Freedman.
Ottenheimer, M. 1996. *Forbidden Relatives: The American Myth of Cousin Marriage.* Urbana and Chicago: University of Illinois Press.
Raz, A. 2003. '*Āysha*: genetics education and community engagement in a consanguineous Arab-Bedouin population in Israel', *Health: The Inter-Disciplinary Journal for the Social Study of Health and Illness* 7(4): 439–461.
———. 2005. *The Gene and the Genie: Tradition, Medicalization and Genetic Counselling in a Bedouin Community in Israel.* Durham, North Carolina: Duke University Press.
———. 2009a. 'Can population-based carrier screening be left to the community?' *Journal of Genetic Counseling* 18(2): 114–119.
———. 2009b. *Community Genetics and Genetic Alliances: Eugenics, Carrier Testing, and Networks of Risk.* New York and London: Routledge.
Raz, A. and Y. Vizner. 2008. 'Carrier matching and collective socialization in community genetics: Dor Yeshorim and the reinforcement of stigma', *Social Science and Medicine* 67(9): 1361–1369.
Reniers, G. 2001. 'The post-migration survival of traditional marriage patterns: consanguineous marriages among Turks and Moroccans in Belgium', *Journal of Comparative Family Studies* 32(1): 21–45.
Richards, M.P.M. and M. Ponder. 1996. 'Lay understanding of genetics: a test of an hypothesis', *Journal of Medical Genetics* 33: 1032–1036.
Rytter, M. 2013. *Family Upheaval: Generation, Mobility and Relatedness among Pakistani Migrants in Denmark.* New York: Berghahn Books.
Sabean, D.W., S. Teuscher and J. Mathieu (eds). 2007. *Kinship in Europe: Approaches to Long-Term Development (1300–1900).* Oxford and New York: Berghahn Books.
Selby, J. 2010. 'Marriage partner preference among Muslims in France: reproducing tradition in the Maghrebian diaspora', *Journal for the Society for the Anthropology of Europe* 9(2): 4–16.

Shaw, A. 2009. *Negotiating Risk: British Pakistani Experiences of Genetics*. Oxford and New York: Berghahn Books.

———. 2011. 'Risk and reproductive decisions: British Pakistani couples' responses to genetic counseling', *Social Science and Medicine* 73: 111–120.

———. 2014. 'Drivers of Cousing Marriages among British Pakistanis', *Human Heredity* 77: 26–36.

Shaw, A., and J.A. Hurst. 2008. '"What is this genetics, anyway?" Understandings of genetics, illness causality and inheritance among British Pakistani users of genetic services', *Journal of Genetic Counseling* 17(5): 459–471.

———. 2009. '"I don't see any point in telling them": attitudes to sharing genetic information in the family and carrier testing of relatives among British Pakistani adults referred to a genetics clinic', *Ethnicity and Health* 13(5): 417–434.

Sheridan, E. et al. 2013. 'Risk factors for congenital anomaly in a multiethnic birth cohort: an analysis of the Born in Bradford study', *Lancet* 382: 1350–1359.

Simpson, B. 2004. 'Acting ethically, responding culturally: framing the new reproductive and genetic technologies in Sri Lanka', *Asia Pacific Journal of Anthropology* 5(3): 227–243.

Tillion, G. 1983 [1966]. *The Republic of Cousins: Women's Oppression in Mediterranean Society*, trans. Quintin Hoare. London: Al Saqi Books, distributed by Zed Press.

Tylor, E.B. 1889. 'On a method of investigating the development of institutions; applied to laws of marriage and descent', *Journal of the Anthropological Institute* 18: 245–272.

Westermarck, E. 1891. *The History of Human Marriage*. London: Macmillan.

Woodley, M. and E. Bell. 2013. 'Consanguinity as a major predictor of levels of democracy: a study of seventy nations', *Journal of Cross-Cultural Psychology* 44(2): 263–280.

Zola, I. 1972. 'Medicine as an institution of social control', *Sociological Review* 20: 487–504.

Chapter 1

THE PREVALENCE AND OUTCOMES OF CONSANGUINEOUS MARRIAGE IN CONTEMPORARY SOCIETIES

Alan H. Bittles

The purpose of this first chapter is to provide readers with background information on consanguineous marriage that is essential for contextualizing the issues discussed in the individual case studies presented across the three parts of this book. After defining consanguineous marriage from a medical genetics perspective, the chapter goes on to describe its current global prevalence; attitudes towards consanguinity in the major world religions; the civil status of consanguineous marriage in different parts of the world; recent trends in rates of consanguineous marriage; and the relationships between close kin marriage, health, and genetic disorders.

Defining Consanguineous Marriage

There is no hard and fast definition of what constitutes a consanguineous marriage but for medical genetics purposes consanguinity is usually described as a union between a couple who are related as second cousins or closer (Bittles 2001). This definition encompasses a number of different levels of consanguinity with first cousin marriages, in which the couple has inherited 1/8 of their genes from a shared ancestor, being the most widespread and common. On average, any children born to such a couple will have inherited identical genes at 1/16 of gene loci, usually described in terms of their coefficient of inbreeding (F) which for the progeny of first cousins is 0.0625 (see also chapters two and ten, this volume, for elaboration). However, in communities with a strong cultural tradition of consanguineous marriage first cousin unions are often contracted over successive generations. As a result, the cumulative coefficient of inbreeding of a first cousin couple can significantly exceed $F = 0.0625$, and marriages between couples nominally related as second ($F = 0.0156$), third ($F = 0.0039$) or more remote cousins may also have significantly greater than expected F values, leading to increased genomic homozygosity and a greater probability of recessive gene expression (Bittles 2009; Bittles 2012: 85–86).

Global Prevalence of Consanguineous Marriage

The common Western stereotype of consanguineous marriages being restricted to small groups living in remote regions of the planet, or to religious and social isolates, is incorrect. As illustrated in Figure 1, unions between close biological kin occur in many parts of the world and data indicate that over 1100 million people live in countries where 20–50 per cent or more of marriages are between couples related as second cousins or closer ($F \geq 0.0156$), equivalent to some 10.4 per cent of the 7.2 billion global population (Bittles and Black 2010).

These figures are lower-bound estimates of the actual global prevalence of consanguineous marriage. In Asia, information on the rates of consanguineous marriage in populous countries such as Indonesia and Bangladesh is fragmentary, even though close kin marriage has been recorded in many indigenous communities of both countries. Similarly, despite many reports in the anthropological and medical genetics literature, remarkably little quantitative information is available on the prevalence or tribal distribution of intra-familial marriage in Sub-Saharan Africa (Murdock 1967; Bittles 2012: 58–59).

Data are also limited on the prevalence of consanguineous unions in migrant communities that originated in countries where consanguinity is traditionally favoured and are now resident in Western Europe, North and South America and Oceania. While a substantial decline in consanguineous unions has been reported in the small Norwegian Pakistani community (Grjibovski et al. 2009),

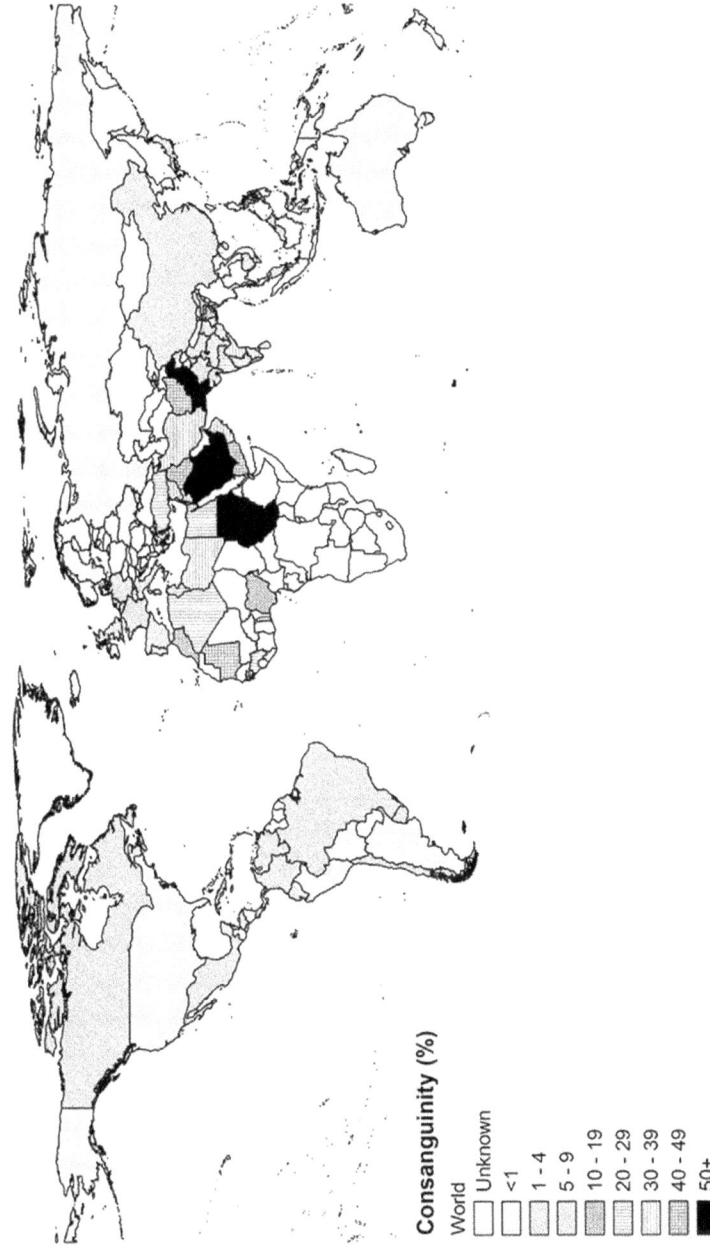

FIGURE 1.1 Global Distribution of Marriages Between Couples Related as Second Cousins or Closer. © 2014 Alan Bittles.

no equivalent major reduction has been apparent in the approximately one million-strong UK Pakistani population (Shaw 2000), although an ongoing study in Bradford in the North of England has suggested a reduction in the prevalence of first cousin unions (Bhopal et al. 2013). Consanguineous unions also continue to be widely contracted within the Turkish and Moroccan migrant communities in Belgium and The Netherlands (Reniers 1998; Waelput and Achterberg 2007), and in the Lebanese community in Australia (de Costa 1988).

As the USA is a major recipient of immigrants, one might expect an equivalent situation there. However, despite a unanimous recommendation by the National Conference of Commissioners on Uniform State Laws (1970) that first cousin marriage should be freely permitted throughout the USA, it remains a civil or criminal offence in thirty-one of the fifty states (Ottenheimer 1996; Paul and Spencer 2008; Bittles and Black 2010). Not surprisingly, under these conditions representative prevalence estimates for consanguineous unions at state or national level have not been collated.

Religious and Cultural Attitudes to Consanguinity

The predominant attitudes towards close kin unions in the major world religions, summarized in Table 1.1, indicate an overall

TABLE 1.1 Religious Attitudes to Consanguineous Marriage

Judaism	Sephardi	Permissive
	Askenazi	Permissive
Christianity	Coptic Orthodox	Permissive
	Greek and Russian Orthodox	Proscribed
	Roman Catholic	Diocesan approval required
	Protestant	Permissive
Islam	Sunni	Permissive
	Shia	Permissive
Hinduism	Indo-European	Proscribed
	Dravidian	Permissive
Buddhism	Theravada	Permissive
	Tibetan	Proscribed
Sikhism		Proscribed
Confucian/Taoist		Partially permissive
Zoroastrian/Parsi		Permissive

correlation with the distribution patterns of consanguineous marriage. In general terms, most of the major faiths at least tolerate consanguineous unions, major exceptions being the Orthodox branch of Christianity, and the Roman Catholic Church which until 1917 required Diocesan dispensation for marriages between couples related as third cousins or closer, with dispensation still needed for the solemnization of first cousin marriages (Cavalli-Sforza et al. 2004; Bittles 2012: 15–19).

Specific exceptions to such general rulings do, however, exist across religions, for example, with first cousin marriage permitted by the Coptic Church, which separated from the other branches of the Orthodox faith on doctrinal grounds in 451 AD. Within the Christian Protestant denominations first cousin marriage is also freely permitted, following the Judaic guidelines on consanguineous marriage listed in the Biblical Book of Leviticus 18: 6–18, yet first cousin unions are not recognized by the Society of Friends (Quakers). By comparison, although there is a general avoidance of consanguineous marriage within the Sikh religion, first cousin unions are contracted by Sikh communities in the predominantly Muslim Pakistani region of Swat (Wahab and Ahmad 2005).

Other than European Muslim populations in Bosnia, Kosovo and Albania, consanguineous marriage is contracted throughout the Islamic world to varying extents, with the highest overall rates in the Gulf region, Sudan, Afghanistan and Pakistan (www.consang.net); for example, in a representative national study in Pakistan 50.3 per cent of marriages were between first cousins and a further 10.9 per cent between second cousins (Ahmed et al. 1992). Besides local cultural preferences, where different branches of Islam coexist the level of consanguineous marriage can be influenced by population size and structure, as illustrated by the significantly higher rate of consanguineous marriage among the minority Sunni Persian community in Iran (52.1 per cent) than in the Shia Persian majority (30.0 per cent) (Saadat et al. 2004).

A major doctrinal schism exists in Hinduism with respect to consanguineous marriage. Prior to marriage in the North Indian Indo-European branch of Hinduism, family records are examined for seven generations on the male side and five generations on the female side to preclude an inadvertent kin relationship (Kapadia 1958). By comparison, in the Dravidian Hindu populations of South India both uncle-niece ($F = 0.125$) and first cousin marriages are traditional and have continued to be favoured in recent generations (Bittles et al. 1991).

Similar but less pronounced divisions exist within Buddhism, with first cousin marriage commonplace in the Theravada branch centred on India and Sri Lanka. In Southeast and East Asia the level of preference for or avoidance of consanguinity varies from country to country. But in the Tibetan branch of Mahayana Buddhism, which also has many adherents in North and Northeast India, consanguineous marriage is strictly avoided.

Civil Legislation on Consanguineous Marriage

In addition to the restrictions on consanguineous marriage that apply at state level in the USA, first cousin marriage is banned in the People's Republic of China, Taiwan, the Republic of Korea, the Democratic People's Republic of Korea, and The Philippines, with the prohibition extending to second and third cousin unions in the two Koreas. In most cases the underlying reason for the prohibition appears to be cultural in origin, although the 1981 Marriage Law of China prohibiting first cousin marriage was more overtly eugenic in its intent and was introduced as part of a suite of laws aimed at minimizing the occurrence of genetic disorders (Bittles 2012: 35–36). Cultural exceptions were, however, included in the Chinese legislation to permit first cousin marriage in ethnic communities (*minzu*) among whom consanguinity was a long-standing tradition. In practical terms the consanguinity restrictions imposed by the 1981 Marriage Law have largely proved to be redundant, since the prior introduction of the One Child Certificate Programme in 1979 has severely restricted the numbers of first cousins available for marriage, exacerbated in many areas by female foeticide and the resultant highly skewed secondary sex ratios.

Global Trends in Consanguineous Marriage

Apart from recent Asian and African immigrant populations, in Western societies there has been a significant general decline in consanguineous marriage from the mid-nineteenth century onwards, with first cousin marriage rates of 0.6 per cent or less in the current populations of these countries (Bittles 2012: 59). In Japan the decline in consanguineous marriage has been both more recent and significantly more rapid (Imaizumi 1986), so that in metropolitan regions the level of consanguineous marriage now approximates to that in Western societies.

Elsewhere in the world the picture is much more mixed, for example, with a reduction in consanguineous marriage reported in some countries of the Middle East, including Lebanon, Saudi Arabia, Kuwait, Jordan and the Palestinian Territories, but an increase in the United Arab Emirates, Yemen and Qatar (Bittles and Hamamy 2010). In South Asia a decline in uncle-niece and to a lesser extent first cousin marriage has been reported in South India (Krishnamoorthy and Audinarayana 2001). But there seems to have been little recent change in the popularity of cousin unions in other South Asian countries, such as Iran (Abbasi-Shavazi et al. 2008) or Afghanistan (Saify and Saadat 2012).

To some extent the explanation for these variant findings lies in the availability of relatives deemed acceptable for marriage, e.g. with a parallel union between a man and his father's brother's daughter preferred in Arab societies but avoided in South India where a cross-cousin marriage between a man and his mother's brother's daughter is the norm (Bittles 2001). However, an additional reason may be the present high levels of political and civil unrest in many parts of the world, resulting in a slower decline in customary intra-familial marriage than had been anticipated or in some cases increased rates of consanguinity, e.g. the Pakistani province of Khyber Pakhtunkhwa (formerly the North-West Frontier Province) adjacent to Afghanistan (Sthanadar et al. 2014). In such regions consanguineous marriage is strongly associated with ensuring personal security through the maintenance of close family ties (Bittles 2012: 63–66).

That said, from a global perspective it does seems inevitable that a combination of rapid urbanization, the associated depopulation of close-knit rural communities, significant reductions in family sizes, and enhanced female as well as male educational and employment opportunities will collectively contribute to a decline in close kin unions, with the closer forms of consanguinity such as uncle-niece or double first cousin unions (both $F = 0.125$) most immediately affected.

Consanguinity-Associated Risks to Offspring Health

Many early reports on morbidity and mortality associated with consanguineous marriage were exaggerated, due to poor individual study design and widespread failure to adequately control for non-genetic variables, such as maternal age and education, birth order and birth intervals. When appropriate data were collected and multivariate analysis was applied to account for non-genetic variables, quite different results were obtained, as in the 1990/91 Pakistan Demographic and Health Survey, where consanguinity at first cousin level (Odds Ratio 1.32) ranked behind birth interval (OR 2.70), maternal education (OR 2.42), and young maternal age (OR 1.52) as a contributory cause of infant deaths, and exerted no significant effect on deaths in children aged two to five years (Grant and Bittles 1997).

Although still imperfect in terms of data collection and control for socio-demographic variables, recent multi-national meta-analyses based on a combined sample size of some 5 million have estimated that the increased mean risk of stillbirth at first cousin level is 0.5 per cent, with infant deaths increased by 1.3 per cent, and deaths from approximately the twenty-eighth week of pregnancy to eight/ten years of age being 3.7 per cent higher than in the children of unrelated parents (Bittles 2012: 123–135).

Consanguinity, Endogamy and Patterns and Prevalence of Genetic Disease

It would be expected that a global decline in consanguineous marriage would be accompanied by a reduction in the expression of recessive disease genes and thus an overall improvement in population health (Campbell et al. 2009). Preliminary data from the USA (Nalls et al. 2009) and the Dalmatian islands of Croatia (Rudan et al. 2003a, 2003b) suggest that these trends are already underway in Western societies, with reduced rates of both single gene disorders and complex diseases of adulthood provisionally identified.

The extent to which this change can reasonably be generalized has, however, been overstated since a large majority of societies which favour close kin marriage also are typified by structured subdivision, e.g. into clans and tribes in Arab society, castes in India, and *biraderi* in Pakistan (Bittles 2008). So whether or not a marriage has been arranged within the family, in these societies it will almost certainly be with another member of one's own sub-community. Besides the social implications, this sub-division is very important from a genetic perspective since, in effect, the difference between a consanguineous and an endogamous marriage is quantitative rather than qualitative, and is primarily indicative of the historical and present-day size and composition of the gene pool from which a spouse is chosen.

A second equally important consideration concerns the division of populations into individual endogamous communities and sub-communities, which over multiple generations would predictably have accumulated specific founder mutations and thus developed unique mutation profiles (Bittles and Black 2010). Failure to acknowledge these often complex levels of sub-division, and instead to treat individual populations as homogeneous entities, can lead to significant over-estimation of the frequency of disease mutations and the numbers of affected individuals (Overall 2009).

In both of these scenarios predictions regarding the beneficial health effects of a shift away from consanguineous marriage will be exaggerated. It could therefore be argued that at least in the short- to medium-term a reduction in family sizes would be a far more efficient way to lessen the burden of inherited diseases, particularly in families where reproductive compensation occurs following the early death of an affected child (Schull and Neel 1972; Overall et al. 2002).

Conclusions

Many important aspects of the impact of consanguinity on human health remain only partially resolved. For example, as previously noted, intra-familial marriage in successive generations can result in greater than expected levels of genomic homozygosity (Woods et al. 2006). Therefore in communities with a strong tradition of consanguineous marriage some upward adjustment of the adverse effects of intra-familial unions on mortality and morbidity may be necessary, but to date no detailed data on this topic have been forthcoming.

From quite a different perspective it is unclear whether the increased levels of homozygosity associated with consanguinity should be regarded as beneficial in terms of the spontaneous elimination of detrimental mutations *in utero*, described in the genetics literature as purging of the gene pool. Pre-implantation losses across all pregnancies are probably very high but information on the subject is largely speculative (Boklage 1990). By comparison, human chorionic gonadotrophin (hCG) studies have clearly indicated overall post-implantation losses of approximately 30–45 per cent (Wilcox et al. 1988; Zinaman et al. 1996), rising very significantly to over 90 per cent in women approaching menopause (Holman and Wood 2001). Studies on miscarriages in the later stages of pregnancy have so far failed to demonstrate convincing evidence of increased consanguinity-associated losses (Bittles 2012: 101–103), possibly because of minimal control for known variables that include the order of pregnancy (Roman et al. 1980), maternal age (Nybo Andersen et al. 2000), and levels of maternal education and family income (Norsker et al. 2012).

The reporting of consanguinity-associated health risks is an especially problematic issue that merits speedy resolution. For example, in the large resident Pakistani community in Bradford the risk of a child being born with a congenital anomaly was 2.6 per cent if the parents were unrelated but 6.2 per cent in first cousin progeny (Sheridan et al. 2013). On the basis of these findings it was widely reported that the children of first cousin couples would be subject to 'a doubling of risk' of a congenital anomaly (Bittles 2013). Rather than 'a doubling of risk', which to many would seem to indicate a highly significant increase in prevalence, the adverse consanguinity-associated outcomes could equally have been expressed as an average excess risk of 3.6 per cent, or conversely that some fifteen of sixteen first cousin progeny would not have a birth defect (see also chapter five, this volume).

Currently there are no reports on the extent to which these quite different approaches to expressing adverse pregnancy outcomes might influence the reproductive plans of first cousin couples. The collection and dissemination of information of this nature could therefore make a valuable contribution towards future genetics education and genetic counselling programmes for consanguineous couples, and possibly also help to improve the frequently ill-informed prejudicial attitudes to legal close kin marriage that exist in most Western countries.

In summary, with a topic as potentially contentious as consanguineous marriage it is essential that health-based studies are well designed and that they incorporate relevant control for non-genetic variables (Hamamy et al. 2011). Of equal importance, the information derived on health risks and provided by health professionals needs to be conveyed in a precise, unambiguous and culturally appropriate manner. Failure to fulfil these basic criteria will predictably result in continued suspicion and misunderstanding of consanguinity, to the detriment of individual cousin couples and communities in which consanguineous unions are customary.

References

Abbasi-Shavazi, M.J., P. McDonald and M. Hosseini-Chavoshi. 2008. 'Modernization or cultural maintenance: the practice of consanguineous marriage in Iran', *Journal of Biosocial Science* 40: 911–933.

Ahmed, T., S.M. Ali, A. Aliaga et al. 1992. *Pakistan Demographic and Health Survey 1990/91*. Islamabad and Columbia, MD: Pakistan National Institute of Population Studies and Macro International.

Bhopal, R.S., E.S. Petherick, J. Wright and N. Small. 2013. 'Potential social, economic and general health benefits of consanguineous marriage: the Born in Bradford Cohort Study', *European Journal of Public Health*, doi: 10.1093/eurpub/ckt166.

Bittles, A.H. 2001. 'Consanguinity and its relevance to clinical genetics', *Clinical Genetics* 60: 89–98.

———. 2008. 'A Community Genetics perspective on consanguineous marriage', *Community Genetics* 11: 324–330.

———. 2009. 'Consanguinity, genetic drift and genetic diseases in populations with reduced numbers of founders', in M. Speicher, S.E. Antonarakis and A.G. Motulsky (eds), *Human Genetics – Principles and Approaches*, 4th edn. Heidelberg: Springer, pp.507–528.

———. 2012. *Consanguinity in Context*. Cambridge: Cambridge University Press.

———. 2013. 'Consanguineous marriages and congenital anomalies', *Lancet* 382: 1316–1317.

Bittles, A.H. and M.L. Black. 2010. 'Evolution in health and medicine Sackler colloquium: consanguinity, human evolution and complex diseases', *Proceedings of the National Academy of Sciences of the United States of America* 107: 1779–1786.

Bittles, A.H. and H. Hamamy. 2010. 'Endogamy and consanguineous marriage in Arab populations', in A. Teebi (ed.), *Genetic Disorders among Arab Populations*, 2nd edn. Heidelberg: Springer, pp.85–108.

Bittles, A.H., W.M. Mason, J. Greene and N. Appaji Rao. 1991. 'Reproductive behavior and health in consanguineous marriages', *Science* 252: 789–794.

Boklage, C.E. 1990. 'Survival probability of human conceptions from fertilization to term', *International Journal of Fertility* 35: 75, 79–80, 81–94.

Campbell, H., I. Rudan, A.H. Bittles and A.F. Wright. 2009. 'Human population structure, genome autozygosity and human health', *Genome Medicine* 1: 91.

Cavalli-Sforza, L.L., A. Moroni and G. Zei. 2004. *Consanguinity, Inbreeding, and Genetic Drift in Italy*. Princeton: Princeton University Press.

de Costa, C. 1988. 'Pregnancy outcomes in Lebanese-born women in Western Sydney', *Medical Journal of Australia* 149: 457–460.

Grant, J.C. and A.H. Bittles. 1997. 'The comparative role of consanguinity in infant and childhood mortality in Pakistan', *Annals of Human Genetics* 61: 143–149.

Grjibovski, A.M., P. Magnus and C. Stoltenberg. 2009. 'Decrease in consanguinity among parents of children born in Norway to women of

Pakistani origin: a registry-based study', *Scandinavian Journal of Public Health* 37: 232–238.

Hamamy, H., et al. 2011. 'Consanguineous marriages, pearls and perils: Geneva International Consanguinity Workshop Report', *Genetics in Medicine* 13: 841–847.

Holman, D.J. and J.W. Wood. 2001. 'Pregnancy loss and fecundability in women', in P. Ellison (ed.), *Reproductive Ecology and Human Evolution*. Hawthorne, NY: Aldine de Gruyter, pp.15–38.

Imaizumi, Y. 1986. 'A recent survey of consanguineous marriages in Japan', *Clinical Genetics* 30: 230–233.

Kapadia, K.M. 1958. *Marriage and Family in India*, 2nd edn. Calcutta: Oxford University Press, pp.117–137.

Krishnamoorthy, S. and N. Audinarayana. 2001. 'Trends in consanguinity in South India', *Journal of Biosocial Science* 33: 185–197.

Murdock, G.P. 1967. *Ethnographic Atlas*. Pittsburgh: University of Pittsburgh Press.

Nalls, M.A., et al. 2009. 'Measures of autozygosity in decline: globalization, urbanization, and its implications for medical genetics', *PLoS Genetics* 5: e1000415.

National Conference of Commissioners. 1970. *Handbook on Uniform State Laws and Proceedings of the Annual Conference Meeting in its Seventy-ninth Year*. Baltimore MD: Port City Press.

Norsker, F.N., L. Espenhain, S. Rogvi, C.S. Morgen, P.K. Andersen and A.M. Nybo Andersen. 2012. 'Socioeconomic position and the risk of spontaneous abortion: a study within the Danish National Birth Cohort', *BMJ Open*, 2: pii: e001077.

Nybo Andersen, A.M., J. Wohlfahrt, P. Christens, J. Olsen and M. Melbye. 2000. 'Maternal age and fetal loss: population based register linkage study', *BMJ* 320: 1708–1712.

Ottenheimer, M. 1996. *Forbidden Relatives – the American Myth of Cousin Marriage*. Chicago: University of Illinois Press.

Overall, A.D.J. 2009. 'The influence of the Wahlund effect on the consanguinity hypothesis: consequences for recessive disease incidence in a socially structured Pakistani population', *Human Heredity* 67: 140–144.

Overall, A.D.J., M. Ahmad and R.A. Nichols. 2002. 'The effect of reproductive compensation on recessive disorders within consanguineous human populations', *Heredity* 88: 474–479.

Paul, D.B. and H.G. Spencer. 2008. '"It's OK, we're not cousins by blood": the cousin marriage controversy in historical perspective', *PLoS Biology* 6: 2627–2630.

Reniers, G. 1998. *Postmigration Survival of Traditional Marriage Patterns: Consanguineous Marriage among Turkish and Moroccan Immigrants in Belgium*. Interuniversity Papers in Demography, PPD-1 Working Paper 1998–1. Ghent: Department of Population Studies, University of Ghent.

Roman, E.A., E. Alberman and P.O. Pharaoh. 1980. 'Pregnancy order and reproductive loss', *British Medical Journal* 280: 715.
Rudan, I., D. Rudan, H. Campbell, A. Carothers, A. Wright, N. Smolej-Narančić, B. Janicijevic, L. Jin, R. Chakraborty, R. Deka and P. Rudan, P. 2003a. 'Inbreeding and the risk of late onset complex disease', *Journal of Medical Genetics* 40: 925–932.
Rudan, I., H. Campbell, A. Carothers, A. Wright, N. Smolej-Narančić, B. Janicijevic and P. Rudan. 2003b. 'Inbreeding and the genetic complexity of human hypertension', *Genetics* 163: 1011–1021.
Saadat, M., M. Ansari-Lari and D.D. Farhud. 2004. 'Consanguineous marriage in Iran', *Annals of Human Biology* 31: 263–269.
Saify, K. and M. Saadat. 2012. 'Consanguineous marriages in Afghanistan', *Journal of Biosocial Science* 44: 72–81.
Schull, W.J. and J.V. Neel. 1972. 'The effects of parental consanguinity and inbreeding in Hirado, Japan. V. Summary and interpretation', *American Journal of Human Genetics* 24: 425–453.
Shaw, A. 2000. 'Kinship, cultural preference and immigration: consanguineous marriage among British Pakistanis', *Journal of the Royal Anthropological Institute* 7: 315–334.
Sheridan, E., J. Wright, N. Small, P.C. Corry, S. Oddie, C. Whibley, E.S. Petherick, T. Malik, N. Pawson, P.A. McKinney and R.C. Parslow. 2013. 'Risk factors for congenital anomaly in a multi-ethnic birth cohort: an analysis of the Born in Bradford study', *Lancet* 382: 1350–1359.
Sthanadar, A.A., A.H. Bittles and M. Zahid. 2014. 'Civil unrest and the current profile of consanguineous marriage in Khyber Pakhtunkhwa Province, Pakistan', *Journal of Biosocial Science* 46: 698–781.
Waelput, A.J.M. and P.W Achterberg. 2007. *Kinderwens van Consanguïne Ouders: Risico's en Erfelijkheidsvoorlichting*, RIVM Rapport 270032003/2007. RIVM: Bilthoven.
Wahab, A. and M. Ahmad. 2005. 'Consanguineous marriages in the Sikh community of Swat, NWFP, Pakistan', *Journal of Social Science* 10: 153–157.
Wilcox, A.J., C.R. Weinberg, J.F. O'Connor, D.D. Baird, J.P. Schlatterer, R.E. Canfield, E.G. Armstrong and B.C. Nisula. 1988. 'Incidence of early loss of pregnancy', *New England Journal of Medicine* 319: 189–194.
Woods, G.C., J. Cox, K. Springell, D.J. Hampshire, M.D. Mohamed, M. McKibbin, R. Stern, F.L. Raymond, R. Sandford, S. Malik Sharif, G. Karbani, M. Ahmed, J. Bond, D. Clayton and C.F. Inglehearn. 2006. 'Quantification of homozygosity in consanguineous individuals with autosomal recessive disease', *American Journal of Human Genetics* 78: 889–896.
Zinaman, M.J., E.D. Clegg, C.C. Brown, J. O'Connor and S.G. Selevan. 1996. 'Estimates of human fertility and pregnancy loss', *Fertility and Sterility* 65: 503–509.

Chapter 2

RISK CALCULATIONS IN CONSANGUINITY

Leo P. ten Kate, Marieke E. Teeuw, Lidewij Henneman and Martina C. Cornel

Lay knowledge holding that consanguinity of parents carries a risk for the health of their children is widespread, especially in Western countries, but the level of this risk is often overestimated. In this chapter we will discuss how to arrive at realistic estimates of these risks. Such estimates are based partly on mathematical reasoning (risk calculation) and partly on empirical data (observational studies). For a proper understanding, we must start with some indispensable basic knowledge of formal genetics and population genetics. Next we will demonstrate how to arrive at consanguinity risk estimates for single diseases. Risk estimates for all autosomal recessive diseases in children of consanguineous parents will then be considered, after which we will summarize how to arrive at the grand total risk for individual couples. Appendix One (Glossary) and Appendix Two (Symbols and Equations) are added for quick reference.

Basic Knowledge

There are many different types of genetic diseases. Some are caused by changes – visible through microscopes or demonstrable through molecular techniques – in the number or structure of chromosomes (chromosomal disorders). Others are caused by alterations in single genes (monogenic disorders), and still others are caused by variants in many genes mostly in combination with environmental factors (multifactorial disorders). The monogenic disorders can be sub-classified according to the type of chromosome on which the gene resides (autosome or sex-chromosome) and pattern of inheritance (dominant or recessive). Although some influence of parental consanguinity on multifactorial disorders cannot be excluded, the clearest risk increase for children of consanguineous parents is for autosomal recessive diseases.

Autosomal genes in humans are located in chromosomes 1–22 (the autosomes), and not in the X- or Y-chromosome (the sex chromosomes). Since everyone with a normal number of chromosomes typically has two copies of each autosome, every individual also has all autosomal genes in duplicate: one copy derived from the father and one from the mother. As a parent, one has an equal chance of passing on the grand paternal or the grand maternal copy to a child. Whichever copy a child receives is a matter of chance and is completely independent of what his or her sibling already obtained.

Autosomal Recessive Diseases

When a gene contains a pathogenic mutation, this may result in a genetic disease. Whether this occurs depends, first of all, on the answer to the question: Is this mutation recessive or dominant? Recessive mutations will not come to expression when the other copy of the gene is normal, i.e. does not contain a pathogenic mutation. The normal copy compensates for the presence of a mutated copy. Persons having one copy with a recessive mutation and one normal copy of the same gene are called carriers. As new mutations only rarely occur, most mutations in carriers are inherited from a parent that is a carrier of this mutation too. As carriership shows no signs or symptoms, without further information or testing it is not possible to determine which one of the two parents of a carrier is the carrier that transmitted the mutated copy.

Individuals with recessive pathogenic mutations on both copies of a gene do not have a normal copy to compensate for the recessive mutation, and will be affected by the associated recessive disease. Since most recessive diseases interfere with the ability to reproduce, most affected children will have parents who are both unaffected, yet carriers. If two carriers mate, every child of theirs has a 1 in 4 (or 25 per cent) chance of becoming affected, a 1 in 2 (50 per cent) chance of becoming a carrier, and a 1 in 4 (25 per cent) chance of inheriting the normal copies of both parents (see Table 2.1).

TABLE 2.1 Autosomal Recessive Inheritance when Both Parents are Carriers

Parents		Carrier Father	
	Gene	Normal copy N	*mutated* copy *m*
Carrier Mother	Normal copy N	NN unaffected, not carrier	N*m* unaffected, carrier
	mutated copy *m*	N*m* unaffected, carrier	*mm* affected

Each parent has a 50 per cent chance of transmitting the normal copy of the gene (N) and 50 per cent of transmitting the mutated copy (*m*). Therefore a child has a 25 per cent probability of inheriting only the two normal copies (NN), a 25 per cent probability of receiving only mutated copies (*mm*), and a 50 per cent probability of getting both the normal and the mutated copy (N*m*).

As these are chances, the actual situation may differ between families. For instance, for a carrier couple with four children, there is a 32 per cent chance that no one will be affected, a 42 per cent chance that precisely one will be affected, a 21 per cent chance that just two will be affected, and so on (see Appendix Three, Part 1).

There are several exceptions to the rule that both parents of a child with an autosomal recessive disorder are carriers. If the disorder is less severe and does not interfere with reproduction, one or even both parents may have two mutated copies of the relevant gene, and be affected too. Families with autosomal recessive deafness provide many examples of this situation. Another, but very rare, exception to the rule is when only one of the parents of a child with an autosomal recessive disease is a carrier, while the other is not a carrier. Apart from non-paternity and new mutations, this situation may occur when both copies of the relevant gene in the patient derive from the carrier parent with no contribution from the other parent. This constellation is known as uniparental disomy. In the rest of this chapter we will ignore these exceptions and stick to the general rule that both parents of a child with an autosomal recessive disease are carriers of a mutation in the relevant gene.

A great many different autosomal recessive diseases are known at present, but new ones are continuously being discovered. The total number of such diseases must be several thousands. Most of these are rare, if not very rare, but their total is still substantial. One in every 400 newborns (0.25 per cent) has an autosomal recessive disease which becomes manifest in early life (UNSCEAR 2001). Well known examples are cystic fibrosis, sickle cell anaemia, the thalassaemias, and many inborn errors of metabolism, several of which are included in newborn screening programmes. A notable example of the last category is phenylketonuria (PKU), where the development of a severe intellectual handicap can be prevented by dietary measures.

Gene Frequency and Carrier Frequency

An important parameter in the context of risk calculation is the so-called gene frequency. By this we mean how often we will find a particular variant of a gene if we draw that gene from the population. For instance, we may want to know the gene frequency of pathogenic mutations in the *CFTR* gene. If present in both copies of the gene, pathogenic *CFTR* mutations cause the cystic fibrosis (CF) disorder. In order to calculate properly, we must bear in mind the fact that every person has two copies of this autosomal gene. So if we study 3000 persons, we are in fact observing 6000 copies of the *CFTR* gene. If we find 100 mutated copies, then the frequency of mutated genes, in this group of 3000 people, is 100 in 6000, or 1 in 60; while conversely the frequency of the normal copy is 59/60.

If one knows the gene frequency of particular mutations in a population, one can deduce how frequently the disorder occurs in newborns in that population. As the disorder only occurs when both copies of the gene are mutated, and as each copy has a chance of 1 in 60 of being mutated, the chance of being affected by the disorder becomes $1/60 \times 1/60$ (=1/3600). [For the sake of comparison, the chance of throwing two sixes with two dice is $1/6 \times 1/6$, or 1/36.]

It can be shown that for serious autosomal disorders the frequency of carriers in the population is twice the gene frequency, i.e. 1/30 in our example. The chance that two partners of a couple are both carriers is then $1/30 \times 1/30$, or 1/900. As children of such couples have a risk of 1 in 4 of being affected, the prevalence of the disease in newborns will be $1/900 \times 1/4$, i.e. 1/3600, a result that complies completely with what we showed above.

Single gene frequencies are population-specific; carrier frequencies are also population-specific. It is for instance well known that gene and carrier frequencies of CF are much higher in populations of European descent than in populations of African or Asian descent.

Risk Estimates for Single Autosomal Recessive Diseases in Children of Consanguineous Parents

When an autosomal recessive disorder occurs in a family, it is clear that there must be several carriers in the family: both parents, at least two grandparents, some aunts and uncles, siblings, etc. So it is not difficult to imagine that someone coming from such a family who marries a family member will have an increased risk of having affected children. However, it can also be shown that marrying a family member when there is no autosomal recessive disorder known in the family also increases the risk of having affected children. We will discuss both situations separately below.

Disorders Already Present in the Family

Suppose a healthy man who has a sister with CF considers marrying the daughter of his father's brother (Figure 2.1). What are the chances of a child of this couple being born with CF? To answer this question we have to know what the chances are that this man and his cousin are carriers. As shown in Table 2.1, two-thirds of the healthy siblings of a patient with an autosomal recessive disease are carriers. So the chance that this man (G in Figure 2.1) is a carrier is 2/3. For his cousin (F) we have to follow the possible track of the mutated allele through the pedigree. We may assume that the father (D) of the man is a carrier: he has a daughter (H) with CF. We may also assume that one of the parents of this father (D) is a carrier. (We ignore in what follows the possibility that both parents are carriers, since this has a low probability and therefore only a small impact on the risk figure.) The chance that the brother (C) of this father has the same mutated gene is therefore 1/2. When this brother of his father is indeed a carrier, there is a 1 in 2 chance that he will pass the mutated gene on to his daughter (F). So her chance of being a carrier is 1/2 (her father is a carrier) times 1/2 (she inherits the mutated gene if present in her father), or 1 in 4. So the chances that the brother of the CF patient and his cousin are both carriers is 2/3 times 1/4, or 1/6, and the chance that a child of theirs will be affected by CF is 1/4 of this 1/6, i.e. 1/24.

How does this compare to a marriage with an unrelated partner? For an unrelated partner, the best estimate of her likelihood of being a carrier is the carrier frequency in the population. For the population in our example this is 1/30, i.e. 7.5 times less than in a first cousin. So the chances of CF in a child of the brother of the CF patient are 7.5 times higher if he marries a first cousin, than if he

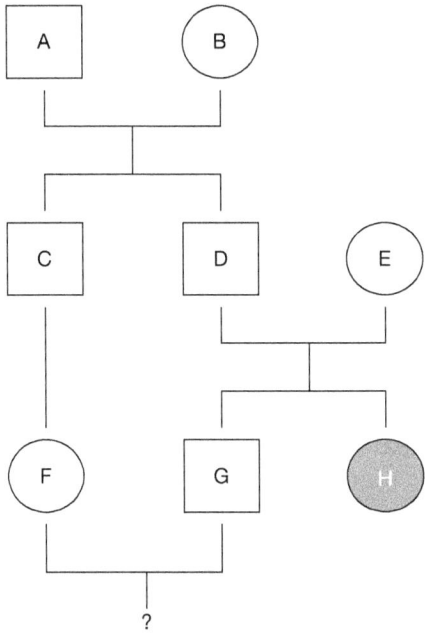

FIGURE 2.1 Pedigree of Family with One Patient with CF (H) whose Brother (G) Wants to Marry his First Cousin (F)
○ = female, □ = male

chooses an unrelated bride: 1/24 compared to 1/180. Fortunately, carrier testing is now available for a large number of recessive diseases, and if both partners turn out to be carriers, reproductive options can be discussed.

In the first situation described above (brother of CF patient marrying his first cousin), apart from neglecting the possibility that both grandparents (A and B) may be carriers instead of only one of them, we also ignored the possibility that the mother of the first cousin could be a carrier of CF. This simplification is justified for the same reason: the risk resulting from taking this possibility into account is very small compared to the risk based on the consanguineous relation between the man and his first cousin. So we do not take the carrier frequency in the population into account. Therefore the risk we calculated (1/24) applies to every other rare autosomal recessive disorder as well.

In the other situation described above (brother of patient marrying an unrelated partner) we cannot ignore the carrier frequency. If the carrier frequency was, for example, 1/300, the risk of the child having the same recessive condition as the sister of the man becomes 1/1800. So here the risk from a consanguineous marriage is 75 times higher than when a sibling of a patient has an unrelated spouse.

Disorders Not Already Present in the Family

Let us consider now the risk of CF in a child if the condition is not known to occur in the family. When both partners of the couple are unrelated, this risk is 1 in 3600. When partners are related, the risk is higher; and the risk increases the closer the relationship.

Figure 2.2 shows a related couple (G and H) with their parents (C, D, E and F), grandparents (A and B), and expected child (the question mark). The main difference with an unrelated couple is the possibility that a particular copy of the *CFTR* gene of one of the grandparents is transmitted to the expected child through both its father and its mother. In this case this grandparental copy of the gene 'meets itself' in the child. It is said to be identical by descent in the child. The probability that a gene is identical by descent in a child of consanguineous parents can be calculated by multiplying the probability of transmission of a particular copy of a gene from one generation to the other through both parents with the total number of copies of this gene in each of the closest common ancestors (see Appendix Three, Part 2). This probability is called the inbreeding coefficient, and is dependent on the type of relatedness of the parents of the expected child. Table 2.2 shows the inbreeding coefficient for a number of situations.

Being identical by descent in itself does not make a gene harmful, but when the gene contains a pathogenic mutation the child having two mutated copies will be affected. If, following common practice, the frequency of a pathogenic mutation in a gene is called q, and the inbreeding coefficient is called F, then the probability of a recessive disease on the basis of identity by descent of the gene will be F x q, or Fq for short. So, in our case, in which F = 1/16 and q = 1/60, there is a probability of 1/16 x 1/60, or 1/960, that the child has CF by this mechanism of identity by descent.

TABLE 2.2 Inbreeding Coefficients for Some Different Types of Consanguineous Marriages

Uncle-niece	First cousins	Double first cousins	First cousins once removed	Second cousins
1/8	1/16	1/8	1/32	1/64

However, this is not the only way in which this child can have two mutated copies. This is also possible when there is no identity by descent, with mutated copies coming from different ancestors. Figure 2.2 shows that there are six different ways to combine copies coming from A, B, C and F. The probability of this event (no identity by descent) is the complement of the probability of identity by descent, and therefore can be written as 1–F, or 15/16 in our case. In this case a recessive disorder can occur only if by chance both copies of the gene are mutated, which is q × q. So the probability of CF in the expected child not being caused by identity by descent in this family is 15/16 × 1/60 × 1/60, or 1/3840. (Although we argued in a previous section of this chapter that in some situations it is permissible to ignore the possibility of multiple independent carriers in the ancestry, ignoring this possibility in the present section would lead us to completely overlook the chance that a disorder in a child of a consanguineous couple may not be due to the consanguinity of its parents.)

We can now calculate the total chance that the expected child will have CF even though the disorder is not known to occur in the family. This chance is the sum of both probabilities of having two

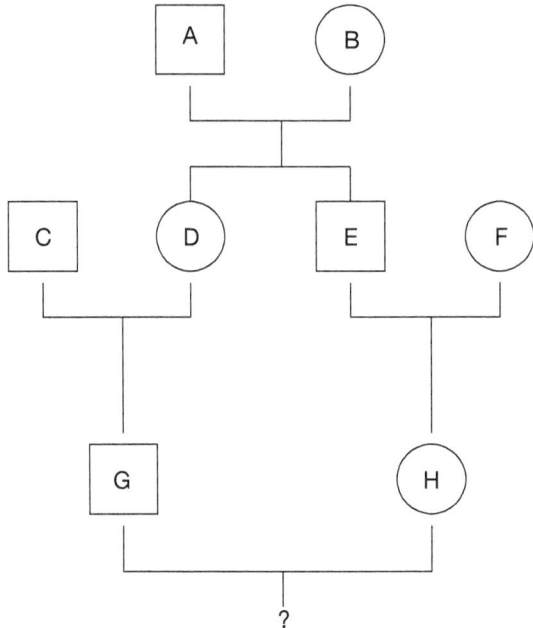

FIGURE 2.2 First-Cousin Marriage in a Family with No Known Patients with Autosomal Recessive Disorders
○ = female, □ = male

mutated copies of the *CFTR* gene, one based on identity by descent and the other in the absence of identity by descent. In our example this is 1/960 + 1/3840, or 1/768. This is almost five times higher than in the absence of consanguinity, where it is 1/3600. So, in general, the equation that allows us to calculate the probability of a particular autosomal recessive disease in a child given a specific consanguineous relation of his or her parents is: $Fq + (1-F)q^2$. In fact, this equation also holds when there is no consanguinity: in that case, F equals zero and the equation reduces to q^2.

As shown above, apart from calculating the probability of disease given the presence of parental consanguinity, we are now also able to calculate the increase in risk caused by this consanguinity. But the equation has more useful properties. For instance, by dividing the first part (Fq) of the equation by the total equation ($Fq + (1-F)q^2$), we can calculate the probability that the disorder of the child is attributable to the consanguinity of the parents, and by dividing the second part $(1-F)q^2$ by the same total equation, we obtain the probability that the disease cannot be attributed to the consanguinity of the parents. In our example, these probabilities are 80 per cent and 20 per cent, respectively. So when observing an autosomal recessive disorder in a child of consanguineous parents, one should not jump to the conclusion that this is the result of the consanguinity (ten Kate et al. 1991). Alternatively, if the disorder is rare, or the child is the result of incest, i.e. has a very high inbreeding coefficient, the chances that it is the result of the relatedness are always higher than the probability that it is not caused by the consanguinity (ten Kate 2010). Table 2.3 lists probabilities for first and second cousins by a number of different gene frequencies. The increase in risk and the fraction attributable to consanguinity are higher as the disorder becomes rarer and as the degree of consanguinity increases.

As shown in Table 2.3, the fraction not attributable to the existing consanguinity is even larger than the fraction due to consanguinity for offspring of second cousins when the gene frequency is 1/60 or higher. It is possible to refine our view on these matters if we know which mutations are involved. For instance, if a CF patient with consanguineous parents has two different mutations of the *CFTR* gene, e.g. delF508 and G542X, it is clear that the parental consanguinity cannot be blamed for the disease in the child. Having two different mutations in the same gene is called compound heterozygosity. If the patient has two similar mutations (homozygosity) the two may be identical by descent, or just identical by state, but not by descent. The relative proportions of compound heterozygotes,

TABLE 2.3 Comparison of Expected Frequencies of Some Selected Autosomal Recessive Diseases in the General Population and in Offspring of First and Second Cousins, with Fractions Attributable to the Consanguinity of the Parents.

Disorder	Gene frequency	Disease frequency	Offspring of first cousins				Offspring of second cousins			
			Disease frequency	Increase in risk	Fraction due to consanguinity	Fraction not due to consanguinity	Disease frequency	Increase in risk	Fraction due to consanguinity	Fraction not due to consanguinity
Cystic fibrosis	1/60	1/3600	1/768	5x	80%	20%	1/1873	2x	49%	51%
PKU	1/126	1/16000	1/1796	9x	89%	11%	1/5404	3x	66%	34%
Pompe disease	1/187	1/35000	1/2770	13x	93%	7%	1/8957	4x	75%	25%

The table is meant to illustrate the importance of gene frequency and degree of consanguinity for disease frequency, increase in risk, and fractions due or not due to consanguinity. As gene frequencies differ by population, the precise figures of disease frequency, risk increase, and fractions due or not due to consanguinity will also differ by population.

homozygotes which are identical by descent, and homozygotes which are identical by state but not by descent, depend on several factors: the inbreeding coefficient, the relative frequencies of different pathogenic mutations and the total gene frequency. If in a sample of patients the inbreeding coefficient and the relative proportion of different mutations are known, it is even possible to estimate from these data the gene frequency in the population to which the patients belong (ten Kate et al. 2010; Gialluissi et al. 2012).

Before we discuss the total risk of autosomal recessive disease in children of consanguineous parents, one should realize that the presence of mutations in different genes can be regarded as independent events. The same independence applies to carriership and the diseases themselves. So the child of the man (G in Figure 2.2), who has a sister with CF and marries his cousin, not only has an increased risk for CF, but also for the many other autosomal recessive diseases that exist and were not already present in their family.

Another final remark for this section: to keep things simple, the above calculations of inbreeding coefficients and risks for offspring of consanguineous parents were applied to rather simple pedigrees in which there is only one consanguineous loop. In practice pedigrees may be more complex, with more than one loop, and in those cases calculations also become more complex.

Risk Estimates for all Autosomal Recessive Diseases in Children of Consanguineous Parents

If we knew all autosomal recessive diseases, and their gene frequencies, in all populations, we could make the above calculations for every disease and arrive at a total estimate of autosomal recessive disease frequency in children of parents with each degree of relatedness. However, as we do not have this knowledge, we have to turn to empirical data that are available on firstly the total risk of congenital and/or genetic diseases in children of unrelated parents, and secondly the additional risk in children of consanguineous parents.

Empirical estimates differ from estimates based on theory, such as Mendelian inheritance, by a certain degree of uncertainty. Empirical estimates have confidence intervals, differ by inclusion and exclusion criteria, and are prone to several sorts of bias. So it is prudent to refer to them in terms that express this uncertainty, using adverbs or prepositions such as 'about', 'approximately' or 'not far from'.

For the rest of this chapter we will assume that the background population risk of medically relevant congenital anomalies is 2–3 per cent and that of serious autosomal recessive diseases, excluding hemochromatosis (a rather frequent late onset and relatively easily treatable condition), is 0.25 per cent (UNSCEAR 2001). Apart from autosomal recessive disorders, congenital anomalies include chromosomal anomalies, autosomal dominant and X-linked disorders, multifactorial, teratogenic disorders and disorders of unknown etiology. As the above risk figures show, autosomal recessive disorders are a small subset of the total of congenital anomalies in the general population. This contrasts sharply with their contribution to the total of congenital anomalies in children of consanguineous parents. As it is easier to obtain data on the total of congenital anomalies than on subgroups like autosomal recessive disorders, research in offspring of consanguineous couples has focused on the prevalence of congenital anomalies. The prevalence of congenital anomalies in offspring of first cousins is estimated to be 1.7–2.8 percentage points higher than the background population risk, mostly attributable to autosomal recessive diseases (Hamamy et al. 2011), So the extra risk for first cousins is about twice the background risk for congenital anomalies, and about ten times the background risk for autosomal recessive diseases. Adding the extra risk of 1.7–2.8 per cent to the population background risk of 0.25 per cent for autosomal recessive disorders results in an overall risk of, say, 2–3 per cent autosomal recessive disorders in children of first cousins.

From First Cousins to Other Degrees of Consanguinity

We stated above that the extra risk of congenital disorders in offspring of first cousins is estimated at 1.7–2.8 per cent above the general population risk. One may wonder what would be the extra risk for other degrees of consanguinity, e.g. second cousins. For a single disorder it can be shown that the extra risk from one degree of consanguinity to another degree changes to the same amount as the change in the inbreeding coefficient (see Appendix Three, Part 3). If this holds true for single disorders then it also holds true for the sum of all disorders. So an extra risk of 1.7–2.8 for the offspring of first cousins ($F = 1/16$) corresponds to an extra risk of 0.4–0.7 in offspring of second cousins (four times less, as $F = 1/64$ is also four times less) and of 3.4–5.6 in offspring of an uncle-niece relation (two times higher since F is here 1/8). When a pedigree has several consanguineous loops the inbreeding coefficient will be much higher than in the case of a simple pedigree with only one loop. Additional loops may not always be evident or known to the consanguineous couple, for instance when they have occurred in earlier generations, making the couple more related than was first assumed.

Which Proportion of Consanguineous Couples is at Risk of an Autosomal Recessive Disorder in their Children?

When we know how frequent a particular autosomal recessive disease is in a population, we can infer from this knowledge the frequency of carrier couples in that population. Since each child of a carrier couple has a one in four risk, the frequency of carrier couples is four times the frequency of the disease in question. If we apply the four times rule (saying that the frequency of carrier couples is four times the frequency of a particular autosomal recessive disease) to this overall risk, we arrive at an estimate of 8–12 per cent for carrier couples among first-cousin marriages. This is, however, an over-estimate as some couples may be carrier couples for more than one disease. Assuming mutual independence of autosomal recessive diseases, one can calculate that 2–3 per cent frequency of autosomal recessive diseases in offspring of first-cousin couples corresponds to 7–10 per cent carrier couples among first-cousin couples. So 7–10 per cent of first-cousin couples have a risk of 25 per cent or higher for autosomal recessive disease in their offspring. Conversely, 90–93 per cent of first-cousin couples have no risk at all of an autosomal recessive disorder in their offspring.

Grand Total Risk for the Individual Consanguineous Couple

From the above, it becomes clear that the risk for consanguineous couples of having affected offspring actually consists of three different risks:

a. The baseline risk for all parents-to-be of having affected offspring;
b. The extra risk due to their consanguineous relation;
c. The risk from disorders already present in the family.

Genetic counselling of consanguineous couples requires a thorough inquiry into the exact pedigree structure and the disorders in the partners and their family – both common and separate branches.

As is usual in genetic counselling, risks should always be put into perspective. Only a minority of consanguineous couples has an increased risk, and if a consanguineous couple has an affected child, this is not always caused by the consanguinity of the parents. Genetic testing of affected and unaffected members may be helpful in some families, and genetic screening of parents-to-be for carriership of the more frequent disorders in a population might be considered.

References

Hamamy, H., et al. 2011. 'Consanguineous marriages, pearls and perils: Geneva International Consanguinity Workshop Report', *Genetics in Medicine* 13: 841–847.

Gialluissi, A., T. Pippucci, Y. Anikster, U. Ozbek, M. Medlej-Hashim, A. Mégarbane and G. Romeo. 2012. 'Estimating the allele frequency of autosomal recessive disorders through mutational records and consanguinity: the homozygosity index (HI)', *Annals of Human Genetics* 76: 159–167.

Ten Kate, L.P. 2010. 'Psychomotor developmental delay and epilepsy in an offspring of father-daughter incest: quantification of the causality probability', *International Journal of Legal Medicine* 124: 667–668.

Ten Kate, L.P., H. Scheffer, M.C. Cornel and J.G. Van Lookeren Campagne. 1991. 'Consanguinity sans reproche', *Human Genetics* 86: 295–296.

Ten Kate, L.P., M. Teeuw, L. Henneman and M.C. Cornel. 2010. 'Autosomal recessive disease in children of consanguineous parents: inference from the proportion of compound heterozygotes', *Journal of Community Genetics* 1: 37–40.

UNSCEAR (United Nations Scientific Committee on the Effects of Atomic Radiation). 2001. Report to the General Assembly. Scientific Annex Hereditary Effects of Radiation.

Appendix One

Glossary

Autosome A chromosome which is not a sex chromosome. Humans typically have 22 pairs of autosomes, numbered 1 to 22, and two sex chromosomes (XX in females, XY in males).

Compound heterozygosity*	see: heterozygosity.
Heterozygosity*	Term to indicate that the two copies of a particular gene are different from each other. If both copies are abnormal, i.e. carry a different pathogenic mutation, the situation is called compound heterozygosity. Heterozygosity without the addition of 'compound' refers to the situation in which only one copy is abnormal while the other one is normal.
Homozygosity*	Term to indicate that both copies of a particular gene are either normal or carry the same pathogenic mutation. If both copies are inherited from the same ancestor (one via the father, and the other via the mother) these copies are said to be identical by descent. If the two copies are inherited from different ancestors they are called identical by state (only).
Identical by descent	see: homozygosity.
Identical by state	see: homozygosity.
Inbreeding coefficient	The probability that the two copies of a gene in a child of consanguineous parents are identical by descent.
Recessive	A copy of a gene is called recessive when it only comes into expression if it is present in duplicate.

* We here assume that different pathogenic mutations can be identified individually and that we can therefore distinguish between them. When one can only distinguish between abnormal and normal, and not between different abnormal copies, compound heterozygosity becomes indistinguishable from homozygosity, and the term homozygosity will include real homozygosity and compound heterozygosity. This was frequently the case in the past, but sometimes still is for some disorders or when resources for molecular diagnosis are missing.

Appendix Two

Symbols and Equations

F	Inbreeding coefficient.
q	Frequency of a particular autosomal recessive pathogenic gene.
$2q$	Frequency of carriers of a particular autosomal recessive pathogenic gene in the population provided that affected patients do not reproduce.*
q^2	Frequency of a particular autosomal recessive disease in a randomly mating population.
Fq	Frequency of a particular autosomal recessive disease in the children of consanguineous couples due to their consanguinity.
$Fq + (1-F)q^2$	Total frequency of a particular autosomal recessive disease in the children of consanguineous couples.
$[Fq + (1-F)q^2]/q^2$	Factor by which the frequency of a particular autosomal recessive disease in the children of consanguineous couples is increased compared to the frequency of the disease in a randomly mating population.
$[Fq + (1-F)q^2] - q^2$	Difference in the frequency of a particular autosomal recessive disease in the children of consanguineous couples and the frequency of the disease in a randomly mating population.
$Fq/[Fq + (1-F)q^2]$	Proportion of affected children with a given autosomal recessive disease due to the consanguinity of the parents compared to the total frequency of this disease among the children of consanguineous parents.
$(1-F)q^2/[Fq + (1-F)q^2]$	Proportion of affected children with a given autosomal recessive disease not due to the consanguinity of the parents compared to the total frequency of this

disease among the children of consanguineous parents.

* When affected patients reproduce normally the carrier frequency will be $2q(1-q)$.

Appendix Three

1. The proportion of families with 0, 1, 2 ... n affected children follows the binomial distribution. So in a family of 4 children the proportions are: for none affected $(3/4)^4 = 81/256 = 31.64$ per cent; for just one affected $4(1/4)(3/4)^3 = 108/256 = 42.19$ per cent; for two affected $6(1/4)^2 (3/4)^2 = 54/256 = 21.09$ per cent; for three affected $4(1/4)^3 (3/4) = 12/256 = 4.69$ per cent; and for all four affected $(1/4)^4 = 1/256 = 0.39$ per cent.
2. The probability of identity by descent of both copies of a particular gene in the expected child (indicated with a question mark) in figure 2.2 is calculated as follows. Step 1: Imagine a copy a of this gene in the grandfather A. The chance that this copy a is transmitted to the expected child through its father (G) is found by multiplying all distinct probabilities of transmission from one generation to the next. Since the probability of transmission from A to D is 1/2, from D to G is also 1/2, and from G to the child again 1/2, the total chance of transmission of gene copy a from the grandfather to the child via G is $(1/2)^3$, i.e. 1/8. Step 2: The same reasoning applies to the transmission of this copy a through E and H to the child. The probability of that event is also 1/8. So the chance that copy a of the gene in grandfather A meets itself in the child is $(1/8) \times (1/8)$, i.e. 1/64. Step 3: So far we have only considered what could happen to copy a of a particular gene of grandfather A. We must, however, take into account that there are three more copies of this gene in the grandparents: one more in the grandfather and two other in the grandmother. So the chance that the two copies of a particular gene in the child are identical by descent is four times the outcome of step 2. So the total probability of identity by descent for any particular autosomal gene for the child in Figure 2.2 is $4 \times 1/64$ or 1/16.
3. For a single disorder, the extra risk is the risk in offspring of consanguineous unions minus the risk in the general population. So, the extra risk is $[Fq + (1-F)q^2]-[q^2]$. This can be reduced to $Fq + q^2-Fq^2-q^2$, and further to $Fq-Fq^2$, and $F(q-q^2)$ or $Fq(1-q)$. So for any given gene frequency q the extra risk is dependent only on F.

PART I

CONTINUITY AND CHANGE
IN TRADITIONAL CONSANGUINEOUS
MARRIAGE

Chapter 3

COUSIN MARRIAGES AND INHERITED BLOOD DISORDERS IN THE SULTANATE OF OMAN

Claire Beaudevin

This chapter uses the case of inherited blood disorders (IBD) as a lens through which to examine the impacts of a global biomedical discourse of genetic risk in cousin marriage in the particular context of implementing genetics services in the Sultanate of Oman, and against the backdrop of a regional public health agenda regarding IBD in the Gulf states. IBD currently represent the very core of the emerging medical genetics services in Oman, as well as in several of the other oil-rich Gulf countries (Bahrain, Qatar, United Arab Emirates, Saudi Arabia). Oman has experienced profound and rather extraordinary social upheavals since the coup that gave the current sultan access to the throne in July 1970. One of them is the healthcare system itself, created *ex-nihilo* during the past few decades. In 1970, there was only one (U.S.-missionary) hospital in the country; in 2000, the healthcare system was ranked first among emergent countries for its 'performance according to the impact on health', and eighth for its 'global performance' (World Health Organization 2000).

IBD have now been made a priority in the creation of genetics services in Oman. Indeed, IBD are new diseases in the country, recognized as diagnostic categories only in the late 1970s; previously, there were no laboratory facilities for diagnosing IBD, and no facilities for managing IBD. Living with sickle-cell anaemia or thalassaemia implies a routine of diverse medical interventions: blood transfusions, treatment reassessment, check-ups and specific blood tests are often necessary on a monthly basis. Besides, the pyramidal organization of the Omani healthcare system also requires patients to go to regional hospitals or even to the capital for treatment (Beaudevin 2013a), as there is only a handful of IBD-specialized units in the country. The public sector provides free healthcare, including certain complex and expensive procedures that can only be performed abroad, for Omani passport-holders, but not for the (mainly male) migrant workers from Asia who comprise 25–30 per cent of the population. The numerous private health institutions do not provide advanced care for people living with IBD (notably regular transfusions and repeated treatment of pain crises) or large-scale screening for IBD (for the disease, or to identify unaffected carriers who risk having an affected child if they marry another carrier).

This chapter is based on anthropological research (Beaudevin 2010, 2013b) that focused on the social dimensions of living with sickle-cell anaemia and thalassaemia, their medical management, and the public health policies related to them. For this research, I conducted long-term fieldwork using ethnographic methods: I spent time with scientists, patients, families and officials, in public and private hospitals and clinics, in and outside the capital (Muscat), in official meetings and conferences, at patients' homes, and with the IBD patient association, etc.

In what follows, I begin by discussing diverse expert and lay discourses about consanguinity, genetic proximity and the local concept of *al-aqārib* ('the closest ones'), in the context of a global medical discourse that stigmatizes consanguineous couples, to show that consanguinity has complex meanings and does not map onto a single social reality in Omani society. I then turn to discuss expert and lay understandings about genetic risk, and to detail the on-going medicalization of cousin marriage that is occurring as a consequence of the Omani public health discourse and policy for managing risk of IBDs in the Sultanate. There are real issues for patients and families in understanding the genetic risk for IBDs, but the common association of cousin marriage with risk for IBDs and the concern with stopping cousin marriage as a means of preventing IBDs is misleading in the light of the high prevalence of IBD carriers in Omani society.

Expert Discourses

Consanguinity as a 'Genetic Burden'

In the early 2000s in Oman, consanguineous marriages characterized around 56 per cent of couples. More precisely, 24.1 per cent of married couples are first cousins, a proportion comparable with neighbouring Saudi Arabia, for example (El-Mouzan et al. 2007). There are no more recent figures, but the proportion may now be lower, since fecundity has decreased from 6.6 children per woman in 1990 to 3.13 in 2007 (Ministry of Health 2008), following the implementation of the 'national birth spacing initiative'.

Omani medical doctors receive six years of training in the Sultanate's two colleges of medicine, but must then study abroad if they wish to obtain their specialist medical qualifications. Most spend several years in the USA or the UK, and a smaller number study in Germany, France, Canada or Australia, where they are exposed to international views about consanguinity that are embedded into their medical training. These views are both ideological and scientific – ideological because they stem from European and North American historical discourses depicting consanguineous marriages as biologically hazardous and socially exceptional (Ottenheimer 1996; see also the Afterword, this volume). The common scientific medical definition considers individuals to be linked by consanguinity when they share at least one ancestor, up to the great-great-grandparents (Susanne et al. 2003). This link is associated with a higher risk of recessively inherited conditions in children compared with children of non-consanguineous couples; thus, marrying a relative is often considered a genetic 'burden'. However, consanguinity rates are notoriously difficult to establish. Social definitions of kin, extended family or tribe do not always correspond to an underlying genetic relatedness. In Oman, for example, contemporary civic status was created only in the 1980s, and so sharing a name (isonomy) does not necessarily indicate shared biological ancestry or traceable tribal origin. Consequently, epidemiological studies of the effects of parental consanguinity on infant health are often based on approximations of consanguinity rates, and are further complicated by the fact that many different factors influence birth outcomes (see chapter one, this volume). Moreover, the abundant literature produced by medicine, public health and biological anthropology on the matter shows a global tendency to stigmatize the 'cultural behaviours' that lead individuals to choose a spouse from among their family members. This has not, however, resulted in globally uniform policy responses; public health goals range from targeted genetic counselling in some countries (Modell and Darr 2002; World Health Organization 1999) to the eradication of this matrimonial practice in others (Mégarbané 2002).

Medical practitioners in Oman are thus caught in the crossfire: on the one hand, they are part of a society where over half of the couples are cousins and over a quarter are first cousins (Nair et al. 2008; Rajab and Patton 2000), and where families value these alliances. On the other hand, the authorities discourage these marriages and the internationally trained medical practitioners have learned in medical school that consanguinity is dangerous. This generates a wide range of sometimes conflicting representations, from 'consanguinity as economic choice' to 'consanguinity as genetic burden' (Bonte 2007; Khlat 1989; Bonte 1994).

Some doctors express extremely critical views. This Omani in his late sixties, living in Muscat, was a young doctor when the current sultan took power:

> I saw a woman, from a rich family. Educated. A very well-known family. One of the daughters was sick [with sickle-cell disease], homozygous and her father wanted her to marry her cousin. He is educated . . . *(sigh)* I told him: 'Do you realize the kind of grand-children you will get?!' [. . .] Marrying one's first cousin, this is not Muslim. The Prophet did not say it. And the diseases and the cousin marriages increase. And there is no social stigma on these marriages, even from the government. (Interview, Muscat, November 2008)

The available official figures do not show any increase in the frequency of cousin marriages, contradicting this doctor's statement. I would also, however, be less sure than this doctor about the lack of stigma from the government. The image of cousin marriages in the media is rather negative. Furthermore, doctors systematically investigate parental consanguinity in cases of congenital abnormality; a mandatory declaration form is available in all maternity units and contains a specific field about consanguinity assessment. In 2003, the regional press (Vaidya 2003) announced the visit to Oman of a renowned European geneticist, who publicly affirmed the impact of consanguinity on the prevalence of genetic disorders in Oman. The negative biomedical view of consanguinity is even endorsed by anthropological publications examining matrimonial behaviours in Arabia and related health matters through the unique lens of the 'consanguineous marriage' (see for instance Al-Kandari 2007).

Consanguinity as 'Causing' Inherited Blood Disorders

Some doctors I observed and interviewed in Oman try to teach patients that cousin marriage is a dangerous practice. The explanatory model of disease that underlies this stand is 'disease as a sanction for prohibited social behaviours' (Zempléni 1985): thus, IBD cases are attributed to the grandparents' and parents' matrimonial choices. For these caregivers, convinced that cousin marriage is a causal factor in the prevalence of IBD, marrying a cousin is incomprehensible, even more so among the most educated groups of the population. An Indian radiologist working in a public hospital in Muscat told me, 'Even if you talk with educated people, it does not change anything. I know doctors who married their first cousin. It's culture. It's deeply rooted. Some even get married without being tested. In India, cousin marriage is forbidden' (Interview, June 2008).

Omani scientists publish notable figures: 7 per cent of Omani newborns are affected by a genetic disorder and a quarter of these cases are due to consanguinity (Rajab and Patton 2000); 10 per cent of Omanis carry an IBD mutation, half of them because of consanguinity (A. Rajab, personal communication, April 2008). These figures are not easily verifiable, but consanguinity cannot be responsible for all IBD cases. Since the frequency of unaffected carriers of IBD (people with IBD traits) is quite high, cousin marriage does not significantly increase the average shared risk of every Omani of having affected offspring.

Since systematic screening for IBD carriers is expensive and arduous, public health specialists tend to focus on defining target groups. In this context, the emphasis is often put on the dangerousness of consanguinity despite its relatively low impact on IBD prevalence in the country. Though they are presented as 'scientific', the criteria used to define these target groups are partly ideological. In the 1990s, a doctor employed by the Ministry of Health started a 'tribal database' linking IBD prevalence in specific families with families' tribal origins, with the aim of assisting future IBD screening campaigns by identifying 'high-risk' family groups and tribes. The protocol for this database, published in a leading peer-reviewed medical journal, reveals an underlying assumption that the 'tribe' is essentially a biological unit deprived of social dimensions. In this publication, this assumption is justified by defining the tribe as a 'genetic as well as social unit', historically intermarrying (supposedly among a paternal lineage, that is, one with the same name indicating common male ancestry) to preserve access to water resources. This database is partly rooted in historical inaccuracies: it is based on a tribal nomenclature written in the early 1900s by a British administrator (Lorimer 1908); it ignores the political fusions and fissions that have occurred in the tribal system since then, as well as the above-noted common disjunction between tribal name and genetics.

This database is probably the most striking indication that cousin marriages and consanguineous marriages in general are targeted by emergent medical genetics public health activity. It is all the more striking for it draws on historical social categories that identify specific tribes with specific diseases. In Doha airport in 2005, I met a young Omani woman who, on learning about my research, immediately exclaimed:

> Ah, *faqr al-dam* [indigence of the blood, i.e., here, inherited anaemia]! ... this is a problem, mainly because of people marrying relatives. You know, there are families where these marriages led to peculiar diseases. The *al-Hinayy*, they are known to have blood disorders; and the *al-Maskariī*, this is mental disorders...

Lay Discourses

Blood Ties and Closeness

There is no Arabic equivalent term for consanguinity. Dictionaries translate it by uncommon phrases such as *rābat al-dam* (blood ties) and by phrases referring to social as well as genetic ties, as *salat al-qarāba* ('kinship relation', which can also encompass alliance) or even `asabiyya*. The latter term – coined by the Arab historian Ibn Khaldūn in the fourteenth century (see Ibn Khaldūn 2004 for an English edition) – focuses on solidarity and loyalty ties that can exist in or outside the kinship network.

Likewise, in Omani common sense usage, consanguinity as biomedically-discouraged cousin marriage is considered one type of proximity (*qarāba*) within a broader range of types of closeness. *Qarāba* is an 'experience-near' practical kinship term (Eickelman 2002) that does not refer to etic analytical categories. This broader whole is called *al-aqārib* (sing. *al-aqrab*), i.e. 'the closest ones'. These are individuals whose proximity is spatial, social, genealogical or all of these at the same time. Thus, neighbours one visits regularly are *aqārib*, as are one's tribe's members (at least those with similar social status) and, above all, the close family members. The nuclear family is called *al-ahl* (people) or *al-hayyān* (*hayy* means neighbourhood). However, as Amal, an Omani teacher in her thirties, states, *al-aqārib* first designates people to whom one is linked by blood or alliance:

> *al-aqārib*, for me, those are all the close relatives: uncles, aunts, cousins, nephews and nieces, brothers-in-law and sisters-in-law. Mainly cousins, actually ... Anyone who is my blood relative; there are some close ones and more distant ones: as my parents' uncles or even more distant, cousins of cousins, for example. (Informal conversation, October 2008)

Biomedical representations are also pervasive within Omani society, notably through the daily use of the English language: most of the patients I met seemed to understand the biomedical meaning of consanguinity. As a result of this integration of biomedical terminology, most lay discourse about consanguinity only refers to first or second cousin marriages. In a conversation held in Arabic, the meaning of *al-aqārib* is thus contextual: when a nurse asks someone who carries an IBD trait if s/he and her/his future spouse are *aqārib*, and when women discuss future spouse choices for one of the family children, the *signifié* is different.

Safety and Backwardness

First cousin marriage in its specific parallel patrilateral form allows an individual to marry his/her closest relative inside the paternal lineage, i.e. the child (*bint ʿamm* or *ibn ʿamm*) of his/her father's brother. A significant body of literature deals with the cultural, social and economic aspects (notably preservation of the paternal lineage legacy) of this matrimonial strategy (see e.g. Bonte 2007). Another pragmatic reason – emotional and material safety – has been described in many societies including in Oman by Christine Eickelman in the 1980s (Eickelman 1984), where her observation remains relevant despite the massive rural exodus that has since occurred. Therefore, discouraging such marriages on public health grounds in contemporary Omani society has consequences that go way beyond health or economic aspects.

Contrary to what some health professionals assert, Omanis are not ignorant about the risks to children of intra-family marriages: cousin marriages may be numerous, but the idea of the dangerousness of a 'lack of external blood' is ancient. Saif, a tribal leader in his late seventies, living in a rural area, told me about his youth (i.e. before there was any public health presence in Oman): 'In some families, we saw their number decreasing. Less children. Dead children, etc. Thus we used to say "they should marry outside, those people. The tribe is drying out" [al-qabīla al-latī bathīf, najtanbūhā], so we avoided them' (Interview, Muscat, June 2008). He then explained that exceptional measures can be taken in such cases: 'One tribe used to want this, to marry outside, but it was not allowed. One day, in the other tribe, a girl was born with a crooked eye, handicapped. However, the tribe asked for her, thinking she could bring in good things'. Indeed, Omanis had observed correlations between endogamy and congenital disorders long before the arrival of biomedicine. Nonetheless, before 1970 and nowadays, they evaluate the risks in ways that are not always congruent with genetic counselling rationality.

Cousin marriage is practised in the Sultanate but not unanimously supported. Some Omanis, following medical advice or wishing to move away from burdensome matrimonial practices, frankly express their opposition. In these cases, marrying a relative is presented as a backward decision, as in the words of Hamad, whose wife is affected by sickle-cell anaemia: 'In Saudi Arabia, they intermarry. This is the reason of the number of sick people there. They do not want to marry outside of the family' (Interview, Seeb, May 2008). Hamad identifies cousin marriage with the Saudi neighbour, i.e. with the country many young Omanis have an aversion to, because of what they call its 'traditionalism'.

Oman's recent history – of internal political conflicts, complex interactions with European powers and tribal dynamics (see for instance Valeri 2009) – has produced a social dichotomy that also reflects the country's topography. While the interior of the Sultanate (al-dākhiliya) is identified with religiosity and attachment to the past, the coastal areas, especially the capital, are considered progressive and developed (Beaudevin 2013a). Hence, many Omanis tend to consider cousin marriages a backward peculiarity of the Interior. Abdulrahman, a young Omani from the Interior, affected by sickle-cell anaemia (as are several of his siblings), laments his parents' lack of foresight before they married: they are first cousins, he suffers this disease, and for him, the causal link is obvious. He even asserts, 'The Ministry of Health does not do anything to decrease the number of births of affected children. It's not complicated: they should only say, "if you marry a relative, this is dangerous for the children"!' (Interview, al-Khoud, May 2005).

Omani Marriage Medicalization Policies in the Pipeline

IBD in the Gulf and in Oman

Genetics has been a regional public health matter in the Gulf for about a decade, and has been energetically discussed in local media, as shown by these newspaper articles' titles: 'Arabs have highest rate of genetic disorders' (Muslim 2006), 'Incidence of genetic blood diseases in Oman among highest worldwide' (Al-Tauqi 2012), 'Congenital anomalies high in Oman' (Vaidya 2003). As the commonest inherited disorders in the region, IBDs are targeted by recent policies. Several countries neighbouring Oman have chosen to implement mandatory premarital screening for IBD: in the United Arab Emirates since 2006, in Qatar since 2009 and in Saudi Arabia since 2004. Newborn screening is also a regional choice: systematic and mandatory in Iran since 1997 and in Saudi Arabia since 2004. In Abu Dhabi (one of the United Arab Emirates), a pilot-study of neonatal sickle-cell screening was launched in 2002 (Al-Hosani et al. 2005). Medical termination following an IBD diagnosis was legalized in Iran in 2003 (Hedayat et al. 2006). It is also allowed in Saudi Arabia, but the authorities advocate pre-implantation genetic diagnosis, considered more in accordance with Islamic jurisprudence (Al-Aqeel 2006; Al-Odaib et al. 2003).

The Dubai-based Centre for Arab Genomic Studies (CAGS), created in 2003, is a leading agent for the regional development of research and public health policies regarding genetics. In 2004, CAGS began to construct a Catalogue of Transmission Genetics in Arabs (CTGA) with the aim of making an inventory of genetic disorders in the region.

Omani health professionals often mention Cyprus as a brilliant example of the quasi-eradication of IBD by voluntarist public health policies. One Omani surgeon told me, 'I heard from a haematologist yesterday that in a European place I don't know, an island, they managed to get a zero incidence. We should do this!' (Interview, Muscat, May 2007). Another doctor, in the University Hospital, spoke admiringly but inaccurately of this strategy: 'In Cyprus, they got a law. They go so far as to sterilize people' (Interview, al-Khoud, December 2008).

In Cyprus in the 1940s, the high prevalence of beta-thalassaemia mutations (about 15 per cent of the population; Angastiniotis et al. 1986) called for prevention policies in order to prevent the bankrupting of a healthcare system unable to afford daily care for thousands of new patients (Weatherall 1998). The prevention programme that was implemented involved the religious authorities, made premarital screening mandatory and allowed medical termination. By the 1980s, the incidence of thalassaemia had decreased by 97 per cent. Although these figures are impressive, few Omani health professionals know the reason for this result: 80 per cent of the pregnancies of affected foetuses had been terminated (Angastiniotis et al. 1986). As mentioned above, medical termination for IBD is allowed in several of Oman's neighbouring countries but not yet in the Sultanate.

In Oman, IBD are specific to Omani nationals, partly because prospective labour migrants must undergo severe mandatory health check-ups and also because of marriages regulations. If the Omani population is not *per se* a genetic isolate, the geography of the Sultanate and its extremely restrictive regulation of bi-national marriages give it an undeniable peculiarity. The legal limitation of these marriages is part of the industrious production of national identity, a process started by the current sultan in the 1970s. An initial 1980 Royal Decree prohibited marriage to a non-Omani, but has been gradually relaxed: in contemporary Personal Status Law, marrying a Gulf Cooperation Council (GCC) national is allowed (the GCC comprising Saudi Arabia, Bahrain, Oman, Kuwait, Qatar and United Arab Emirates). Since 1993, marrying a non-GCC national can be allowed by a special dispensation from an *ad-hoc* ministerial committee, but the process commonly takes more than three years, and disregarding this rule can lead to deprivation of Omani citizenship. Meantime, governmental discourse tends to discourage consanguinity, believing – erroneously, given the prevalence of IBD traits in the general population – that banning cousin marriages would solve the IBD problem.

Regarding IBD – and genetics more broadly – the Omani government stands at a crossroads. Given the concomitance of dwindling oil resources and the growing prevalence of IBD, the Ministry of Health began some years ago to conceive a national screening policy, aiming at spotting individuals carrying the IBD genetic mutations. However, decisions have not yet been made regarding the practical organization of screening. Several screening and counselling programmes are being trialled in public institutions, mainly in the capital and on a voluntary basis: electrophoresis equipment has been purchased for several primary healthcare facilities and any Omani can request a blood test for free. Many come with some of their siblings or with their future spouse. The entire process lasts about two weeks, with a final mandatory visit to the healthcare centre to be given the results by one of the few nurses trained in genetic counselling.

IBD Screening: For Whom, and Why?

One important technical consideration influences IBD policy-making: population screening is simpler, and cheaper, than genetic testing, since it does not involve genomic investigations *per se* but a characterization and quantification of haemoglobin variants, used as a proxy for genetic status for IBD. Detecting IBD-carriers only requires haemoglobin electrophoresis, which is a widely known, relatively cheap and easy-to-perform laboratory technique. Most of the patients, families and health practitioners I met favoured mandatory IBD screening, which young Omanis have discussed in internet forums since the early 2000s (English Sabla 2004). There is, however, no consensus on who should be screened. IBD are not minority-specific disorders in the Sultanate, but are widespread all over the country. The 'tribal database' mentioned above is not (yet?) an official screening tool.

Some advocate screening adolescents at school, but my observation is that currently blood tests are often omitted during mandatory medical check-ups for Omani school children. Since more than 95 per cent of women give birth in hospitals (Ministry of Health 2008), it would be possible to create a systematic neonatal screening programme, but doctors are concerned that parents will forget the carrier status of their children decades later, when the spouse selection process would start. Moreover, there are practical concerns about neonatal screening: detecting abnormal haemoglobin is impossible with simple tests in infants before six to eight months and would thus incur significant laboratory expense.

Looking at the experiences of neighbouring countries, many patients and caregivers favour premarital screening, given that almost all births in Omani society occur within marriage. In 2008, premarital tests for HIV/AIDS and hepatitis B, already compulsory for the few foreigners authorized to marry Omanis, became mandatory for Omanis. This implies the existence of a 'prenuptial medical frame' into which IBD screening would be integrated. Yet, as a haematologist very relevantly told me, 'there is a timing in marriage here, and it is difficult to slow it down' (Interview, al-Khoud, December 2008).

It may seem surprising that some families are reluctant to request screening during the engagement negotiations. However, planning a marriage is a significant symbolic and financial investment:

choosing a spouse is a long process that can sometimes be similar to a reciprocal 'investigation' conducted by families. The aim is to ensure the future couple complies with the *kafā`a* rules that their status similarity is sufficient. In Oman, *kafā'a* is both sustained by Ibadi jurisprudence and Personal Status Law (article 20). And yet, it stands in contradiction to the Fundamental Law (article 17) that prohibits any kind of discrimination. Most of the time, *kafā`a* is assessed on a financial and social status basis, but health matters can also constitute additional criteria (see Al-Azri 2012 about these criteria and their everyday application in Oman). In principle it is thus acceptable to request information about a future spouse before the dowry is brought to the groom's house.

Policy-makers in Oman have not yet defined the ultimate goal of a potential screening programme. As Claire Julian-Reynier comments, there are different issues at stake:

> The interest of heterozygous individuals screening is different from the one of disease screening. First, it means the identification of high-risk couples; secondly, informing them about their risk; thirdly, giving them access to prenatal diagnosis or pre-implantation genetic diagnosis for further pregnancies. (Julian-Reynier 2003, my translation)

Moreover, screening for high-risk couples is really only practicable in social contexts where prenatal examinations and pre-implantation genetic diagnosis (PGD) are available to complement the screening, which is not the case in Oman. PGD is available in Saudi Arabia for couples who carry IBD mutations, but Oman currently has no public infrastructure to support the use of assisted reproduction technologies. Furthermore, for some doctors, the fact that Oman has a comparatively small population complicates the situation as this doctor involved in the new national genetics centre remarks:

> There is a PGD lab in the plans [of the genetics centre], but people have no idea of realities. It's just like for bone marrow transplantation: everything seems too perfect. There is always a risk to miss affected embryos and the best European success rate are around 30 per cent [...] In Saudi Arabia, they have 50 million inhabitants [Oman has 2.8], it is absolutely different. (Interview, Darsayt, April 2008)

Amniocentesis and chorionic villus sampling are also currently unavailable in the Sultanate, mainly because of the scarcity of appropriate cytogenetics facilities. The university hospital and the Ministry of Health lab where such analysis would be possible are overwhelmed by requests from all over the country, mostly related to voluntary adult IBD screening and pre-bone marrow transplantation check-ups. As a result, couples who can afford it sometimes choose to obtain PGD abroad – the current price of the procedure is approximately 20 000 US$ in the USA.

The bioethics of medical termination in Muslim societies is a complex issue beyond the scope of this chapter. In Oman, it is theoretically allowed only if the pregnant woman's life is endangered (Ministry of Health and Unicef 1999). In practice, although it is rarely performed, medical termination may be offered when foetuses suffer severe cerebral or cardiac abnormalities (and not for IBD or Down syndrome); doctors may advise couples they believe able to afford the expense to go abroad for termination, and will provide precise lists of hospitals. Since the late 1990s, the Ministry of Health has been considering legalizing medical termination on the grounds of parental suffering, neonatal pain and mortality and health expenses (Ministry of Health and Unicef 1999).

The Omani healthcare system thus provides couples with only limited choices in the management of their risk of having affected children, despite the fact that a national mandatory screening programme is an official priority in the current governmental five-year plan. Health and educational facilities dedicated to disabled children are also extremely scarce in Oman.

Lay Perceptions of Genetic Risk

On being identified as carriers, individuals must anticipate not their own future sickness but the potential birth of an affected child, in a process which implicates an entire family and its procreative choices. In this process, IBD are considered to be deficiencies (*faqr al-dam*, i.e. 'indigence of the blood'), since they put a serious strain on one's own 'value on the matrimonial market' (Fassin 2000) and on that of one's children. Risking giving birth to an affected child is thus partly also risking not finding a spouse for him/her, i.e. fathering a pariah.

Being a Carrier

A new social category appeared in Oman with the use of haemoglobin electrophoresis: that of 'carriers' of IBD, whose 'abnormal haemoglobin' level is elevated but not pathological, and who were socially invisible beforehand since there is no exterior sign of their genetic status. For carriers of an IBD mutation, the idea of being the vehicle of a disease that could – or perhaps already does – affect one of their children is often difficult to understand. Indeed, sickle cell and thalassaemia mutations, in heterozygous form, very rarely cause symptoms. Admitting their inheritability and their role in the birth of an affected child has to be experienced as an act of faith.

Rayan, a thirty-year-old Omani, tells about the moment she discovered she was a thalassaemia carrier:

> I had to undergo thyroid exams, they took blood for this, in the university [hospital]. And after two weeks, they told me I had no thyroid problem but I had *ānīmīa thalāsīmīa* [one of the Arabic phrases for beta-thalassaemia], I was a carrier. They did not tell me anything, did not prescribe any medication, nothing. They only told me I should do some tests before getting married and I shouldn't marry a carrier. They were students, and this was a scary story [she laughs and seems embarrassed]. First, I was really frightened. I didn't understand why they were talking about. Then, they explained me again and I understood. (Interview, Mawaleh, December 2008)

Rayan's difficulty in understanding her genetic status, something she does not feel in her body, is partly related to the ambiguity of the phrasing through which she first learnt she was a carrier:

> Drawings, that would be useful. The doctor could first say what it is, thalassaemia, what it means to have this disease, something about my own situation, the way I got it. Not only, 'You got it. Do not marry someone like you. No need of treatment. Goodbye.' If she had explained in a better way, I would have understood, I wouldn't have been so terrified. She tells me I'm a carrier of thalassaemia, I hear 'pregnant' . . . [the Arabic term *hāmal* means both 'carrier' and 'pregnant']. I didn't know *hāmal* meant this too. (Interview, Mawaleh, December 2008)

The disturbing intangibility of the idea of having a mutation but not being ill means people sometimes reject the biomedical discourse. This is all the more likely when there are no affected people in the family, when healthy children embody the 'biomedical mistake'. Once the inheritability is thus obliterated, the management of risk is no longer necessary. One young father of a sick infant exclaimed in despair, 'No one is sick in the family! I do not understand'! (Direct observation, Muscat, December 2006).

Interpreting Numbers

Though autosomal recessive inheritance is a simple mechanism for geneticists, making it clear and understandable for non-specialists is arduous. I frequently observed scenes that could be described thus:

a health professional explains the risk as 'one risk upon four' (rarely as '25 per cent'); parents hear this figure, but conceive it as 'given once and for all', i.e. the birth of one affected child would guarantee the subsequent births of three unaffected siblings. Every pregnancy is a new throw of the dice, but is thus not taken into account. Indeed, the single occurrence is seen as protective of other family members. This conception of risk echoes the notion of social recessivity of disease, in Zempléni's phrase (coined in another context): 'The best known examples are elective disorders attributed to certain authorities or divinities who protect the community under the sole condition that they physically invade one member of each generation' (Zempléni 1985). This form of risk perception has been described in the Caribbean too, where some families, rejecting genetic aetiology, question the 'unicity of a sickle-cell child [. . .]: why him and not the others?' (Benoît 2004).

Another common interpretation of numerical risk entails its gradual relativization: for some parents, whatever risk has been announced by health practitioners, and without questioning the genetic aetiology, the birth of several unaffected children is somehow seen to 'cancel' the risk. A 'stroke of good fortune' thus eliminates the everyday reality of the risk. This has also been described elsewhere, such as in the infectious disease department of a French hospital, where the absence of vertical transmission of HIV from mother to child is a 'local reassurance' for staff members (Desclaux and Egrot 2003). Moreover, a risk value is meaningful contextually, and is not acceptable in the absolute. Rayan, the young woman mentioned above, asked me to explain to her again the recessive inheritance where both partners in a couple are carriers. Once I finished, she exclaimed, 'Ah! But then it's not 50 per cent? It's 25 per cent?! If I had known if was 25 and not 50, I wouldn't have said anything and the first guy who proposed me wouldn't have run away!' (Interview, Mawaleh, December 2008).

Looking for a Spouse

Few interviewees had experienced premarital IBD screening, partly due to the small scale of the pilot programmes in the country, and partly due to a frequent mix-up: the relatively recent genetic screening is commonly confused with screening for sexually transmitted diseases, which also requires a blood sample. Thus, mentioning tests during the pre-engagement period of a marriage negotiation is often considered as an ill-concealed accusation of depravation towards the other family.

Another misunderstanding that can occur during this period arises from the biomedical discourse, mentioned above, that erroneously presents consanguinity as the main cause of IBD. Many Omanis, having integrated the message that consanguinity is dangerous, decide not to get tested on the grounds of this aetiological model, thinking that not marrying a cousin is therefore the best prevention. Umm Safiya, a young Omani woman, told me that a '[test] is not needed for those who marry outside of their family' (Interview, al-Khoud, April 2008).

The status of carrier can constitute a 'damaged identity' that periodically resurfaces (Atkin and Ahmad 1998). Indeed, as 'epilepsy is dormant between seizures, carrier status [. . .] is dormant between two reproductive episodes' (Parsons and Atkinson 1992). Finding a spouse is the first of these moments and represents a dilemma, for the future couple's parents, between divulging their child's genetic status and risking not finding a spouse, especially if carrying a mutation is considered pathological in their community. Being a carrier makes the individual 'discreditable' since their 'differentness is not immediately apparent and is not known beforehand' (Goffman 1986). The dilemma for parents thus lies in the decision to 'discredit' their child or not. Rayan, who is carrier of a thalassaemia mutation, relates how she chose her husband, after having been told about the risk:

> I wasn't engaged yet at that time and I decided to put this first. My husband, I told him to get tested before we decided anything. [I wonder if she asked by herself] Oh yes, it was me! My parents? Impossible. They would have kicked my ass if they had known that I asked him such a thing! They didn't know. My husband is the third one. The first one ran away even before getting tested, maybe he did not understand, maybe he thought I was sick [she laughs]. The second one didn't get tested and said 'it's nothing, we get married and we'll see'. And my husband, him, the third one, he got tested. He's not a carrier. (Interview, Mawaleh, December 2008)

Rayan was so scared of stigmatization (including from her own family) that she did not risk asking her parents to impose screening upon potential sons-in-law:

> I was scared they would think I was sick, I couldn't have children, or things like this. And that they would have said 'Allah will provide' and wouldn't accept my fiancé to get tests. Allah, Allah, always Allah. OK, but we also have minds ... My parents would have dared to say to my fiancé's family 'she wants a house, she wants a diamond',

but they would never have said 'she wants a blood test'. (Interview, Mawaleh, December 2008)

Yusuf has a son affected by sickle-cell anaemia. His cousin tells me that before Yusuf got married, Yusuf was informed about his carrier status but had no choice at that time – everything was already decided and impossible to cancel. The perceived inescapability of the marriage process after engagement weighs down IBD mutation carriers more heavily than their potential 'genetic responsibility' (Novas and Rose 2000) towards future children.

For people affected by IBD, finding a spouse is of course even more difficult. Their coping strategies are various: some, like Abdulrahman (a sickle-cell anaemia patient) abandon the idea of getting married because of the risk of having affected children. In 2008, he was offered in marriage a cousin unable to find a husband because of a partial paralysis affecting her legs. Abdulrahman first agreed but then categorically withdrew his consent, after learning she was a sickle-cell mutation carrier and wanted children. Asila, a mother of two affected by a mild form of thalassaemia, chose to marry a very religious man, someone she told me 'would never divorce [her]', and decided not to inform him about her disease before the birth of their first child.

Salma is a young sickle-cell patient who had already forced two potential husbands to get tested and refused their proposals after their carrier status was confirmed. Her story casts light on the collective management of risk inside families:

> With my husband, finally, we didn't get tested. Because in case it has been positive ... we couldn't have got married and he absolutely wanted to marry me. If you ask me why I let him do this ... I think that twice, it was too much. I was scared. And my parents told me not to do the tests, because they really liked him and wanted him as a son-in-law. He didn't want to say to him 'she wants a house, jewellery and a blood test'. (Interview, Seeb, December 2008)

In her work about African-American mothers who carry sickle-cell trait, Shirley Hill shows that it is partly erroneous to base public health policies on the assumption that it is the women's duty to avoid transmitting the trait to their children. Imposing a screening test on the future husband, or abandoning their wish to be parents, 'may be viable strategies for groups with access to and confidence in medical knowledge and with patterns of marriage, childbearing, and gender relations coincide with the assumptions of the health belief model' (Hill 1994).

Asila's choosing secrecy and Salma's eventual succumbing to social and emotional pressure show that gender asymmetry persists among affected individuals.

The Social Context of Childbearing

The possible recurrence of an IBD within a family after the birth of an affected child has to be contextualized within local representations of a 'normal' family. Rayan, pregnant, holds her one-year-old and tells me, 'I can't wait! [I seem puzzled, she laughs.] I'm in a hurry to give him four! Yes, the four standard children. But my husband wants six, or maybe twelve. The Omani family ... [she laughs] But I told him it won't be with me! I think four is ok' (Interview, Mawaleh, December 2008). In many families, any procreative 'pause' imposed on a woman by the birth of an affected child or by the evaluation of risks to future pregnancies is seen as a 'breach' of this woman's fertility. Such pauses may threaten women's social status, since the father of several affected children can easily obtain a divorce or take a second wife.

Many carrier couples have more children despite the birth of an affected child. This risk-taking attitude partly reflects the procreative pressure of contemporary Omani society. However, there is no broad consensus on this, as the following conversation between Yusuf (Y.), who recently had an affected son, and his sister (S.), who is also a nurse, shows:

> S. [to me] – When their first daughter was born, I was staying with them and I knew they both were carriers. We were scared. I pushed my sister-in-law to get the daughters screened. Thank God, they are ok. But the boy ... he got oedemas ... I understood.
> [She turns to her brother and asks:]
> S. – So. What is your plan?
> Y. – I will wait.
> S. – Wait for what?
> Y. – ...
> S. [calling me to witness] – I know this family with four affected children. And they don't do anything. No birth spacing [euphemism for birth control, originating in the name of the 'National Birth Spacing Initiative' launched by the Omani Ministry of Health]. (Interview, Seeb, May 2007)

Fatma, whose two sons have thalassaemia, could afford a choice. She tried to control the risk, without breaching religious law: 'For my third son, I asked a sheikh in Saudi Arabia if it was allowed to do termination for thalassaemia. He said yes. Thus, when leaving to India for the amniocentesis, I got myself prepared to this. But he's not sick' (Interview, Sūhar, April 2008).

Some families appear as 'risk takers' (Shaw 2009) who may seem to not take the risk seriously. Yet, their decisions are not necessarily misunderstandings of genetic aetiology. Rather, the criteria on which reproductive decisions are made are not inevitably those favoured by biomedicine: the preservation of social structure seems more assured by maintaining the matrimonial system than by avoiding giving birth to affected children. As Sylvie Fainzang states: 'preserving health is not the only rationality, and divergent rationalities do exist, "alternative" to utilitarist rationality' (Fainzang 2001).

Concluding Remarks

In this chapter, the case of inherited blood disorders in Oman offers a lens through which to investigate the implementation of genetics services and the expert and lay representations of heritability and consanguinity. The 'young' Omani healthcare system, created *ex-nihilo* since 1970, is the scene of conflicting discourses about cousin marriage. Health practitioners are torn between international public health views learned in Western universities and that often demonize this practice, and local perceptions that approve it for social, economical and historical reasons. Moreover, the very concept of consanguinity does not echo a single, simple and finite social reality in the Omani society, where proximity is composite – it includes blood ties, but also entails alliances and shared territories.

Ethnographic fieldwork carried out with doctors and patients in Oman's public healthcare facilities showed the variety of local modes of risk construction and perception. For patients, the novel availability of genetic information about potential spouses and in-laws creates new dilemmas during the spouse selection process. It also raises questions about how genetic information should best be communicated to patients, given the potential stigmatization of carriers, and the misunderstandings of statistical risk information that are possible. It also shows how, even when patients understand the risks, alternative (non-biomedical) rationalities can prevail throughout marriage negotiations and in the matter of reproductive decision-making.

Examining the wider context of policy debate concerning the management of IBDs in the country also reveals the irony of focusing on consanguineous marriage, a practice that has considerable social significance, in a population where the prevalence of IBD carriers is high and which is also genetically 'closed' due to restrictive bi-national marriage policies. In this context, banning cousin marriage would not have a significant impact on the prevalence of IBD.

Compared to its neighbouring countries, the peculiarity of the Omani context lies in its current public health situation regarding genetics: the Sultanate is still experiencing an ongoing process of policies implementation, since no decision has yet been made regarding the national screening strategies. The Cypriot ideal of quasi eradication of an IBD appears tempting for many health and public health professionals, but the means used in this achievement – mandatory premarital screening and legalization of medical termination for IBD – are problematic in the Sultanate. The medicalization of spouse selection is certainly beginning in Oman, but its final form still has to be determined.

Acknowledgements

The French Ministry of Higher Education and Research, the French Society for Perinatal Medicine (SFMP), the French Centre for Archaeology and Social Sciences of Sana'a (CEFAS, Yemen) and the French Embassy in Oman funded this research. Fieldwork has been supported by the College of Arts and Social Sciences, Sultan Qaboos University, Muscat, Oman. Ethical approval was obtained from the Research and Ethical Committee of the Omani Ministry of Health. The author would like to express her gratitude to patients, families and health practitioners in Oman whom she worked with. She is indebted to them for their trust and for the way in which they let her settle into their everyday lives, in hospitals or at home. She would also like to thank the editors of this volume for their beneficial feedback, as well as Dr Sultan M. Al-Hashmi for his unfailing support in Oman, and Professor Anne Marie Moulin and Dr Mary-Ashley Ouvrier for their highly valuable comments on earlier versions of this chapter.

References

Al-Aqeel, A.I. 2006. 'Ethical guidelines in genetics and genomics: an Islamic perspective', *Saudi Medical Journal* 26(12): 1862–1870.

Al-Azri, K. 2012. *Social and Gender Inequality in Oman: The Power of Religious and Political Tradition*. Oxford and New York: Routledge.

Al-Hosani, H., M. Salah, H.M. Osman, H.M. Farag and S.M. Anvery. 2005. 'Incidence of haemoglobinopathies detected through neonatal screening in the United Arab Emirates', *La Revue de Santé de la Méditerranée orientale* 11(3): 300–307.

Al-Kandari, Y.Y. 2007. 'The health consequences of consanguineous marriage in Kuwait', *Anthropology of the Middle East* 2(2): 74–86.

Al-Odaib, A.N., K.K. Abu-Amero, P.T. Ozand and A.M. Al-Hellani. 2003. 'A new era for preventive genetic programs in the Arabian Peninsula', *Saudi Medical Journal* 24(11): 1168–1175.

Al-Tauqi, Z. 2012. 'Incidence of genetic blood diseases in Oman among highest worldwide', *Muscat Daily*, 16 October.

Angastiniotis, M., S. Kyriakidou and M. Hadjiminas. 1986. 'How thalassaemia was controlled in Cyprus', *World Health Forum* 7: 291–297.

Atkin, K. and W.I.U. Ahmad. 1998. 'Genetic screening and haemoglobinopathies: ethics, politics and practice', *Social Science and Medicine* 46(3): 445–458.

Beaudevin, C. 2010. 'Faqr al-dam, "l'indigence du sang", comme héritage. Représentations et enjeux sociaux des hémoglobinopathies héréditaires au sultanat d'Oman' [Faqr al-dam (indigence of the blood) as inheritance. Representations and social stakes of hereditary haemoglobinopathies in the Sultanate of Oman]. PhD thesis in Social Anthropology, College of Law and Political Science, Aix-Marseille University (France).

———. 2013a. 'Of red cells, translocality and origins: inherited blood disorders in Oman', in S. Wippel (ed.), *Regionalizing Oman. Political, Economic and Social Dynamics*. Dordrecht, Heidelberg, New York and London: Springer Science, pp.91–105.

———. 2013b. 'Old diseases and contemporary crisis. Inherited blood disorders in Oman', *Anthropology and Medicine* 20(2): 175–189.

Benoît, C. 2004. 'Circuit de soins des enfants drépanocytaires à Saint-Martin/Sint Marteen (FWI/DWI). Santé, migrations et exclusion sociale dans la Caraïbe', in A. Lainé, D. Bonnet, L. Keclard and M. Romana (eds), *La Drépanocytose: Regards croisés sur une maladie orpheline*. Paris: Karthala, pp.116–140.

Bonte, P. 2007. 'Le choix du conjoint dans les sociétés musulmanes maghrébines contemporaines. Evolutions sociales et réformes juridiques', *Anthropology of the Middle East* 2(1): 1–19.

——— (ed.). 1994. *Epouser au plus proche. Inceste, prohibitions et stratégies matrimoniales autour de la Méditerranée*. Paris: Editions de l'EHESS.

Desclaux, A. and M. Egrot. 2003. 'Le chiffre et ses interprétations. Logiques sous-jacentes aux discours médicaux contemporains sur le risque VIH', in A. Leca and F. Vialla (eds), *Le risque épidémique: droit, histoire, médecine et pharmacie*. Aix-en-Provence: Presses Universitaires d'Aix-Marseille, pp.435–446.

Eickelman, C. 1984. *Women and Community in Oman*. New York and London: New York University Press.
Eickelman, D.F. 2002. *The Middle East and Central Asia. An Anthropological Approach*, 4th edn. Upper Saddle River: Prentice Hall.
El-Mouzan, M.I., A.A. Al-Salloum, A.S. Al-Herbish, M.M. Qurachi and A.A. Al-Omar. 2007. 'Regional variations in the prevalence of consanguinity in Saudi Arabia', *Saudi Medical Journal* 28(12): 1881–1884.
English Sabla. 'Should or shouldn't pre-marriage blood tests be compulsory in Oman?', 28 November 2004. Available from http://www.englishsabla.com/forum/showthread.php?s=d2a1332661c0ea14d323d60e3d13c153&t=27092&highlight=sickle.
Fainzang, S. 2001. 'Cohérence, raison et paradoxe. L'anthropologie de la maladie aux prises avec la question de la rationalité', in *Ethnologies Comparées*, 3. Available from http://alor.univ-montp3.fr/cerce/r3/s.f.htm.
Fassin, D. 2000. *Les Enjeux politiques de la santé. Etudes sénégalaises*, équatoriennes *et françaises*. Paris: Karthala.
Goffman, E. 1986. *Stigma: Notes on the Management of Spoiled Identity*. Touchstone: Simon & Schuster.
Hedayat, K.M., P. Shooshtarizadeh and M. Raza. 2006. 'Therapeutic abortion in Islam: contemporary views of Muslim Shiite scholars and effect of recent Iranian legislation', *Journal of Medical Ethics* 32: 652–657.
Hill, S.A. 1994. 'Motherhood and the obfuscation of medical knowledge: the case of sickle cell disease', *Gender and Society* 8(1): 29–47.
Ibn Khaldūn. 2004. *The Muqaddimah: An Introduction to History*. Princeton: Princeton University Press.
Julian-Reynier, C. 2003. 'Les enjeux sociaux du dépistage génétique en population', in *L'Observatoire de la Génétique*. IRCM (Institut de Recherches Cliniques de Montréal).
Khlat, M. 1989. *Les Mariages consanguins à Beyrouth. Traditions matrimoniales et santé publiques*. Paris: PUF.
Lorimer, J. 1908. 'Gazetteer of the Persian Gulf, Oman, and Central Arabia', in *Geographical and Statistical*. Calcutta: Superintendent Government Printing.
Mégarbané, A. 2002. 'Mariage entre cousins ... que conseiller?', in *L'Observatoire de la Génétique*. IRCM (Institut de Recherches Cliniques de Montréal).
Ministry of Health. 2008. Annual Health Report 2007. Mascate: Department of Health Information & Statistics, Directorate General of Planning.
Ministry of Health, and Unicef. 1999. Report on Perinatal / Neonatal infant mortality – Sultanate of Oman. Muscat, 56.
Modell, B. and A. Darr. 2002. 'Genetic counselling and customary consanguineous marriage', *Nature Reviews Genetics* 3: 225–229.
Muslim, N. 2006. 'Arabs have highest rate of genetic disorders', *Gulf News* 21 February 2006, http://gulfnews.com/news/gulf/uae/health/arabs-have-highest-rate-of-genetic-disorders-1.226021.

Nair, P., E. Ibrahim, T. Obeid, A. Farid and G.O. Tadmouri. 2008. 'Genetic disorders in Oman: a CTGA perspective', in Centre for Arab Genomics Studies (ed.), *Genetic Disorders in the Arab World: Oman*. Dubai, Centre for Arab Genomics Studies, pp.44–57.

Novas, C. and N. Rose. 2000. 'Genetic risk and the birth of the somatic individual', *Economy and Society* 29(4): 485–513.

Ottenheimer, M. 1996. *Forbidden Relatives: The American Myth of Cousin Marriage*. Champaign: University of Illinois Press.

Parsons, E. and P. Atkinson. 1992. 'Lay constructions of genetic risk', *Sociology of Health and Illness* 14(4): 437–455.

Rajab, A. and M.A. Patton. 2000. 'A study of consanguinity in the Sultanate of Oman', *Annals of Human Biology* 27(3): 321–326.

Shaw, A. 2009. *Negotiating Risk. British Pakistani Experiences of Genetics*. Oxford and New York: Berghahn Books.

Susanne, C., E. Rebato and B. Chiarelli (eds). 2003. *Anthropologie biologique. Evolution et biologie humaine*. Brussels: De Boeck.

Vaidya, S.K. 2003. 'Congenital anomalies high in Oman', *Gulf News*, 18 February.

Valeri, M. 2009. *Oman. Politics and Society in the Qaboos State*. London and New York: Hurst / Columbia University Press.

Weatherall, D.J. 1998. 'Thalassemia in the next millennium'. Keynote address. *Annals of the New York Academy of Sciences* 30(850): 1–9.

World Health Organization. 1999. *Services for the prevention and management of genetic disorders and birth defects in developing countries*. Geneva: WHO.

———. 2000. *World Health Report*. Geneva: WHO.

Zempléni, A. 1985. 'La Maladie et ses causes. Introduction', *L'Ethnographie* 1985(2): 13–44.

Chapter 4

'Dangerous Liaisons'
Modern Biomedical Discourses and Changing Practices of Cousin Marriage in Southeastern Turkey

Laila Prager

In recent years there have been public debates in some European countries on the genetic risks of so-called 'customary marriages', especially marriages between cousins. The European media maintain that in Western Europe cousin marriages have noticeably increased, as a result of the influx of migrants from the Middle East who – as many of the commentators declare with utter conviction – remain devoted to the 'traditional' marriage practices of their countries of origin (cf. Elderen et al. 2010; Giordano et al. 1998: 244; Port and Bittles 2001: 97–98; 415–416). In the UK and in Germany, debate has centred on whether European states should implement special laws in order to prohibit marital relations among various categories of relatives and to make prenatal screening obligatory (Bahnsen 2011; BBC News 2008; Beckford 2010; Dyer 2005; Rowlatt 2005). Such discussions are predicated on twentieth-century Western biomedical assumptions according to which cousin marriages are supposed to entail a high risk of hereditary diseases (cf. Paul and Spencer 2008).

As a matter of fact, the same biomedical ideas about the genetic dangers resulting from cousin marriages are nowadays propagated in many of the migrants' countries of origin in the Middle East (cf. Bener and Hussain 2006; Bittles 2008; el-Hamzi 2006; The National

2009). Although contemporary biologists and medical researchers have come to quite different conclusions about the actual degree of the genetic risks emerging from cousin marriages (see the Introduction and chapters one and two), the general idea that such 'dangerous liaisons' are in one way or another detrimental to the health of the offspring increasingly acquires the status of common sense knowledge in the Middle East, with Turkey standing out as a prime example.

In Turkey, approximately 25–30 per cent of marriages are conducted among consanguineous kin (Fışloğlu 2001; Tunçbilek 2001: 277) and 66.3 per cent of these consanguineous marriages are first cousin marriages. The prevalence of consanguineous marriages varies from region to region in Turkey, and is highest (39 per cent) in East Turkey (Tunçbilek 2001: 277). For the Alawi regions in Turkey, the reported rate of consanguineous marriage is 35 per cent (Tunçbilek 2001).

From the 1980s onwards, the Republic of Turkey has launched a public campaign against the practice of cousin marriage, the alleged genetic risks of which are continuously propagated by the newspapers, radio, and television (Bellér-Hann and Hann 2001: 145; Delaney 1991: 155; Gokalp 2011: 406) and by state institutions including schools and hospitals, and by medical scientists (cf. Arpacı et al. 2003; Canatan 2011; Canatan et al. 2006; Guler and Karacan 2007; Gülleroğlu et al. 2007; Tunçbilek 1997). Moreover, since the 1990s, particularly in the Mediterranean parts of Turkey, there have been warnings that consanguineous marriages – which are understood in this public health discourse as cousin marriages – may lead to the disease of *Akdeniz Anemisi* (Mediterranean Anaemia) among children (cf. Altay and Başak 1995; Canatan et al. 2003; Tunçbilek and Özgüç 2007). In 1993 the Ministry of Health implemented a premarital screening programme in the Turkish Mediterranean region to manage this perceived risk. Moreover, in the Mediterranean cities of Adana, Antakya, Antalya and Muğla prenatal diagnostic centres have been established, where potential marriage partners, particularly those who are consanguineously related, are expected to attend to determine any genetic risk. This campaign against consanguineous marriage and potential concomitant diseases such as *Akdeniz Anemisi* as propagated in the media, in school and local medical facilities, has had a profound impact on the way in which local, social and religious groups in contemporary Turkey conceptualize marriage choices.

In this chapter I shall discuss how one of the major ethnic/religious groups living in the Southeastern Mediterranean region of Turkey has responded to this campaign by reshaping its traditional marriage system. The focus is on the Alawi, a so-called 'heterodox' Islamic group living in the Mersin, Çukurova and Hatay region of Turkey. Because they practice FBD marriage, the Alawi have been among the major targets of the Turkish state campaign against hereditary diseases. Having been confronted with this campaign the Alawi have arrived at an astonishing solution by replacing the former preference for FBD marriage with a preferential MZD marriage, a phenomenon which is quite unexpected since in the anthropological literature MZD marriages are usually considered an anathema in societies where FBD marriage is the rule or, more precisely, FBD marriages are usually associated with a statistical absence or lower rate of MZD marriages (cf. Ayoub 1959; Barry 1998; Chelhod 1965; Holy 1989). Moreover, in the framework of the Turkish campaign against cousin marriage, the MZD is considered as dangerous as the FBD in terms of genetic risk. Nevertheless, many Alawi informants maintain that the MZD is genetically the least dangerous of all cousins and therefore perfectly suited as a marriage partner. Why, for the Alawi, under the impact of modern biomedical concepts, should a marriage with the MZD be less likely to produce genetic disorders in children than a FBD marriage, although both types of cousin marriages are considered by the Turkish state to entail the same degree of genetic risk?

In the following, I will shed some light on this seeming paradox by contextualizing the shift from FBD to MZD marriages within traditional Alawi ideas about kinship and relatedness. It will become evident that the Alawi have not simply assimilated modern biomedical discourses, but have actually adapted this knowledge to their own culture specific ideas. I draw on information given by female and male Alawi informants among whom I undertook field research from 2006 to 2008 in different villages in the Hatay region and in the cities of Antakya and Adana. Additional data are based on interviews that I conducted with physicians from Antakya (Hatay) and Antalya.

The Alawi in Turkey

The Alawi should not be confused with the better-known Turkish Alevi who constitute 20 per cent of the population in Turkey. Although the term Alevi also derives from Ali, the cousin and son-in-law of Muhammad, the beliefs and ritual practices of the Alevi differ greatly from those of the Alawi (cf. Prager 2010b: 3). Since the tenth century, the Alawi – or Nusairi, as they are also known – have inhabited a mountain range (Ğabel Ansayri) that nowadays forms part of Southeastern Turkey (Çukurova, Mersin and Hatay region), Syria, and North Lebanon. In Syria and Turkey, the Alawi constitute an Islamic heterodox religious minority whose most prominent and controversial member is the president (at the time of writing) of Syria, Bashar al-Assad. According to official statistics, they account for 10–13 per cent of the total population of Syria (Engin and Franz 2000: 157), whereas Lebanon hardly has more than 9000 Alawi (Halm 1982: 383n. 604). In Turkey, they number between 700,000 and one million (Brawer 1988: 96). Since the 1960s, the Alawi have also settled in Western European countries such as Germany, France and the Netherlands, as well as in the Arab Gulf States (Prager 2010b: 38–40).

The origin of the Alawi can be traced back to religious movements of ninth-century Iraq, where Ibn Nusair, the founder of the Alawi religion and companion of the 11th Imam, heralded his doctrines (Azzi 2002). While there is ongoing debate in Islamic studies about whether the Alawi should be classified as belonging either to the Seveners, Eleveners or Twelver Shi'ites (cf. Halm 1982: 284ff; Nimier 1987; Khuri 1991: 49–61), contemporary Alawi in Turkey clearly associate themselves with the Twelver group (Merwin 2007: 363; Prager 2010b: 41). A major difference between the Shia and the Alawi, however, is that the latter worship Ali as a manifestation of the divine essence and believe in the reincarnation and transmigration of souls (see Prager 2013; Prager forthcoming). Generally, the Alawi religion can be considered as a syncretistic system of ideas, involving Islamic, Christian and Jewish influences along with ideas from Persian, Indian and Greek philosophies (Khuri 1991: 50–51; Prager 2010b: 43–45). Moreover, Alawi religious doctrines are only transmitted in a secretive initiation ritual to young men, while women are normatively excluded from religious knowledge.

The ethnonym *Alawi*, which derives from Ali, the cousin and son-in-law of Muhammad, is nowadays used within the group as an autodesignation. This term came into use when the short-lived Alawi state was established in 1925 under French mandate. In Turkish state reports from the 1930s onwards, the Alawi were also designated as *Eti Türkleri* ('Hittite Turks'), in order to conceal their Arab origins. Today, the term Eti-Turk is almost obsolete, but the term *Arap Alevileri* is quite commonly used in Turkey to designate the Alawi. The core region of the Alawi state was later incorporated into Syria, while a smaller part in the North, along with the Sanjak of Alexandretta, was annexed by Turkey in 1939. Differing greatly from normative Sunni Islam in religious beliefs and ritual practices, the Alawi have been regarded with suspicion by governments from the age of the Ottoman Empire to the modern Turkish nation state, leading to a variety of religious, social and economic pressures.

I conducted fieldwork mainly in the Çucurova region (Adana, Mersin) and in the Hatay province, where a majority of the Alawi population has settled, in the urban centres of Antakya and Iskenderun, and in the surrounding rural areas. The older generations still speak Arabic as the mother language, whereas younger people mostly use Turkish, while partly still speaking and understanding the local Arabic dialect. Bilingualism is important as the Alawi of Turkey use not one but four different kinship terminologies, depending on the age of the speaker and the region of origin (cf. Prager 2010b). Moreover, the use of Arabic or Turkish as the main language and of specific terminologies has a great impact on how the Alawi have actually incorporated the biomedical ideas propagated by the Turkish state (cf. Prager 2010b: 131–157, 179–194).

Premarital Testing and Haemoglobinopathy Prevention Programmes in Turkey

In 'Laws on Health and Marriage', an article comparing different premarital examination regimes of the 1930s, Blacker (1935: 191) notes 'it is perhaps a surprising fact that the most comprehensive law is that which operates in Turkey'. Even during the 1920s, in Turkey's early republican period, obligatory prenuptial examinations were implemented: according to Article 122 of the Law on Public Hygiene (1925), 'Every man and women who intends to marry must undergo a medical examination' (Somersan 1938: 261). From 1930 premarital health examinations were canonized in Articles 123 and 124 of the Public Health Law (*Umumī Hıfzısıhha Kanunu*) (Blacker 1935: 191; Evered and Evered 2011: 21).

From this foundation period of the new Turkish nation state onwards, health was considered not an individual task, but the business of government, and included the selection of 'healthy' marriage partners. Consanguineous marriages were not yet the target of state sponsored prenuptial examinations, but syphilis, gonorrhoea, soft chancre, leprosy, tuberculosis and mental diseases were (Blacker 1935: 191). These were considered social diseases (*içtimaī hastalıklar*) and syphilis in particular was targeted as a disease of decadence destroying the health of the state, thus evoking a set of ideas that Foucault (1994) would later subsume under the term 'governmentality'. The belief was that these diseases were primarily transmitted through prostitutes and alcoholics, who thereby constituted a major threat to future generations of the 'Turkish race' (Salgırlı 2010: 293).

During the 1930s, the Ministry of Health installed an ambitious project to compile regional surveys at the provincial level, and register every potential disease, as part of the state's attempts, during the Turkization period, to achieve a comprehensive knowledge of its many provinces and of its citizens' health and fitness (Evered and Evered 2011: 4–5). Simultaneously, Western style eugenic ideas were disseminated through the Turkish school system and by radio (Salgırlı 2010: 283), potentially enabling every Turkish citizen who attended high school to acquire a basic knowledge of genetics/eugenics. However, it was not until the 1980s that the idea of public health among the Turkish citizens was officially linked with the question of avoiding consanguineous marriages. During this period, the Republic of Turkey began to launch public campaigns against the practice of cousin marriage, the alleged genetic risks of which were continuously propagated in school education and by the newspapers, radio, and television (Bellér-Hann and Hann 2001: 145; Gokalp 2011: 406). The press in the 1980s regularly reported stories about married cousins who were unable to beget children, or whose offspring were seriously handicapped/disabled, one report maintaining that the risk of having a handicapped child through 'inbreeding' would be around 30 per cent (Bellér-Hann and Hann 2001: 145). Many Turkish medical scientists supported this state campaign by producing alleged scientific evidence that parental consanguinity leads to higher infant mortality, sterility, congenital malformations, and other diseases (Fışloğlu 2001: 217; Tunçbilek 2001: 777). The reports use widely differing definitions of 'consanguineous marriage'; the latter can – depending on the author – range from first to fourth cousins and sometimes the genealogical range is not specified (see Canatan et al. 2003; Fışloğlu 2001: 215; Guler and Karacan 2007; Jaber et al. 1998). Furthermore the articles do not specify the problem that continuous 'cousin marriages' over generations would actually result in closer relationships in terms of genetics and might therefore increase the potential health risks (cf. Prager 2012; Sheridan et al. 2013). The vagueness of these publications with regard to the identification of kin types and genealogical depth actually gives the impression that these medical reports have to be understood primarily as part of a state propaganda on marriage issues and modernity and less as independent and reflexive research on genetics and consanguinity.

Moreover, in recent years, *Akdeniz Anemisi* (Mediterranean Anemia), a kind of haemoglobinopathy called *Thalassemia* has been added to the list of diseases believed to be linked to cousin marriage (Arpacı et al. 2003; Gülleroğlu et al. 2007; Savaş et al. 2010; Tunçbilek 1997; Vural et al. 2009). Haemoglobinopathies are hereditary autosomal recessive genetic blood disorders resulting from structural changes or abnormal synthesis of the polypeptide chain of the haemoglobin molecule, a protein that carries oxygen (Sonati and Costa 2008: 40–41). They can be classified into the thalassaemias (due to an imbalance in the rate of synthesis of the globin chain) and the abnormal haemoglobins (including sickle-cell anaemia), the latter group characterized by amino acid changes on the alpha and beta globin chain of the haemoglobin molecule (Arıca et al. 2012: 147). In sickle-cell anaemia (SCA), abnormal haemoglobin causes red cells to become sickle- or crescent-shaped under certain conditions, clogging blood vessels, preventing oxygen from reaching tissues, and leading to blood clots and other problems (Rothfeld and Romaine 2005: 19). β-thalassaemia is characterized by the deficiency or absence of beta globulin production (Guler and Karacan 2007: 783).

SCA and β-thalassaemia constitute the major part of the haemoglobin disorders in Turkey with a frequency of 2.3 per cent among the whole Turkish population, corresponding to 1,300,000 carriers and 4000 patients. Nowadays, both forms of the haemoglobinopathies are considered to be the biggest health problem in contemporary Turkey (Arıca et al. 2012: 146). It is said that thalassaemia and SCA can lead to serious medical, social, and economic problems for patients and their families and, as most studies state, 'financial burdens for health services' (e.g. Ayçiçek et al. 2011: 267; Guler and Karacan 2007: 783). Since the 1990s, the Ministry of Health has launched numerous prevention programmes, entailing premarital screening in order to eradicate haemoglobinopathies in Turkey (Canatan 2011). As with the so-called syphilis problem of the 1930s, when prostitutes and alcoholics were believed to be responsible for the decline of public health, nowadays the non-modern, 'traditional', seemingly 'archaic' and economically disadvantaged segments of the society are believed to be those who, by indulging in consanguineous marriages, are responsible for the prevalence of haemoglobinopathies (Canatan et al. 2003: 58; Cogulu et al. 2011:

291; Tunçbilek 2001: 277). The Arabic-speaking Turks in particular, the so-called Eti-Turks with whom the Alawi are usually identified, have been stigmatized by medical researchers as the main carriers of haemoglobinopathies because, as the scientific studies usually assert, they mainly practise consanguineous marriages (cf. Aksoy 1957, 1961; Altay 2002; Altay et al. 1978; Aluoch et al. 1986; Çürük et al. 2008; Özsoylu and Sahinoglu 1975; Tosun et al. 2006). Some specific forms of haemoglobinopathies are actually found among Eti-Turks (Çürük et al. 2008: 526). In this context it is important, however, to note that none of these studies has produced convincing statistical data indicating a clear correlation between the practice of consanguineous marriages and the frequency of haemoglobinopathies.

In accordance with these allegations, the highest rates for ß-thalassaemia were found in the Antakya Hatay (13.1 per cent) and Çukurova region (10 per cent), and for SCA were detected in Çukurova (10 per cent), in Mersin (13.6 per cent) and in Hatay (8 per cent). In all these regions, the Alawi constitute the majority of the local population (cf. Arıca et al. 2012: 147, 149; Savaş et al. 2010: 413). Not surprisingly, Hatay and Mersin were among the first regions in which prevention centres were established in line with the 1993 law about the 'Fight Against Hereditary Blood Disease', aiming to implement premarital screening programmes and genetic counselling. Other provinces were included in 2000 at the initiative of the Turkish National Haemoglobinpathy Council (TNHC) in order to provide for treatment and control of the disease throughout Turkey (Guler and Karacan 2007: 784). In 1999, premarital testing of haemoglobinopathies was made obligatory in Hatay, at the Mother and Child Health Care Center, in Mersin and in Adana (Tosun et al. 2006: 85). Moreover, diseases such as HIV, hepatitis A, B, C and syphilis were also included in the premarital testing. However, not all of these additional diseases had previously been screened for, since patients had to pay for the examinations and could not afford them (Başer et al. 2011: 336).

In order to achieve a more comprehensive screening, in Hatay all premarital and prenatal tests for haemoglobinopathies were provided free of charge from 2002 onwards. In 2002, written regulations for the 'Fight Against Hereditary Blood Diseases' were published and a state funded Haemoglobinopathy Prevention Program (HPP) was implemented in the 'high risk provinces' of Turkey (Canatan 2011: 9). This programme aimed to collect data on thalassaemia carrier prevalence and disease incidence, to establish referral centres for prevention and treatment, to educate health personnel in genetic counselling, to conduct public education and to screen for carriers and offer genetic counselling to couples at risk (Canatan 2010). A report on the screening programme in Hatay maintains that 87,830 couples during 2004–2009 came forward for such a premarital blood test (Arıca et al. 2012: 150).

In regions like Adana, Mersin and Hatay where the premarital screening programme was firmly implemented and prenatal diagnosis centres were established, the local inhabitants were increasingly confronted with modern forms of genetic knowledge and became alerted to warnings against the negative effects of consanguineous marriages. Moreover, surveys have shown that the local inhabitants acquire their knowledge about thalassaemia primarily from television (14.2 per cent), school (13.5 per cent), and newspapers (16.4 per cent) (Gülleroğlu et al. 2007: 167). In any case, irrespective of whether the medical prevention centres or the media broadcastings were more influential, the reaction of the Alawi does not correspond to the solution conceived by the Turkish government. Due to the screening programmes and the media campaign, the Alawi have indeed become very much aware of diseases like *Akdeniz Anemisi* and their potential link with consanguineous marriage. Instead of abandoning cousin marriage altogether, however, as the Turkish state had intended, they have shifted from FBD to MZD marriage, arguing that the MZD/MZS union is not dangerous at all in terms of 'genetic risk'. As a result, most spouses relating to each other as MZD/MZS do not attend premarital screenings at all. Yet from the perspective of the Turkish state such marriages are as dangerous as any other type of cousin marriage.

In order to understand this seemingly bizarre Alawi idea that marriage to the MZD is 'genetically' less dangerous than marriage to other first cousins, I will shed further light on how modern genetic knowledge has mingled with traditional concepts of kinship and relatedness in Alawi thought.

Shared Substances: 'Blood' and 'Genes'

Up to the 1990s, the Alawi described kinship relations above all in terms of shared substances such as 'blood' (*dam*), 'sperm' (*bidar*) and 'milk' (*halīb min al-imm*) (Prager 2010a). Consanguinity was conceptualized as being established by the equal transmission of blood (*dam*) from both parents to the child, the father providing 'male blood' (*dam min ar-riǧāl*), the mother giving 'female blood' (*dam min an-nisā*). Due to this equal transmission of male and female blood (*nufs-nufs* 'half-half'), a given Ego acquires what the Alawi call 'resemblance' (*tašaba mithlu*) to his parents and to his parents' siblings, a resemblance in a physical sense and/or with regard to personal traits. In terms of *tašaba* Ego thus can share similarities with any cognatic relative in G1 (first ascending generation), be it with the Father (F), the Mother (M), the Mother's Brother (MB), Mother's Sister (MZ), Father's Sister (FZ) or with the Father's Brother (FB).

The Alawi give these consanguinal relations a certain patrilineal stress by further differentiating among the blood deriving from the parents. Although the mother and father transfer their blood in equal parts to the child, the Alawi informants say that Ego participates in the blood of his/her father with two thirds, and in the mother's blood with one third. This implies that the parents' blood is in itself differentiated according to these principles, so that the mother's blood consists of two thirds of the blood from her father and of one third from her mother. The same holds true, of course, for Ego's father. In terms of relatedness Ego is thus more related to his/her father than to his/her mother, and on the matrilateral side Ego is more related to his/her mother's father than to his/her mother's mother. This differentiation within the male and female blood gives the Alawi kinship system a clear focus on patrilineality, as Figure 4.1 illustrates.

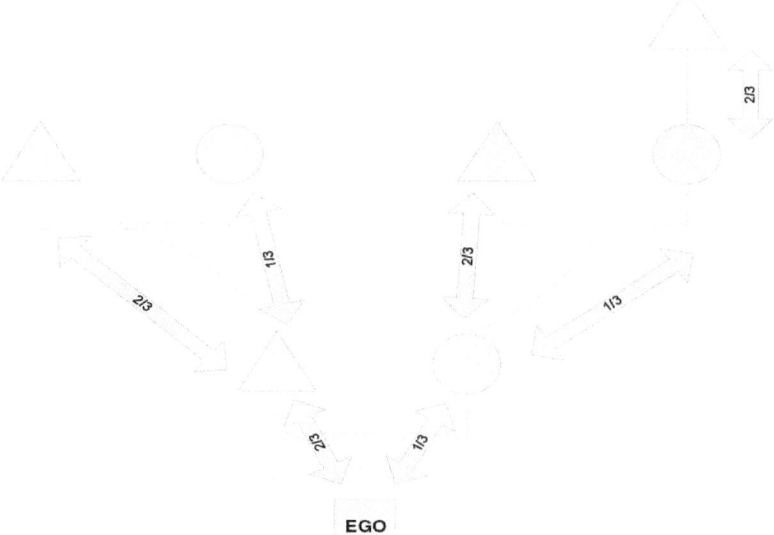

FIGURE 4.1 Two Thirds-One Third Differentiation of Male and Female Blood
○ = female, △ = male, □ = female or male

If one applies this principle of the differentiation of male and female blood to the ascending generations, one immediately observes that there is a continuous separation between patrilineally transmitted blood on the patrilateral and on the matrilateral side. One also observes, however, that the 'amount' of patrilineal blood that Ego shares with his male ascendants becomes weaker in every ascending generation. If one translates the two thirds-one third differentiation of the male and female blood in terms of percentages (2/3 = 66.6 per cent; 1/3 = 33.3 per cent) – although the Alawi informants themselves would not express the differentiation in this way – one would arrive at the diagram shown in Figure 4.2.

Full patrilineal identity thus only exists between a father and his children, as well as between the latter and the father's brother (FB) and the father's brother's children (FBCh) (that is, Ego's patrilateral parallel cousins). For instance, if Ego is male, his own children will be identical with him in terms of shared patrilineal blood, his children will be different however from the children of his patrilateral parallel cousins, because the latter's blood has already mixed (at one third) with the patrilineal blood transmitted by another woman (FBW). Patrilineal succession in terms of fully shared blood thus can only be articulated within the range of two consecutive generations, whereas Ego's patrilineal relations already start to become weaker in G +2 (second ascending generation e.g. grand-parents) and G –2 (second descending generation e.g. grand-children). Therefore the

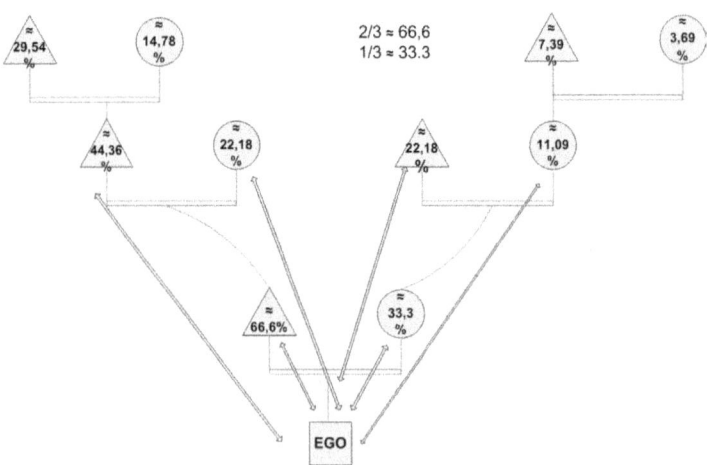

FIGURE 4.2 The Decrease of Patrilineal Relatedness in Consecutive Ascending Generations (in percentages)
○ = female, △ = male, □ = female or male

Alawi kinship system could never take the form of a classical segmentary system, because the patrilines – as far as the identity of the blood is concerned – immediately start to fade in the ascending and descending generations (Prager 2010a). Accordingly, the Alawi only consider persons to be closely related if they belong to two consecutive generations.

Due to the impact of the modern biological discourses advocated at Turkish schools, in the media and in medical institutions, including the prenatal screening centres, younger members of the Alawi community no longer speak of shared blood but of shared 'genes' (*genler*). Up to now, however, the idea of the proportional transmission of male and female substances has remained unaffected. Younger Alawi therefore still claim that they are genetically related with the father by two thirds, and with the mother by one third, even though Mendel would turn in his grave and the Turkish medical scientists would be convinced that their educational programmes about modern genetics and the concomitant dangers of consanguineous marriages have largely failed.[1] However, while in the domain of consanguinity the Alawi appropriation of biomedical concepts simply amounted to a terminological replacement (blood → genes), the Turkish campaign against cousin marriage left the Alawi with a more difficult problem.

Therefore, in the following I shall discuss and explain the astonishing solution that emerged – the replacement of FBD by MZD marriage – by drawing on ethnographic data about marriage choices that I collected in three Alawi villages in the Hatay region.

From FBD to MZD Marriages

As a general rule the Alawi practise religious endogamy, that is, both marriage partners should belong to the Alawi religious community; a person cannot convert to the Alawi religion but acquires membership by being born into an Alawi family. Moreover, as stated above, until the beginning of the 1990s the Alawi practised above all FBD marriage with a post-marital residential pattern based on viri/patrilocality or neolocality. The majority of the members of the older generations are married with the FBD/FBS, as these categories are considered to be the closest potential marriage partners a person can have. Under the impact of the Turkish campaign against consanguineous marriage this marriage pattern changed radically, with the majority of the younger Alawi nowadays practising MZD marriage.

TABLE 4.1 Marriage Partner Choices among First Cousins (according to different age groups) Based on Data Collected in Three Villages in Hatay from 2006 to 2008

Age	FBD/ FBS	FZD/ FZS	MBD/ MBS	MZD/ MZS
18–34	5%	12%	18%	65%
35–49	55%	20%	18%	7%
50–65	73%	19%	7%	1%
> 65	69%	17%	11%	3%

Table 4.1 presents statistical data on changing marriage partner choices across four different age groups in three villages in the Hatay regions.[2] According to census data available through the village mayors (*mukhtar*) in 2007, the three villages together had in total 3082 inhabitants (Village A: 572; Village B: 834; Village C: 1676), of which 2279 are or were married (including widow[er]s, divorcees). Seventy-one per cent of these persons are/were married to a first cousin (the others being married to second or third cousins, neighbours, or other non-consanguinals). The sample thus consisted of 1981 persons. Of these, 486 persons were asked directly about their marriage choices as well as those of their relatives (brothers, sisters, children, parents, etc.). The identification of the relevant kin types (i.e. FBD, MZD, etc.) for the questionnaires was based on former extensive research on Alawi relationship terminologies (see Prager 2010b). The data on the marriage choices were then stratified according to age.

While Turkish medical scientists in Hatay would maintain that the Alawi marriage system has not 'improved' at all in terms of genetic risk because cousin marriage is still practised, the Alawi themselves argue that by choosing the MZD they marry a person to whom one is only vaguely genetically related. They explain this statement by specifying an order of ideal marriage partners, which usually takes the form of the following list, ranked according to a decrease in preference, from left to right:

FBD/FBS > FZD/FZS > MBD/MBS > MZD/MZS

The preferential order stipulated in the list is based on the value of patrilineal endogamy which accords with the already mentioned idea that Ego is more closely related to the patrilateral than to the matrilateral side. It is exactly this idea that is expressed in the rank order, because by starting with the FBD, and moving further from the FZD to the MBD and the MZD, the relative distance to one's own patriline continuously increases.

The logic behind this idea of an increase in distance to one's own patriline is of course based on the aforementioned concept of the differential transmission of male and female blood/genes and therefore on the culture-specific Alawi model of relatedness. The marriage partners in the list are ranked according to the degree at which Ego shares patrilineally transmitted substances with them. If one projects the Alawi system of blood transmission (or 'genetic' relatedness), i.e. the idea that two thirds derive from the paternal, one third from the maternal side, on the rank order of the marriage partners, one observes that

- FBD marriage: Ego shares with his marriage partner two thirds of patrilineally transmitted substance, i.e. maximal accordance with Ego's own patriline
- FZD marriage: Ego still shares patrilineal substance (blood/genes) with his marriage partner at one third (transmitted by the FZ)
- MBD marriage: Ego no longer shares substance with his marriage partner deriving from his own patriline, but both marriage partners are still related via the patriline of the MF (at two thirds)
- MZD marriage: Ego is related only at one third to his marriage partner via the patriline of the MF.

Thus by marrying the MZD/MZS instead of the FBD/FBS, the Alawi nowadays practise what formerly was considered to be the least preferred type of marriage. Whereas according to medical scientists the MZD would still be classified genetically as a full cousin, the Alawi believe that they are fully complying with the demands of the Turkish state campaign by marrying a person who is only vaguely related to Ego in terms of shared genes. The differential degrees of relatedness among first cousins in Alawi understandings of shared substance (blood/genes) are shown in Figure 4.3, again expressed in percentages for a better visualization.[3]

Therefore, viewed from the Alawi perspective, the MZD/MZS is a person with whom one has close contact (in rituals, through visits and emotionally) but with whom one only shares a minimum of identical 'genetic' substance.

Since the MZD/MZS is thus not dangerous at all, the Alawi informants are convinced that premarital/prenatal testing of haemoglobinopathies is unnecessary in such cases. This is also reflected in a study on the efficacy of premarital screening in Hatay, Turkey, showing that only 17.5 per cent of pregnant high risk couples

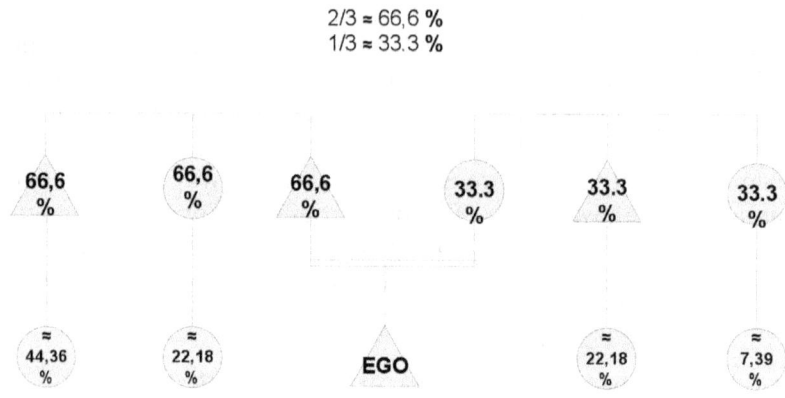

FIGURE 4.3 Relative Closeness among First Cousins According to Alawi 'Genetics'
○ = female, △ = male, □ = female or male

underwent prenatal diagnosis, despite receiving genetic counseling (Ayçiçek et al. 2011: 267).

By contrast, however, the FBD/FBS marriage is nowadays said – by younger and even older Alawi – to bring forward illnesses, particularly *Akdeniz Anemisi*, because the marriage partners are genetically too close. This statement is corroborated by stories told in almost every household in Hatay. These stories concern children who, after having been born from a FBD marriage, soon fell ill with a form of haemoglobinopathy and either died or turned out to be a financial 'burden' to their families, since they frequently required hospital treatment. At women's gatherings, particularly in the wake of marriage arrangements, I often heard the women uttering the phrase that 'if one marries a *qarīb* (close consanguineous relative) one's child is in danger of getting *Akdeniz Anemisi* and will not live long, since it loses all its blood'. Thus, if a marriage among cousins is at stake, all the women openly discuss and calculate the relative closeness of the prospective marriage partners. However, only in case of FBD/FBS marriage would all the women agree that the young couple has to attend a premarital blood test prior to their engagement.

In the few cases in which FZD/FZS and MBD/MBS marriages are contracted, it is often the girls who push to be tested together with their fiancés. As they explained to me, this is not only because they are afraid of potential genetically-transmitted diseases, but also because they are aware of the stigmatization which is nowadays attributed to first cousin marriages in public discourses. Therefore, by subjecting themselves to a premarital blood test (for haemoglobinopathies) these couples want to prove their modernity. For example, when Mayla, a seventeen-year-old girl, became engaged to her FZS, the first thing she told me was that she was really in love with her fiancé and she was not marrying him because of the 'old tradition' or from social pressure from their families; she further explained that she herself had requested a blood test in order to prevent people from thinking that she was not modern. In other words, nowadays, for young Alawi requesting a premarital test in Hatay may be a form of emancipation from tradition and a way of showing one's modernity.

Conclusion

While the Turkish state campaign against cousin marriage and the popularization of biomedical concepts of genetic risk have definitely had an impact on the marriage practices of local societies, as the Alawi case demonstrates, they do not necessarily entail a complete decline of traditional notions of kinship, relatedness and affinity. By shifting from FBD to MZD marriage instead of abandoning cousin marriage altogether and by arguing that the MZD is not dangerous since she shares with oneself only a small amount of patrilineal transmitted 'genetic' identity, the Alawi testify to the importance of a once commonly known anthropological idea that kinship/relatedness and biology may partly converge, but are never identical. Therefore, as has been done for other regions (c.f. Richards and Ponder 1996; Shaw and Hurst 2008; Simpson 2004), more in-depth research among different ethnic, religious and social groups in Turkey should be undertaken, in order to investigate how biomedical knowledge is culturally adopted and integrated at the local level.

In the Alawi case, the appropriation of modern biomedical terms such as 'genes', 'hereditary diseases', 'genetic risk' and 'Akdeniz Anemisi' has led to an amalgamation of traditional and modern ideas – at least for the time being. It is an open question, however, as to how long the practice of marrying the MZD/MZS as a means of preventing *Akdeniz Anemisi* will prevail. In the Çucurova region, particularly in the city of Adana, younger generations of the Alawi have already abandoned cousin marriage altogether. Apart from the screening programmes and the media campaign against cousin marriage, the Alawi from this region are also influenced by the fact that their *lingua franca* is Turkish and that they have shifted to a kinship terminology which is based on a modern Western-derived Turkish form of classifying relatives. According to this terminology every first cousin – as in the so-called *Eskimo system* – is designated with the same term, 'kuzen' (i.e. cousin, see also Gokalp 2011: 81), thereby classifying all PSbCh (Parents' Siblings' Children) as showing the same degree of relative closeness/distance and thus declaring them an unmarriageable category. This contrasts sharply with the Arabic terminology of the Alawi from Hatay where every first cousin is designated with a different term (cf. Prager 2010b: 140–157).

It is a timely question whether the younger generations of the Alawi from Hatay who are increasingly influenced by the Turkish language will soon follow the same path by avoiding cousin marriages altogether. Moreover, it remains to be seen for how long the Turkish Alawi may still uphold their marriage law of religious endogamy. Comparable to the warnings against cousin marriage, some medical scientists in Turkey have already maintained that intermarrying constantly within a specific ethnic/religious group might entail a high degree of genetic risks (e.g. Ayçiçek et al. 2011: 265; Elderen et al. 2010: 416; Gökçe 1991, cited in Fışloğlu 2010: 215). It would not come as a surprise if the Turkish government soon declares such types of religious and/or ethnic endogamy as new forms of 'dangerous liasions' threatening the public health. A respective state sponsored campaign stigmatizing endogamy would confront the Alawi and other concerned ethnic/religious groups of the Republic of Turkey with a series of epistemological problems, the outcomes of which cannot yet be foreseen.

Notes

1. The Alawi physicians with whom I conducted interviews were of course very much aware of scientific discussions about genetics. However, they explained to me that they would not usually convey genetic knowledge to their Alawi patients, as the latter were already educated about genetics at school or by the media. The physicians were also aware of the local concepts concerning the 1/3 and 2/3 division of blood/genes, but they would not interfere with these ideas, taking the view that the latter have no impact on the genetic risk. Most of the physicians themselves were actually married to first cousins.
2. When visiting other Alawi villages in the Hatay region, I usually asked my informants randomly about the prevalence of cousin marriages and respective changes in the conception of marriageable persons. The

answers given seem to corroborate the trend that emerges from the statistical data given in Table 4.1.
3. The Alawi do not consider (cousin) marriages among the ascending generations when calculating 'genetic' risks.

References

Aksoy, M. 1957. 'Sickle-cell-thalassaemia disease', *British Medical Journal* 30: 734–738.

———. 1961. 'Brief note: Hemoglobin S in Eti-Turks and the Allewits in Lebanon', *Blood* 17: 657–659.

Altay, Ç. 2002. 'Abnormal hemoglobins in Turkey', *Turkish Journal of Haematology* 19(1): 63–74.

Altay, Ç. et al. 1978. 'Hemoglobin S and some other hemoglobinopathies in Eti-Turks', *Human Heredity* 28: 56–61.

Altay, Ç. and N. Başak. 1995. 'Molecular basis and prenatal diagnosis of hemoglobinopathies in Turkey', *International Journal of Pediatric Hematlogy/Oncology* 2: 283–290.

Aluoch, J.R. et al. 1986. '␣ickle cell anaemia among Eti-Turks: haematological, clinical and genetic observations', *British Journal of Haematology* 64(1): 45–55.

Arıca. S.G. et al. 2012. 'Evaluation of hemoglobinopathy screening results of a six year period in Turkey', *International Journal of Collaborative Research on Internal Medicine and Public Health* 4(2): 145–151.

Arpacı, A. et al. 2003. 'An education programme on sickle cell anemia an ß-thalassemia for the 8th grade students', *Turkish Journal of Hematology* 20(1): 19–24.

Ayçiçek, A. et al. 2011. 'Beta-globin gene mutations in children with beta-thalassemia major from şanlıurfa Province, Turkey', *Turkish Journal of Hematology* 28: 264–268.

Ayoub, M.R. 1959. 'Parallel cousin marriage and endogamy: a study of sociometry', *Southwestern Journal of Anthropology* 15: 266–275.

Azzi, J. 2002. *Les Noussairites-Alaouites (histoire, doctrine et coutumes)*. Clamecy: Editions Publisud.

Bahnsen, U. 2011. 'Drum prüfe, wer sich bindet: Neuartige Gentests sollen Paaren die Angst nehmen, ihre Kinder könnten mit schweren Erbkrankheiten zur Welt kommen. Eine medizinische Revolution, ethisch umstritten', *Zeit online* 3 February. http://pdf.zeit.de/2011/06/M-Gentest.pdf. Accessed 2 June 2012.

Barry, L. 1998. 'Les modes de composition de l'alliance. Le "mariage arabe"', *L'Homme* 147: 17–50.

Başar, M., et al. 2011. 'Services provided at the Premarital Counseling Center and characteristics of the clients, in Kayseri, Turkey', *Health* 3(6): 333–337.

Blacker, C.P. 1935. 'Laws on health and marriage', *The Eugenics Review* 27(3): 191–196.
BBC News. 2008. 'Birth defects warning sparks row', 10 February.
Beckford, M. 2010. 'Baroness Deech: risks of cousin marriage not discussed for fear of offending Muslims', *Daily Telegraph Online* 23 March. http://www.telegraph.co.uk/news/religion/7497906/Baroness-Deech-Risks-of-cousin-marriage-not-discussed-for-fear-of-offending-Muslims.html. Accessed 3 July 2012.
Bellér-Hann, I. and C. Hann. 2001. *Turkish Region: State, Market & Social Identities on the East Black Sea Coast*. Santa Fe: School of American Research Press.
Bener, A. and Hussain, R. 2006. 'Consanguineous unions and child health in the state of Qatar', *Paediatric and Perinatal Epidemiology* 20(5): 372–378.
Bittles, A.H. 2008. 'A community genetics perspective on consanguineous marriage', *Community Genetics* 11: 324–330.
Brawer, M. 1988. *Atlas of the Middle East*. New York: Macmillan Publishing Company.
Canatan, D. 2006. 'Hemoglobinopathy Control Program in Turkey', *Community Genetics* 9: 124–126.
———. 2010. 'Mother and Child Health General Director. Hemoglobinopathy Control Program', *Journal of Hermatology/Oncology Special Topics* 3: 5–8.
Canatan, D., et al. 2003. 'Frequency of consanguineous marriages in patients with hereditary blood disorders in Southern Turkey', *Community Genetics* 6: 58.
——— 2011. 'Haemoglobinopathy Prevention Program in Turkey', *Thalassemia Reports* 1: 9–11.
Chelhod, J. 1965. 'Le marriage avec la cousin parallèle dans le système arabe', *L'Homme* 5(3–4): 113–173.
Cogulu, O. et al. 2011. 'Reasons for adult referrals for genetic counseling at a genetic center in Izmir, Turkey: analysis of 8965 cases over an eleven-year period', *Journal of Genetic Counseling* 20: 287–293.
Çürük, M.A. et al. 2008. 'Prenatal diagnosis of sickle cell anemia and β-thalassemia in Southern Turkey', *Hemoglobin* 32(6): 525–530.
Delaney, C. 1991. *The Seed and the Soil: Gender and Cosmology in Turkish Village Society*. 2nd edn. New York and Berkeley: University of California Press.
Dyer, O. 2005. 'MP is criticized for saying that marriage of first cousins is a health risk', *British Medical Journal* 331: 1292.
Elderen, T. van, et al. 2010. 'Turkish female immigrants' intentions to participate in preconception carrier screening for hemoglobinopathies in the Netherlands: an empirical study', *Public Health Genomics* 13: 415–423.
Engin, I. and F. Erhard (eds). 2000. *Aleviler/Alewiten*. Hamburg: Deutsches Orient-Institut.

Evered, E.Ö. and K.T. Evered. 2011. 'Sex and the capital city: the political framing of syphilis and prostitution in early Republican Ankara', *Journal of the History of Medicine and Allied Sciences* 66: online doi:10.1093/jhmas/jrr054 [1–34].

Fışloğlu, H. 2001. 'Consanguineous marriage and marital adjustment in Turkey', *The Family Journal* 9(2): 215–222.

Foucault, M. 1994. *Dits et Écrits (vol. III)*. Paris: Gallimard.

Giordano, P. et al. 1998. 'The molecular spectrum of beta-thalassemia and abnormal hemoglobins in the allochthonous and authochthonous Dutch population', *Community Genetics* 1: 243–251.

Gokalp, A. 2011. 'Mariage de parents: entre l'échange généralisé et le mariage parallèle. Le cas de la Turquie', in F. Georgeon and M. Timour (eds), *Altan Gokalp – Têtes rouges et bouches noires et autres écrits*. Paris: Centre National de la Recherche Scientifique.

Guler, E. and M. Karacan 2007. 'Prevalence of beta-thalassemia and sickle cell anemia trait in premarital screening in Konya Urban Area, Turkey', *Pediatric Hematology Oncology* 29(11): 783–785.

Gülleroğlu, S.K. et al. 2007. 'Public education for the prevention of hemoglobinopathies: a study targeting Kocaeli University students', *Turkish Journal of Hematology* 24(2): 164–170.

Halm, H. 1982. *Die islamische Gnosis. Die Extreme Schia und die 'Alawiten*. Zurich and Munich: Artemis Verlag.

el-Hamzi, M.A.F. 2006. 'Pre-marital examination as a method of prevention from blood genetic disorders', *Saudi Medical Journal* 27(9): 1291–1295.

Holy, L. 1989. *Kinship, Honor and Solidarity: Cousin Marriage in the Middle East*. Manchester and New York: Manchester University Press.

Jaber, L. et al. 1998. 'The impact of consanguinity worldwide', *Community Genetics* (1): 12–17.

Khuri, F.I. 1991. 'The Alawis of Syria: religious ideology and organization', in R.T. Antoun and D. Quataert (eds), *Syria: Society, Culture, and Polity*. New York: University of New York Press, pp.49–61.

Merwin, S. 2007. 'Des Nosayris aux Ja'farites: le processus de "Chiitisation" des Alaouites', in B. Dupret et al. (eds), *La Syrie au Présent: Reflets d'une Société*. Beirut: Actes Sud, pp.359–364.

Nimier, A. 1987. *Les Alawites*. Paris: Édition Asfar.

Özsoylu, S. and M. Sahinoglu. 1975. 'Haemoglobinopathy survey in an Eti-Turk village', *Human Heredity* 25: 50–59.

Paul, D.B. and H.G. Spencer. 2008. '"It's ok, we're not cousins by blood": the cousin marriage controversy in historical perspective', *PLoS Biol* 6(12). http://www.plosbiology.org/article/info:doi/10.1371/journal.pbio.0060320. Accessed 2 June 2012.

Port, K. and A.H. Bittles. 2001. 'A population-based estimate of the prevalence of consanguineous marriage in Western Australia', *Community Genetics* 4: 97–101.

Prager, L. 2010a. 'Âmes sexuées et idées de procréation chez les Alawites/ Nousairites (en Turquie)', *Anthropology of the Middle East* 5(2): 77–99.

———. 2010b. *Die Gemeinschaft des Hauses: Religion, Heiratsstrategien und transnationale Identität türkischer Alawi-/Nusairi-Migranten in Deutschland*. Berlin: LITVerlag.

———. 2012. 'Customary marriage', in S.Loue and M. Sajatovic (eds), *Encyclopedia of Immigrant Health*. Heidelberg and New York: Springer Verlag, pp.526–527.

———. 2013. 'Die Zeichen der Wiedergeburt: Körper, Stigmata und Seelenwanderung bei den Alawiten/Nusairiern der Südosttürkei', *Paideuma* 59: 237–260.

———. forthcoming. 'The mnemonic body: cycles of rebirth and the remembrance of former lives in Alawi religion', in P. Franke et al. (eds), *Körper, Sexualität und Medizin in muslimischen Gesellschaften*. Bamberg: Bamberg University Press.

Richards, M. and M. Ponder. 1996. 'Lay understanding of genetics: a test of an hypothesis', *Journal of Medical Genetics* 33: 1032–1036.

Rothfeld, G.S. and D.S. Romaine. 2005. *The Encyclopedia of Men's Health*. Amaranth: Facts on File.

Rowlatt, J. 2005. 'The risks of cousin marriage', BBC News. http://news.bbc.co.uk/2/hi/programmes/newsnight/4442010.stm. Accessed 2 June 2012.

Salgırlı, S.G. 2010. 'Eugenics for the doctors: medicine and social control in 1930s Turkey', *Journal of the History of Medicine and Allied Sciences* 66(3): 281–312.

Savaş, N. et al. 2010. 'Hemoglobinopathy awareness among high school students in Antakya (Antioch), Turkey', *International Journal of Hematology* 91: 413–418.

Shaw, A. and J.A. Hurst. 2008. '"What is this genetics, anyway?" Understandings of genetics, illness causality and inheritance among British Pakistani users of genetic services', *Journal of Genetic Counseling* 17(4): 373–382.

Sheridan, E. 2013. 'Risk factors for congenital anomaly in a multiethnic birth cohort: an analysis of the Born in Bradford Study', *The Lancet* 382: 1350–1359.

Simpson, B. 2004. 'Acting ethically, responding culturally: framing the new reproductive and genetic technologies in Sri Lanka', *Asia Pacific Journal of Anthropology* 5(3): 227–243.

Somersan, N. 1938. 'Prenuptial medical examination in Turkey', *The Eugenics Review* 29(4): 261–263.

Sonati, M.F. and F.F. Costa. 2008. 'The genetics of blood disorders: the hereditary hemoglobinopathies', *Jornal de Pediatria* 84(4): 40–51.

The National. 2009. 'Qatar starts premarital genetic screening for all', 8 December.

Tosun, F. et al. 2006. 'Five-year evaluation of premarital screening program for hemoglobinpathies in the Province of Mersin, Turkey', *Turkish Journal of Hematology* 23: 84–89.

Tunçbilek, E. 1997. 'Genetic services in Turkey', *European Journal of Human Genetics* 5(2): 178–182.

———. 2001. 'Clinical outcomes of consanguineous marriages in Turkey', *The Turkish Journal of Pediatrics* 43(4): 277–279.

Tunçbilek, E. and M. Özgüç. 2007. 'Application of medical genetics in Turkey', *Turkish Journal of Pediatrics* 49: 353–359.

Vural, B. et al. 2009. 'Nursing students' self-reported knowledge of genetics and genetic education', *Public Health Genomics* 12: 225–232.

PART II

COUSIN MARRIAGES WITHIN MIGRANT POPULATIONS IN EUROPE

Chapter 5

BRITISH PAKISTANI COUSIN MARRIAGES AND THE NEGOTIATION OF REPRODUCTIVE RISK

Alison Shaw

Fifty years after substantial Pakistani migration to Britain began, there is no firm evidence of any significant decline in the rate of consanguineous and especially first cousin marriage among the children and grandchildren of pioneer-generation migrants. This contradicts the general expectation that cousin marriage will decline with urbanization, modernization and the transition to smaller families (see Introduction and chapter one of this volume). Since the 1980s, evidence has also accumulated showing that consanguineous marriage among British Pakistanis confers a significant health risk for children: the prevalence of many mostly very rare recessive genetic conditions is higher among British Pakistanis than among other ethnic groups. Policy and media debate over the implications of this evidence has centred on whether cousin marriage should be actively discouraged and on whether consanguineous couples should be singled out for genetic advice and screening. The state shoulders the financial costs of caring for children with serious medical problems, disabilities and special needs.

To date, consanguineous couples have not been targeted in UK health policies for genetic risk advice or premarital, preconception or prenatal screening on the basis of consanguinity alone. Carrier screening for thalassaemia is provided to all pregnant women in high prevalence areas of the UK, and is provided to targeted groups in low prevalence areas, as the prevalence of unaffected carriers of thalassaemia is higher among people of Mediterranean, South Asian and African ancestry (http://sct.screening.nhs.uk; last accessed on 8 November 2013). The risk for rare recessive conditions associated with parental consanguinity is managed on a case-by-case basis through the existing maternity, genetic and other services. Usually at-risk couples are identified only after they have had an affected child; when the child is referred for diagnosis and therapy, the parents are offered genetic counselling to manage risk to future pregnancies. Individuals or couples may also seek or be referred for genetic counselling on the basis of a family history of a genetic condition. Additionally, some local schemes supporting Pakistani families with recessive conditions for which the mutations have been identified seek to 'cascade' preconception or premarital genetic counselling to other members of the extended family, encouraging them to seek carrier testing (Alwan and Modell 2007; Modell and Darr 2002).

In this chapter, I discuss why consanguineous marriage has continued to be practised by British Pakistanis and describe how some consanguineous couples with children diagnosed with recessive genetic conditions have engaged with medical genetics services. I begin by describing trends in consanguineous Pakistani marriages and summarizing the scientific and media reporting of the adverse health outcomes associated with parental consanguinity among British Pakistanis. Then, using one family as an illustrative case study, I discuss the socio-economic and emotional significance of cousin marriage not just for the parents who conventionally arrange such marriages but also for many young people themselves. In this family, a couple reflected on genetic risk while deliberating over the marriages of their unaffected children. Finally, I draw on fieldwork undertaken with Pakistani Punjabi and Mirpuri families referred to a genetics clinic (Shaw 2009, 2011) to show that, contrary to the prevailing media stereotype that British Pakistanis are 'in denial' (Cryer 2005) about genetic risk and do not engage with clinical genetics services or techniques of risk management, Pakistani couples do engage with clinical genetics services in a variety of ways. Families' responses to genetic risk are not fixed but change over time, according to life stage and experience. This, I conclude, represents negotiated engagements with discourses of risk rather than a straightforward cultural convergence towards the marriage patterns of the majority society.

Birādarī Endogamy and Consanguineous Marriages

British Pakistanis numbered 747,205 people or 1.3 per cent of the total British population according to the 2001 Census, and are residentially concentrated in parts of London, West Yorkshire, notably in Bradford and Leeds, the Midlands and the North. Their origins in Pakistan are diverse but the majority originate from the Punjab region of Pakistan and from Mirpur district in Azad Kashmir, bordering northern Punjab. For most British Pakistanis, membership of a *birādarī* or extended kinship group has an important influence over life decisions, including marriage. *Birādarī* names indicate *quom* (tribe) or *zāt* (caste, or subcaste) identities (Shaw 2000: 69–71) and carry connotations of hierarchy, indicating an *ashraf* (noble, respectable), *zamīndār* (landowning) or *kammi* (artisan) status. These identities intersect with and may cut across heterogeneity by urban, rural and regional origins and social class (Shaw 2000: 116–117; Werbner 1990).

During my fieldwork, I was often told that marriages 'in the family' are preferred because a young woman is more likely to be comfortable, safe and well-treated if she marries into a household of people whom she already knows and trusts, rather than into a household of outsiders. Relatives are recognized as *apne log* (our own people) as opposed to people who are *bahar se* (from outside), while consanguineous kin are *khunī rishte* (blood connections). A *birādarī* tends to be endogamous, but *birādarī* endogamy is preferential not prescriptive. A *birādarī* is not necessarily a biologically homogeneous entity because *birādarī* membership can also be extended to previously unrelated people through alliances, most especially alliances of marriage. In Pakistan overall, between a third and a half of marriages are with cousins, the rest occurring with more distantly related or unrelated people (Hussain and Bittles 1999; Shami et al. 1989).

Families vary in the importance they attach to *birādarī* or caste endogamy. Concerns to maintain the purity of the *birādarī* may be greater for families such as the Sayeds, who claim descent from the Prophet Mohammed, than for people from middle ranking or artisan castes, but hierarchy with respect to caste, *birādarī* and wealth also enables various forms of social mobility, including across *zāt* and *birādarī* boundaries (Shaw 2000: 131; Werbner 1990: 113–119). Marriage choices are strategic: they concern reputation and socio-economic interest, and to understand a particular choice it is necessary to understand all the relationships – historical and current – between those involved (Donnan 1985, 1988). On this basis, some but not all marriages will be with relatives of the same *birādarī*. Marriages create links between households and particularly successful marriages may be followed by further marriages connecting the same two households. In Pakistan, higher frequencies of consanguineous marriage are associated with rural areas, lower levels of education and younger age at marriage, while lower frequencies are associated with urban areas and higher levels of education (Hussain and Bittles 1999; Afzal et al. 1994). Given this prevalence pattern in Pakistan, it would be reasonable to expect that the frequency of consanguineous marriage among British Pakistanis would show signs of declining over one or two generations, even though some marriages will continue to be between first cousins, for example to consolidate a business established by two brothers (Shaw 2000: 147).

In fact, there is some evidence that the opposite has occurred: that consanguineous marriage among British Pakistanis has increased rather than declined. A West Yorkshire study from the late 1980s found an increase from 33 per cent to 55 per cent in the proportion of first cousin marriages by comparing the marriages of 100 young mothers with the marriages these women reported for their mothers' generation (Darr and Modell 1988). In the late 1990s, I compared the marriages of twenty-four couples of the pioneer generation in Oxford with the marriages of seventy adult children and found an increase from 37 per cent to 59 per cent in first cousin marriages (Shaw 2001). Significantly, as I discuss below, nearly all of these first cousin marriages involved cousins from Pakistan. Larger-scale survey data also indicate that consanguineous marriage was common in the 1990s among second generation Pakistanis (Modood et al. 1997: 319). In these studies, no distinction is made between Pakistan-born and UK-born in the category 'second generation'.

A recent Norwegian study, by contrast, is 'the first to demonstrate a decrease in the proportion of consanguineously related parents in an immigrant population of Pakistani origin and their descendants in a European country' (Grijibovski et al. 2009: 237). Norway's Pakistani population is just over a quarter of the size of the Pakistani population of Bradford alone. Comparing data from nearly 2,000 women in two cohorts, the study demonstrated a significant decline in parental consanguinity, most dramatic among Norwegian-born Pakistani women (from 48.3 per cent in 1995–1997 to 18.8 per cent in 2002–2005) and occurring mostly in first cousin marriages. Overall there was a 25 per cent increase in marriages to unrelated partners. Consanguinity was most prevalent, and more likely to persist over time, among women whose parents were consanguineous; the study suggests that this represents the continuity of family traditions whereby parents make the main marital decisions (Grijibovski et al. 2009).

To date, there appear to be no such clear indications of a decline in cousin marriage among British Pakistanis. The most recent data are from the city of Bradford, which is home to 10 per cent of Britain's Pakistani population and where one fifth of the city's population is of Pakistani origin (2001 Census). Data collected from approximately 5,000 Pakistani-origin mothers of babies born between 2007 and 2011 show that over half (59 per cent) of the babies have consanguineously married parents (Sheridan et al. 2013). This consanguinity rate is similar to that reported for Pakistanis in Birmingham twenty years ago (Bundey and Alam 1993). It also represents an approximately 10 per cent increase in the reported parental consanguinity of the babies' maternal and paternal grandparents (Born in Bradford).

Genetic Epidemiology and Media Reporting

Research from the 1980s onwards in the UK (and also in Norway; see Stolenberg 1997) has shown higher rates of infant mortality and morbidity among Pakistanis compared with other ethnic groups. In Bradford between 1996 and 2003, the rate of infant death and illness exceeded national averages, at 9.1 per 1,000 live births compared with 5.3 per 1,000 live births recorded for England and Wales, and the rate was higher for infants of Pakistani ancestry than for those of other ethnicities (Born in Bradford). Attempts have been made to assess the contribution of parental consanguinity to these outcomes. In Birmingham, a five-year prospective study of the health of 4,934 babies noted that although Pakistani babies comprised 20 per cent of the study population, they accounted for 40 per cent of the observed ill health, most of this arising from a wide range of rare recessive genetic conditions. The study also observed that 69 per cent of the Pakistani couples were consanguineous, and that infant mortality and morbidity was three times higher among the babies of consanguineous compared with non-consanguineous Pakistani couples. The authors concluded that if Pakistanis stopped marrying relatives, infant death and illness would decrease by 60 per cent (Bundey and Alam 1993).

More recent studies have continued to report significantly higher risks of infant death and long-term illness in children of consanguineous couples. A national review of children with progressive intellectual and neurological deterioration found unexpectedly high numbers of cases in districts such as Bradford, and many of these cases concerned children of consanguineous Pakistani parents (Devereux et al. 2004). The most recent reported data on consanguinity and risk of congenital anomalies are from the above-mentioned Born in Bradford study, a prospective multi-ethnic birth cohort study of 23,776 babies born between 2007 and 2011 (Sheridan et al. 2013). The study identified parental consanguinity as a statistically significant risk factor for congenital anomalies, independent of socio-economic deprivation: parental consanguinity increased the risk for congenital abnormalities by 2 per cent, an elevated risk similar to that for British mothers aged over thirty-four years. The study notes also that in some cousin couples the degree of genetic relatedness may be higher than that expected from first cousins because of complex consanguinity in the family (Sheridan et al. 2013: 8; chapter two, this volume).

Media accounts have often been alarmist, stigmatizing 'South Asians', 'Asians' and more recently 'Muslims' as the perpetrators of the practice of cousin marriage. A national newspaper described close kin marriage as customary 'in Britain's Muslim community' and claimed it has been practised by Muslims 'since the fourteenth century' and is only now producing a 'genetic backlash' from which children are suffering (Haslam 2001). In a Newsnight television documentary on 16 November 2005, Member of Parliament Ann Cryer maintained that cousin marriage is a cultural tradition that is 'unacceptable in the twenty-first century'. Later that year, Cryer described cousin marriage as an unhealthy lifestyle choice. She argued that just as having unprotected sex, drinking alcohol, eating greasy food and smoking cigarettes are discouraged in order to reduce both individual health risks and the social and economic costs of HIV, Chlamydia, liver damage, obesity and lung cancer, so too cousin marriages should be discouraged: 'Prevention is better – and cheaper – than cure. The NHS [National Health Service] is one of our greatest assets and everyone can expect the best of care whatever their problem, but it does not have unlimited resources' (Cryer 2005). In 2008, a national paper carried the headline, 'Minister warns of "inbred" Muslims', and reported that another Member of Parliament had called for a debate over the 'surge of birth defects' resulting from 'inbreeding among immigrants' (*Sunday Times*, 10 February

2008). On 21 April that year in the House of Lords, reproductive law professor Baroness Ruth Deech asked, 'what steps is Government taking to address genetic problems arising from marriages between first cousins?' In her 2010 Gresham lecture, Baroness Deech called for a 'vigorous campaign' to deter cousin marriages on the grounds of genetic risk, since an outright ban would fail to respect human rights (Deech 2010). The public health concerns were followed up in 2011 in a Radio programme in April and a television documentary in June. In 2011, a national paper reported on the 'heartbreaking issue that multicultural Britain scandalously ignores', namely that 'marriage between cousins in Muslim communities is causing terrible disabilities in children' (*Daily Mail*, 4 June 2011).

In the media reporting, the health risks of cousin marriage are usually quickly linked with debates over multiculturalism, the politics of integration, immigration and even terrorism, particularly in relation to Muslim minorities. In these portrayals, there are echoes of the nineteenth-century concerns that cousin marriage among linguistic and religious minorities in the United States would threaten 'social progress', concerns that resulted in thirty-one states making cousin marriages illegal (Ottenheimer 1996: 113). Similar concerns are echoed in contemporary debates elsewhere in Europe (chapters six and seven, this volume). But whereas in Denmark consanguineous marriage has been defined as forced marriage and linked with immigration politics, in the UK debates the emphasis has been on defining the degree of genetic risk in consanguineous marriage and finding ways to manage it through existing local genetic counselling provisions, avoiding what might be perceived as 'ethnic profiling' with its potential to stigmatize a minority group.

In much of this reporting, too, the extent of the risk is presented in an alarming manner. The 'doubling' of a background risk is frequently stressed, but in absolute terms, this amounts to an approximately 4–6 per cent, rather than 2–3 per cent, risk of an affected child (Bennett et al. 2002; Firth and Hurst 2005; chapter two, this volume). If this risk is about equivalent to the risk of a woman over thirty-four years of age having a child with a congenital or genetic abnormality, this hardly justifies a public health policy aimed at discouraging cousin marriage. In the House of Lords debate (21 April 2008), one questioner asked the then health minister if some ethnic communities have a higher risk than others; Lord Darzi's response was 'no', that the risk is 'double' the background risk, but that this is low. A public health campaign may be inappropriate, but some practitioners consider it insufficient to continue to manage the risk with current provisions – by providing genetic counselling only to couples after they have had an affected child, or to people who seek genetic advice because of their family history. Clinicians could, and in some localities do, for some disorders, manage the risk for a known recessive condition more proactively by maintaining a register of families with affected children and inviting 'at risk' individuals or couples for preconception counselling and screening (see for comparison chapter eight, this volume). This strategy requires ethics consent for the disclosure of patient information to relatives, because currently the onus is on patients, not clinicians, to communicate risk information in the family. Moreover, for some first cousin couples whose families have practised consanguineous marriage for generations there will be a higher risk even if there is no known family history of disease (Sheridan et al. 2013: 8; chapter two, this volume). New genetic sequencing technologies for consanguineous couples in the absence of a family history may soon enable more precise preconception genetic risk assessment (chapter ten, this volume).

Marriage as a Risky Business

It is also important to contextualize these policy questions with reference to how marriage patterns among Pakistanis in Britain have changed over the past fifty years. It remains the case that nearly all British Pakistanis marry, and like other British South Asians, they tend to marry earlier and be less likely to separate or divorce than White or African-Caribbean British people. But there are indications of change towards later marriage (Berrington 1994: 530) and of increasing marital instability; the small proportion of lone parents has doubled since the mid-1990s (Babb, Butcher et al. 2006: 24–25). Pakistanis themselves usually justify arranged marriages by saying they are less risky than 'love marriages', with which they are usually contrasted. They may say that parents are better judges of a good match than are young people, and parents will consequently share some responsibility for the success of an arranged marriage. A couple can expect support from their wider kinship network if problems arise and this inhibits separation and divorce. But there are also indications of change in how Pakistani parents and young adults are thinking about the risks and benefits of conventionally arranged marriages. There has been much public discussion of forced marriages, and parents and young people are increasingly concerned to emphasize that an arranged marriage requires the couple's freely given consent, even if this marriage meets with parental approval (Shaw 2009: 103). Some so-called arranged marriages, whether to kin or unrelated people, are in fact initiated by the couple and assisted by parents and the wider family. Indeed, young adults today utilize a range of strategies to find spouses or new partners, ranging from dating people they meet at college to using internet dating sites, such as shadi.com.

The observed increase in the rate of consanguineous marriage among British Pakistanis, noted above, is connected to the fact that these marriages are usually transnational. In Western Europe, spousal immigration is a common consequence of transnational marriage within minority groups originating outside Western Europe (Beck-Gernsheim 2007). In Bradford during 1992–1994, approximately 57.6 per cent of Pakistani marriages were to spouses from Pakistan (Simpson 1997). Immigration statistics indicate that approximately half of British-born Pakistanis aged between nineteen and fifty has a Pakistan-born spouse (Dudley and Harvey 2001). For kin in Pakistan, there is a strategic motivation in the opportunity to migrate to Britain, while for relatives in the UK transnational marriage helps to maintain links with and fulfil obligations to kin, especially siblings, in Pakistan. Yet the separation and distance produced by international migration can undermine trust and introduce new dangers. British women risk being viewed as 'passports' – as a means of gaining an entry visa – by uncommitted husbands, or else they risk becoming 'immigration widows' should a husband's entry application be rejected. Incoming spouses are vulnerable in ways that reflect changing gender dynamics in processes of settlement and adjustment; the incoming son-in-law in particular is in a weak position as he is dependent on his wife and her family, reversing the conventional South Asian pattern of patrilocal residence after marriage (Charsley 2006, 2008). Arranged transnational consanguineous marriages thus entail complex risks and benefits which individuals and families assess and reassess, as is illustrated in the case study below of marriages over two generations in a family from northern Punjab.

Zahida came to England to join her husband, who is her first cousin, in the 1970s, bringing their Pakistan-born children. In 1979, the elder son married his father's sister's daughter (his FZD), according to his father's wishes. The bride, Shamim, came to England from the Middle East where her parents were living. In 1986, the second son married his mother's younger brother's daughter (his MBD), according to his mother's preference. This bride came to England from Pakistan. Then in 1987, the daughter married her mother's brother's son (her MBS), who is also her brother's wife's brother. Zahida's household in Britain and her brother's household in Pakistan were now connected through two marriages, in a *watta satta* or 'sibling exchange' (Shaw 2009: 94–95, 98). This son-in-law also came to Britain. This marriage did not last, with the husband remaining in the UK but leaving his wife for a new partner. Sibling exchange marriages are considered to carry risks for the other marriage if one of the marriages fails, but in this case there was no serious impact on Zahida's younger son's marriage.

In the next generation, a similar pattern of selecting spouses from the children of the parents' closest siblings emerged, but with two new elements: the parents' awareness of aspects of genetic risk, and the younger generation's personal preferences seemingly playing a larger part in the process. I illustrate this with a discussion of Shamim's children's marriages. Shamim had six children: three now married, and three who died before the age of five years, having been born with severe physical and intellectual abnormalities. The affected children required round-the-clock care, suffered fits and recurrent infections and were never able to sit unsupported; caring for them took a considerable toll on the family, particularly on Shamim. Doctors diagnosed an underlying but unknown condition, probably arising from a rare recessive but unidentified mutation; they gave a recurrence risk of 1 in 4, but explained that there was no prenatal genetic test. At first, the parents believed that the health of their babies was entirely in God's hands. Having lost three children to the condition and with two healthy children to care for, they considered terminating their sixth pregnancy to avoid the suffering to all concerned that would follow should this baby be affected, but finally chose not to, on religious grounds, and had a healthy son.

Contemplating her children's marriages, Shamim did not want her daughters to suffer as she had by giving birth to and caring for infants with fatal congenital problems: 'I do not want my daughters to go through what I have gone through, or to have a child with thalassaemia, I know I am carrier for that'. Shamim had been tested for thalassaemia after her sister had given birth to an affected child, and showed me a card indicating her carrier status. Shamim told me her children had been tested for thalassaemia carrier status, and she took these results into account when considering *rishta*s (marriage partners) for her children. She also told me that avoiding marriages 'on the father's side' of the family and choosing a relative from her side of the family would reduce the risk of these rare genetic problems in her grandchildren. This, she explained, is because blood connections between people related through their mothers are weaker than those between people related through their fathers: 'if the fathers [of the boy and girl] are brothers, there is the most danger'.

This construction of genetic risk is linked to indigenous ideas about the strength of patrilineal blood ties. During my fieldwork, my accounts of the Mendelian notion of an equal genetic contribution from the mother and the father to a child sometimes elicited surprised reactions from Pakistani women, who sometimes asked, 'but isn't the blood stronger on the father's side', or else asserted that the genetic link between people related through their mothers is 'weaker' than between people related through their fathers (Shaw and Hurst 2008). I have also heard it said that people in Pakistan believe that British Pakistanis are marrying maternal rather than paternal relatives in order to reduce the risk of genetic problems in children. This seems to be an extension of the idea that men, rather than women, are the perpetrators of lineage or *birādarī* identity, and that a father's 'genetic' contribution to a child, through the substance of blood, is stronger than that of the mother's because semen is concentrated blood: 'every drop of semen is made from 100 drops of blood' (Shaw 2000: 218). This, then, is one of the ways in which modern notions of genetic risk may be incorporated into indigenous ideas about biological inheritance (see also chapter four, this volume).

These medical considerations took their place alongside social and emotional ones, chiefly concerning the fact that Shamim had closer links with her siblings in urban Pakistan and in the Middle East than her husband had with his siblings in the UK or his more distant kin in Pakistan. Thus, the elder daughter was married to the son of one of Shamim's distant relatives, a woman who has only one child, because, Shamim said, 'She will treat my daughter like her own daughter, not a daughter-in-law, and the boy does not have any brothers, so my daughter will have no sisters-in-law to order her about and treat her harshly'. The second daughter, Ayesha, married a relative of her mother's 'side' of the family, the son of her mother's brother (her MBS). Ayesha was studying at university when Shamim first told me that she was discussing the *rishta* with her brother, saying, 'they have asked us, and we are talking to him about it. It is making us ... closer'. Shamin and her brother discussed the risk of thalassaemia in the light of Ayesha's carrier status, and Shamim's brother's son had a genetic test showing he was not a carrier. A few years later, Shamim's son (not a thalassaemia carrier) married his MZD, who was raised in the Middle East.

The other new element in these negotiations was the attention given to children's preferences. As noted, young adults increasingly emphasize that it is their individual responsibility to accept or reject a particular match, and parents have had to accept a child's refusal of a particular match on grounds that may include genetic risk, saying, for instance, 'and there is this thing about blood' (Shaw 2009: 106). Equally, they may actively prefer, and view in quite romantic terms, marriage to a relative from Pakistan who they view as someone who knows their culture and religion (Shaw and Charsley 2006). As Charsley notes, 'the possibility of transnational marriage introduces potential spouses who are equally close in terms of kinship, but distant enough in other ways to be acceptable partners, whilst fulfilling the criteria of connection needed to be confident of social approval and the reduction of risk involved in such arrangements' (2013: 152).

Before Shamim's brother raised the subject of his son marrying Ayesha, Ayesha and her cousin had chosen to marry, and Ayesha stressed that this was her choice, her decision:

> I met him at my sister's wedding in Pakistan, four years ago – he was there from Kuwait and I was there from England – and we have been in touch even since. I liked him as soon as I met him. We spoke to each other first, and he told me he liked me. Then I let my parents know and he let his parents know, and our parents they got on with it then. So I couldn't say it was totally an arranged marriage. Actually, it was just him and me to start with . . . It was my decision at the end of the day. Living in this day and age, I wanted to marry someone who I would be comfortable with. It's a coincidence that it's him, my cousin. It could have been someone out of the family. He is educated – he is studying, in Pakistan, for a masters' degree in business and finance – and we don't have any major differences.

Ayesha may have been distancing herself from the dominant discourse that views arranged cousin marriage disapprovingly, both for being 'arranged', implying lack of choice, and on genetic grounds, by saying that, in her case, it is a 'coincidence' that her husband is her cousin. She had high hopes for this marriage, thinking it might also give her the option of living in the Middle East. Quite early into the marriage, it became clear that her husband had different expectations of the marriage, and the birth of a baby did not prevent the couple from eventually separating. Ayesha's parents now feel a burden of guilt and responsibility for having encouraged this match. This story is not unique; other cases indicate that changing and conflicting expectations of marriage are a factor in destabilizing British Pakistani marriages, and that there are signs that some young people and their parents may be coming to view arranged transnational consanguineous marriages as 'riskier' than love marriages (Qureshi et al. 2014).

Engagements with Clinical Genetics Services

The case study above illustrates two ways in which perceptions of genetic risk can feature in marriage choices without necessarily being overriding considerations. In this section, I summarize the responses of fifty-one couples to being given a numerical recurrence risk for a genetic problem in a child, by comparing their initial responses with their attitudes to genetic risk and genetic risk management four years later (Shaw 2011). These couples were in most cases young (of the same generation as Ayesha whose case was discussed above), consanguineous, and had transnational marriages. Across the sample of fifty-one couples, clinicians had identified fifty-four genetic conditions (three couples were carriers of two recessive conditions). Most of these conditions were rare recessives, yielding a 1 in 4 recurrence risk, with varying degrees of severity, fourteen of them fatal. For about half of the recessive conditions the mutation was unknown, which meant that a genetic test was not available, although some of the conditions could be identified prenatally by ultrasound.

The factors known to influence couples' responses to recurrence risk and risk management information include: their understandings of the diagnosis and of genetic risk; the availability of a prenatal test; the severity of the condition for which there is risk; their experience of the condition in question; and their attitudes to prenatal diagnosis and abortion. For this sample of Pakistani couples, I identified four categories of responses to recurrence risk and risk management information: 'taking the risk', 'postponing', 'managing', or 'exempt', the latter meaning that parents dismissed the risk, saying it was irrelevant to them. Initially, about half of the couples were risk-takers, broadly sceptical of the diagnosis as genetic and that it might recur, and anxious to have another child. Four years later, however, the responses of fifteen couples had changed, the most striking change being the increase in the number of couples opting for risk management. The number of risk-takers and the number of postponers decreased. The analysis indicated the importance of couples' reproductive experiences in shaping both their initial responses and the direction of change. Two factors were particularly important in influencing these changes: the births of more fatally affected infants and the availability of a prenatal genetic test. Over the four-year period, six more affected infants were born to couples in this sample, and genetic scientists identified the mutations causing two of the rare recessive conditions. These changes may seem small from the perspective of clinical epidemiology, but they are, I think, important in showing that risk response is not only socially and culturally shaped but can change over time, both with new personal experiences of genetic conditions and with developments in scientific knowledge and diagnostic and management possibilities.

Conclusion

The apparently continuing popularity of consanguineous and especially first cousin marriages among British Pakistanis can be understood in terms of both strategy and trust – that is, their socio-economic benefits and the strong cultural, religious and emotional connections linking British Pakistanis with relatives in Pakistan. These connections are then reinforced in the next generation through transnational marriages. However, young British-raised adults are increasingly aware of the discourse of risk in relation to cousin marriage, and are also aware of the popular equation of arranged with forced marriage. They may seek to distance themselves from these discourses by emphasizing individual choice in marriage, and in exercising personal choice in spouse selection to a greater extent than their parents did. They may actively favour a Pakistan-raised spouse, considering that such a partner will have a better knowledge of Islam and of Pakistani cultural norms than they do, as well as because of the apparent 'distance' introduced by marrying cousins from Pakistan, sometimes using the argument about genetic risk as a reason for refusing a particular cousin.

At least within families directly affected by genetic conditions, and among the professionals who provide clinical genetics services for them, there is a gradually increasing awareness that at least some of the elevated risk for recessive conditions can be managed medically without banning cousin marriage. Differences exist between and within extended families in how individuals and couples understand both genetic inheritance and the implications of a genetic diagnosis for other family members (Shaw and Hurst 2008, 2009), but there is also evidence that these perceptions are not static and that some couples and families who have had affected children do make greater use of clinical genetics services over time (Shaw 2011). In the UK, these clinical processes are part of the broader medicalization of reproduction that has occurred within modern societies rather than a specific medicalization of cousin marriage, despite the wider public and media discourse of genetic risk.

Pakistani marriage negotiations also need to be situated within the context of broader continuities and change in marital dynamics and family forms in British society. Evidence of an increase in Pakistani lone parenthood, for instance, implies conflicting expectations of marriage and separation if not formal divorce. There is also evidence that whereas previously 'arranged' marriages were viewed as safer, especially for women, than the 'love' marriages with which they are conventionally contrasted, transnationally arranged consanguineous marriage may now be being seen as carrying greater social and emotional risks (Qureshi et al. 2014). Perceptions of the practice of arranged marriage are becoming increasingly multidimensional and contradictory, open to dispute and debate, even within one family. There is scope here for further research to investigate the motivations underlying particular marriage choices within particular families and to examine generational change in these motivations, including the role of considerations of genetic risk.

References

Afzal, M., S.M. Ali and H.B. Siyal. 1994. 'Consanguineous marriages in Pakistan', *Pakistan Development Review* 33: 663–674.

Alwan, A. and B. Modell. 1997. 'Community control of genetic and congenital disorders', *EMRO Technical Publications Series* 24. Alexandria: World Health Organisation Regional Office for the Eastern Mediterranean.

Babb, P., H. Butcher et al. 2006. *Social Trends: Office for National Statistics* 36: 26–30.

Beck-Gernsheim, E. 2007. 'Transnational lives, transnational marriages: a review of the evidence from migrant communities in Europe', *Global Networks* 7(3): 271–288.

Bennett, R.L., A.G. Motulsky, A.H. Bittles, L. Hudgins, S. Uhrich, D. Doyle, et al. 2002. 'Genetic counseling and screening of consanguineous couples and their offspring: recommendations of the National Society of Genetic Counselors', *Journal of Genetic Counseling* 11: 97–119.

Berrington, A. 1994. 'Marriage and family formation among the white and ethnic minority populations in Britain', *Ethnic and Racial Studies* 17(3): 517–546.

Born in Bradford: http://www.borninbradford.nhs.uk/uploads/downloads/research_and_scientific/cohort_information/Baseline%20Summary%20Factsheet%20BiB.pdf

Bundey, S. and H. Alam. 1993. 'A five-year prospective study of the health of children in different ethnic groups, with particular reference to the effect of inbreeding', *European Journal of Human Genetics* 1: 206–219.

Charsley, K. 2006. 'Risk and ritual: the protection of British Pakistani women in transnational marriage', *Journal of Ethnic and Migration Studies* 32(7): 1169–1187.

———. 2008. 'Vulnerable brides and transnational ghar damads: gender, risk and "adjustment" among Pakistani marriage migrants to Britain', in R. Palriwala and P. Uberoi (eds), *Marriage, Migration and Gender*. Sage: New Delhi, pp.261–285.

———. 2013. *Rishta*s: *Transnational Pakistani Connections: Marrying 'Back Home'*. London: Routledge.

Cryer, A. 2005. 'First cousin marriages: a public health issue?' *Bio News* 337 (28/11/2005-4/12/2005). Last accessed 11 November 2013.

Darr, A. and B. Modell. 1988. 'The frequency of consanguineous marriage among British Pakistanis', *Journal of Medical Genetics* 25: 191–194.

Deech, R. 2010. 'Family relationships and the law since the '60s: cousin marriage', *Gresham College Lecture* 23 March.

Devereux, G., L. Stellitano, C.M. Verity, A. Nicholl, R.G. Will and P. Rogers. 2004.'Variations in neurodegenerative disease across the UK: findings from the national study of Progressive Intellectual and Neurological Deterioration (PIND)', *Archives of Diseases of Childhood* 89: 8–12.

Donnan, H. 1985. 'The rules and rhetoric of marriage negotiations among the Dhund Abbasi of North East Pakistan', *Ethnology* XXIV(3): 183–196.

———. 1988. *Marriage among Muslims: Preference and Choice in Northern Pakistan*. Delhi: Hindustan Publishing Corporation.

Dudley, J. and P. Harvey. 2001. *Control of Immigration Statistics: United Kingdom, 2000*. Home Office, 14/01.

Firth, H.V. and J.A. Hurst. 2005. *Oxford Desk Reference: Clinical Genetics*. Oxford: Oxford University Press.

Grjibovski, A., P. Magnus and C. Stoltenberg. 2009.'Decrease in consanguinity among parents of children born in Norway to women of Pakistani origin: a registry-based study', *Scandinavian Journal of Public Health* 37(3). ISSN 1403-4948.s 232 - 238.s doi: 10.1177/1403494808100939.

Haslam, J. 2001. 'Harsh Troth', *Guardian Society* 14 March: 6–7.

Hussain, R. and A.H. Bittles. 1999. 'Consanguinity and differentials in age at marriage, contraceptive use and fertility in Pakistan', *Journal of Biosocial Science* 31: 121–138.

Modell B. and A. Darr. 2002. 'Genetic counselling and customary consanguineous marriage', *Nature Reviews* 3: 225–229.
Modood, T., R. Berthoud, J. Lakey, J. Nazroo, P. Smith, S. Virdee and S. Beishon. 1997. *Ethnic Minorities in Britain: Diversity and Disadvantage.* London: Policy Studies Institute.
Ottenheimer, Martin. 1996. *Forbidden Relatives: The American Myth of Cousin Marriage.* Urbana and Chicago: University of Illinois Press.
Qureshi, K., K. Charsley and A. Shaw. 2014. 'Marital instability among British Pakistanis: transnationality, conjugalities and Islam', *Ethnic and Racial Studies* 37(2): 261–279.
Shami, S.A., L.H. Schmidt and A. Bittles. 1989. 'Consanguinity related prenatal and postnatal mortality of the populations of seven Pakistani Punjab cities', *Journal of Medical Genetics* 26: 267–271.
Shaw, A. 2000. *Kinship and Continuity: Pakistani Families in Britain.* London and Amsterdam: Routledge/Harwood.
———. 2001. 'Kinship, cultural preference and immigration: consanguineous marriage among British Pakistanis', *Journal of the Royal Anthropological Institute* 7(2): 315–334.
———. 2009. *Negotiating Risk: British Pakistani Experiences of Genetics.* Oxford: Berghahn.
———. 2011. 'Risk and reproductive decisions: British Pakistani couples' responses to genetic counselling', *Social Science and Medicine* 73: 111–120.
Shaw, A. and K. Charsley. 2006. 'Rishtas: adding emotion to strategy in understanding British Pakistani transnational marriages', *Global Networks: A Journal of Transnational Affairs* 6(4): 405–421.
Shaw, A. and J.A. Hurst. 2008. '"What is this genetics, anyway?" Understandings of genetics, illness causality and inheritance among British Pakistani users of genetic services', *Journal of Genetic Counseling* 17(4): 373–382.
———. 2009. '"I don't see any point in telling them": attitudes to sharing genetic information in the family and carrier testing of relatives among British Pakistani adults referred to a genetics clinic', *Ethnicity and Health* 14(2): 205–224.
Sheridan, E., J. Wright, N. Small, P.C. Corry, S. Oddie, C. Whibley et al. 2013. 'Risk factors for congenital anomaly in a multiethnic birth cohort: an analysis of the Born in Bradford study', *The Lancet* 382: 1350–1359.
Simpson, S. 1997. 'Demography and ethnicity: case studies from Bradford', *New Community* 23: 89–107.
Stoltenberg, C., P. Magnus, R.T. Lie, A.K. Daltveit and L.M. Irgens. 1997. 'Birth defects and parental consanguinity in Norway', *American Journal of Epidemiology* 145(5): 439–448.
Werbner, P. 1990. *The Migration Process.* Oxford: Berg.

Chapter 6

A Cousin Marriage Equals a Forced Marriage
Transnational Marriages between Closely Related Spouses in Denmark

Anika Liversage and Mikkel Rytter

In some Western European countries immigrants' transnational consanguineous marriages have been debated from the perspective of genetic risk (see chapter five, this volume). In Denmark, consanguineous immigrant marriages have also been the topic of public and political debate. However, the discussions have primarily centred not on health issues but on the risk that transnational consanguineous marriages are forced marriages. To counter this concern, the Danish Parliament in 2003 introduced the 'rule of supposition of forced marriage' – often referred to simply as either the 'rule of supposition' or as 'the cousin rule' – which made it very difficult for a married couple to be united in Denmark if they are biologically related. Statistics indicate that it used to be common, for example for Turkish and Pakistani immigrants and their descendants living in Denmark, to marry spouses from the extended family found in the country of origin (Schmidt and Jakobsen 2004: 127). However, the rule of supposition of forced marriage has most likely reduced the number of these marriages significantly.

The rule of supposition is a policy that concerns the distribution of the right to family reunification. Thus it concerns the right for Danish residents to marry individuals from other countries, and their subsequent ability to bring these spouses to live with them in Denmark – that is, to reunite in Denmark. To our knowledge, the rule is unique, as it – contrary to normal legal procedures – *a priori* supposes that a transnational marriage between two relatives is a forced marriage, that is, a criminal act and abuse of the young couple involved perpetrated by the parents and perhaps the wider family.

This chapter outlines the recent historical and political context of Denmark in which this specific rule of supposition took shape. Before 2001, there was heated debate concerning how to distinguish between 'forced marriages' and 'arranged marriages' in certain immigrant groups. With the introduction of the rule of supposition in 2003, the deciding factor now became whether couples were 'closely related, and otherwise closer related relatives' (relationships presented as highly problematic ones, with strong indications of enforcement) or not. In this respect both the problem and the potential political solution changed within a few years. We then present two extended cases, that of the Danish-Pakistani couple Hamid and Aisha and of the Danish-Turkish couple Baha and Gülser, to shed light on the experiences that transnational couples may have to face with the rule of supposition.[1] Last, to illustrate the clash between the views of the authorities on one side and those of an affected couple on the other about the character of their marriage, we present a third exemplary adjudication, taken from the home page of the Ministry of Social Affairs and Integration.

Throughout, the chapter discusses the workings of state classification. Here, transnationally married couples may undergo the experience of having their own understandings of their marriages overturned, and their life trajectories redirected in the confrontation with bureaucratic classifications (cf. Bowker and Star 2000). The chapter also presents strategies that transnational couple may use or seek to use to put their life trajectories back on track and establish their desired family life.

The Danish Context – A Historical Overview

Denmark is a relatively small northern European country with 5.5 million inhabitants and no significant colonial past or history of pronounced immigration. Larger-scale immigration occurred during the late 1960s and early 1970s, as labour migrants entered from Turkey, Pakistan, Morocco and the former Yugoslavia. In 1973, as a consequence of the oil crisis, the Danish Parliament put a stop to further labour migration. However, many labour migrants had already settled in Denmark and started to bring in their spouses and children. In the 1980s and 1990s in particular, Denmark also received refugees from numerous countries. Hence, in 2011, nearly 7 per cent of the population in Denmark were classified in national statistics as either 'immigrants' or 'descendants of immigrants' from non-Western countries (Statistics Denmark 2011).

A substantial proportion of the increase in the non-Danish population over the last three decades stems from family reunification. Not only did the initial labour migrants bring in their families, but their children – the so-called 'second generation' – also began to marry spouses from their parents' countries of origin. Thus studies show that 80–90 per cent of immigrants of Pakistani or Turkish descent, marrying in the late 1990s, chose spouses who were resident in their parents' country of origin (Celikaksoy Mortensen 2006; Schmidt and Jakobsen 2004).

During the 1990s, transnational marriages played a prominent part in an increasingly heated public debate on immigrants and immigration (cf. Rytter 2003; Hervik 2011). This debate was also a central theme in the national election in November 2001, where a new Liberal-Conservative government came into power, backed by the votes and support of the right-wing Danish People's Party. The latter party's strong anti-immigration agenda, along with the general securitization of external borders following the terrorist attacks of 11 September 2001, became central in the 2002 passage of a number of laws restricting immigration to Denmark dramatically (cf. Pedersen and Rytter 2011).

To reduce the number of family reunifications, the new government introduced five requirements related to age, accommodation, financial support, collateral and 'national attachment'. Thus, for transnational couples to be united in Denmark, they both had to be older than twenty-four years; they had to place a deposit of approximately 7,000 Euros as collateral in a savings account; they had to own or rent accommodation of a specified size in their own name; they had to prove that they had a specified minimum income; and they had to show an 'attachment' to Denmark – based on factors such as linguistic capability, employment and length of residency – greater than their attachment to any other country. These regulations have been called 'the strictest in the world' (Schmidt 2011: 259). In addition, at the end of 2003, the government passed the specific rule of supposition.

Before we proceed to this specific piece of legislation, we need to clarify our conceptual approach to classification processes.

Politics and Classifications

The crucial aspect of the rule of supposition is how and with what consequences state authorities classify transnational marriages. Any system of classification is both a model of and model for the world; it reflects the idea of an already ordered and objective social reality that can be captured and represented by the specific system of classification. At the same time the very process of definition and organization implies the will and power to construct social reality in specific ways. The generative aspects and dynamics of power inherent in processes of classification become salient when we turn to state bureaucracy that uses categorization as a significant tool of 'governmentality' (Foucault 2002). For modern nation-states, policies and procedures of classification are fundamental organizing principles that provide a way of conceptualizing social relations around which people structure their lives.

Processes of classification generally involve the perspectives of both 'internal identification' and 'external categorization' (Jenkins 2004): in social interaction we are always categorized in different ways by our surroundings, and we identify ourselves in different ways in relation to significant others. Sometimes the external categorization and the internal identification may be similar, because the same scales or systems of evaluation are being applied, but such is not always the case. We can be put in the categories of 'beautiful' or 'sloppy', while we might identify ourselves as being 'ordinary looking' or 'systematic'. In everyday encounters the discrepancy between external categorization and internal identification can often be negotiated.

However, in situations where it is the state that categorizes citizens, a fundamental discrepancy may exist between the two perspectives. In such cases, it becomes evident that the state has the definitional power to construct the social world, with potentially severe consequences for the ordinary people involved. One extreme case is the way in which the South African apartheid system classified every citizen according to four race-based categories. Families who considered themselves 'white' could risk suddenly being categorized as 'coloured', with dire consequences for their everyday lives, in terms of whom they could marry, where they could go to school or work, and how they were received by their surroundings in general (Bowker and Star 2000). In this respect citizens' life opportunities may largely be created and distributed by the classification procedures of the state. Power is vested in such bureaucratic categorization, as it is often consequential and may have very concrete material effects, regardless of whether the bureaucratic categorization corresponds with how the implicated individuals identify themselves (Jenkins 2000).

As this chapter will show, the immigration regime of the Danish nation-state since 2003 has created substantial problems for some Danes with immigrant backgrounds who have married a foreign family member, because it classifies some marriages as 'forced' regardless of the couple's own explanations to the contrary. However, just as South Africans who felt they had been put in the wrong bureaucratic box had various strategies for attempting to be reclassified (Bowker and Star 2000), transnational couples also have various more or less successful strategies for navigating the state bureaucracy and changing the external categorizations of their marriages to correspond with their own understandings of them. Such cases show that whilst governments may use policy as an instrument for imposing their ordering principles upon those they seek to govern, reflexive subjects will often attempt to answer back (Shore and Wright 2011: 17).

To understand why different Danish governments have defined the marriage practices of ethnic minorities as so problematic, the next section covers the political situation in Denmark in the years preceding the introduction of the rule of supposition.

Debates and Discourses Concerning Immigrants' Transnational Marriages

In Denmark, the public and political focus on immigrant transnational marriages intensified considerably during the 1990s. Here, two discourses, one of humanism and one of nationalism, gained prominence and were used (and abused) within the public debate (Hervik and Rytter 2004).

The discourse of humanism concerned forced marriages. The debate rose in response to national media coverage of a number of cases in which young women revealed that their immigrant parents had forced them into transnational marriages against their will. Crisis shelters also reported increasing numbers of immigrant women asking for help (Bredal 1999, 2006; Rytter 2003). Within the discourse of humanism any legal measures that could help young people (mostly women) from being forced into marriage were considered reasonable.

Parallel to the growing concerns for the safety and well-being of young immigrant women was a discourse of nationalism. This discourse stressed the need to tighten the state borders in order to protect the Danish nation from the influx of immigrants, perceived as undermining not only the Danish economy and social cohesion but also national security. In the 1990s the right-wing Danish People's Party in particular voiced this position; but after 11 September 2001, the discourse of nationalism and the advocacy of stricter legislation on family reunification to regulate the inflow of especially Muslims soon became a legitimate position across a broader section of the political spectrum (cf. Gad 2011: 61). A radical reduction of the number of non-Western spouses was also presented as a necessary means of improving the integration of the immigrants and descendants already living in Denmark.

Thus two discourses coexisted, each reinforcing the other. According to the discourse of humanism, young immigrant women were vulnerable victims to be protected from their repressive patriarchal families. According to the discourse of nationalism, Danish values and territory should be protected from the threat of the Muslim 'Other'.

Forced Marriages and Arranged Marriages – Separate Categories or Not?

The coexistence of these two discourses came together in the understanding that transnational marriages were often also forced marriages, fuelled by the wishes of non-Western family members to gain access to wealthy Europe. Thus, purportedly, daughters in immigrant families were sometimes used as 'human visas' – as an influential Norwegian book was entitled (Storhaug 2003) – simply to provide an entry into Europe through marriage. Even though the size of the problem of forced marriages could not be objectively ascertained, the public concern with the marriage patterns of immigrants took the form of a moral panic (cf. Rytter 2003: 43) and the political desire to curb the phenomenon increased.

While to be anything but against forced marriage was generally difficult, a central question in this debate amongst politicians,

NGOs, researchers and feminists became how the categories of forced marriages and of arranged marriages related to one another (cf. Bredal 1999). Should they be understood as separate categories, or were they fundamentally alike and thus both to be considered problematic?

One position in the debate insisted that the two types of marriages differed: whilst an arranged marriage involves the active engagement of parents and sometimes other family members it also requires the acceptance and consent of the young individuals involved. Furthermore, different degrees of arrangements in marriages are common worldwide. Forced marriages are here seen as an aberration – a marriage arranged against the wishes and consent of the young people involved (Gullestad 2002: 33). The opposite position in the debate argued that forced and arranged marriages cannot (and should not) be dissociated, as all types of arrangements imply degrees of pressure and force from the family, with the young people having no free will or real choice. From this perspective arranged marriages are about as problematic as forced marriages.

Given these conflicting understandings, clauses on immigrant marriages had to be omitted when the government of the Social Democrats and the Social Liberals in 1999 passed a Law of Integration. Formulating clear statements on this subject was simply not possible (Bredal 1999: 75). Instead, the government of the time tried to use legislation to prevent transnational forced marriages, even though the existing Danish law on marriage already made it illegal to force anybody into marriage. Thus in 1998 and 2000 the government passed rules to prevent entry visas from being issued when young people had been forced or pressured into a transnational marriage. A rule from 2000, for example, stated that non-Danish citizens aged between eighteen and twenty-five were to be interviewed when applying for family reunification with their foreign spouses, to assess whether the marriage could, without doubt, be considered to have been contracted according to the [Danish] resident's own wishes.[2]

These rules, however, led to only very few visa rejections. Politically, their low impact was interpreted not as an absence of forced marriages but as being due to young people's fears of opposing their parents.[3] According to the Danish political understanding, the evident inefficacy of the rules arose from young people not daring to identify themselves as being forced to marry even though 'in reality' they had been forced. Consequently, the authorities could not categorize their marriages as forced or deny them family reunification.

For the authorities to deal effectively with the problem, the problem itself thus had to be redefined.

The political disagreement as to whether forced and arranged marriages were separate categories changed after the 2001 election. Brought to power on promises of reducing immigration, the new Liberal-Conservative government soon explicitly conflated voluntary arranged marriages and forced marriages. Thus the first action plan in the area is entitled *The Government's Plan of Action against Forced, Quasi-forced and Arranged Marriages 2003–2005*. This action plan states the following:

> In Denmark it is customary for young people to choose their own marriage partner and enter a marriage based on a loving relationship [...] The practice of arranged marriages is a violation of the right of the individual to freely find and choose a spouse. (Action Plan 2003: 5)

As both the title and this statement confirm, the official state definitions of legitimate marriages had changed: forced marriages and arranged marriages were now two of a kind, constituting a continuum of marriages all of which were to be prevented. However, by enlarging the categories of problematic marriages, the government had also dramatically enlarged the presumed problem at hand (Hervik and Rytter 2004: 136), by making a large proportion of transnational marriages amongst immigrants unacceptable. This extension of the problem, by the fusion of marriage categories that had heretofore been considered different, paved the way for the introduction of a strict national immigration regime.

The Rule of Supposition of Forced Marriage

Entangled in the political desire to redefine 'the problem' was the issue of cousin marriages. Such marriages were generally considered problematic, even though marriages between the children of siblings – i.e. first cousins – are legal in Denmark. In contrast to Danish majority practices, consanguineous marriages are common in countries such as Pakistan and Turkey, and migrant families from these countries often continue this marital practice after moving to Europe. In line with the broad range of motives underlying transnational marriages more generally, a range of reasons exists for such consanguineous marriages, including the wish to renew family relations, to keep resources within the family, and to find spouses believed to embody the norms and values of the country of origin (Beck-Gernsheim 2007; Charsley 2006; Rytter 2012b; chapter five, this volume).

As to the extent of extended family marriages among immigrants, a Danish survey based on data from 2003 showed that 24 per cent of the young Turkish and 47 per cent of the young Pakistani informants had married a relative (Schmidt and Jakobsen 2004: 127).[4] These numbers match the results of a large study amongst immigrants in Norway. Findings showed that 26 per cent of the first and 22 per cent of the second generation of Turks in Norway had married within the extended family, and 54 per cent of the first generation and 47 per cent of the second generation of Pakistanis had done the same, making endogamous marriages especially important in the latter group (Suren, Grjibovski and Stoltenberg 2007: 24ff.).

When the Danish government in 2003 passed the rule of supposition its explicit intention was to reduce the number of forced marriages by targeting transnational marriages between relatives. The rule states the following.

> Leave to remain . . . cannot be granted, if it can be deemed questionable whether the marriage has been contracted, or the cohabitation has been established, according to the wishes of both spouses. . . . If the marriage has been contracted between closely related, or otherwise closer related relatives, it is considered questionable – unless specific reasons mandate otherwise – if the marriage has been contracted according to the wishes of both parties. (Aliens Act § 9, stk. 8, pkt. 2)

According to this rule, a transnational marriage within the extended family of 'closely related and otherwise closer related relatives' equals a forced marriage. Consequently, leave of entry for this kind of foreign spouse is denied.

One important aspect of the rule is that it introduces a new way for state officials to identify 'forced marriages'; officials no longer have to interview young spouses about the character of their marriage. Instead, the officials are now instructed to use a kinship diagram to accept or reject applications for family unification. The significant category of 'closely related and otherwise closer related relatives' not only aims at extended family networks but also:

> encompasses relatives in the direct descent of the spouse's grandparents' and the spouse's grandparents' siblings. . . . That means that the two persons [who wish to live together in Denmark] cannot have the same great-grandparents, and that one person's great-grandparents

cannot be the other person's great-great grandparents. (Danish Immigration Service 2009: 4)

This delineation of a broad part of the extended family makes it clear that the 'problem' of immigrant transnational marriage has exceeded concerns of genetic risks. The categories of relatives seen as problematic thus include not only such distant relatives as 'the grandchildren of grandparents' siblings', but also relatives of stepparents (Jørgensen 2012).[5]

Figure 6.1 illustrates that the applicant (in the lower left corner) cannot obtain a visa if marrying a spouse within the box. A marriage to an individual outside of the box ('sponsor' in the lower right corner), however, will not be considered 'forced'.

But how do the Danish authorities justify their equation of transnational marriages within the extended family with forced marriages? The following section covers this issue.

The Political Rationale behind the Rule of Supposition of Forced Marriage

In his 2003 introduction of the bill in the Danish parliament, Minister of Integration Bertel Haarder, representing the Liberal Party, presented three arguments for the bill. Notably, none of the three referred to genetic or health concerns.

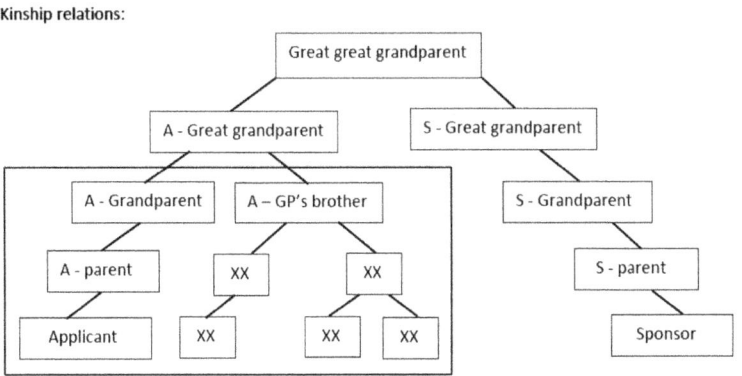

FIGURE 6.1 Categories of Kin with whom Marriage is Considered Forced by the Danish Immigration Authorities (from Danish Immigration Service 2009: 5, authors' translation)

Haarder grounded his first argument in the number of applications for entry visas that the Danish authorities turned down due to suspicion of forced marriage: from the start of 2001 through the middle of 2003, twenty-seven couples received such rejections. Haarder then proceeded to say the following:

> In 11 of the 27 cases, the information provided shows that the marriages were contracted with a close or otherwise closely related relative ... In the present Danish society, it is uncommon for young people to wish to marry a relative ... especially if the parties, prior to the marriage, have had no contact other than what stems from their being related. Studies show that cousin marriages are often forced marriages, contracted because the families in the home country – to ensure a future in the West for their children – pressure the Danish immigrants into entering the marriage.[6]

Haarder's first argument is numerical: a considerable proportion of transnational couples whose applications were rejected due to suspicions of forced marriages were married to relatives. Taking this observation as documenting a substantial overlap between marriages within the extended family and forced marriages, Haarder thus argued that preventing the former type would prevent the latter type from occurring. However, the total number of cases to which he referred is small (27), amounting to less than one case per month in the period investigated. Furthermore, the majority of the rejections based on suspicion of forced marriage were issued in marriage where the couples were not relatives.

Haarder's second argument was the claim that in Danish society both cousin marriages and arranged marriages (where spouses have had little contact prior to the wedding) are 'uncommon'. Apparently the differences between the marriage practices of the majority and arranged cousin marriages within Muslim minorities makes the latter less legitimate. The argument, however, does not concern whether arranged cousin marriages are also due to force.

Haarder's third argument was the claim that 'studies show' that cousin marriages are often the result of enforcement, centrally motivated by extended family wishing to send their children to the affluent West. While Haarder does not specify what studies he is referring to, we know of no such studies other than a brief in the weekly magazine *Monday Morning* (2002). The brief uses anthropological studies from Norway, the UK and elsewhere to argue that consanguineous marriages are often forced marriages. However, several of the scholars quoted in the brief disagreed strongly with the conclusions drawn (Fischer 2003; Bladet Forskning 2004).

In the same parliamentary speech, Haarder also underscored that he is aware that not all marriages between relatives are forced. Haarder stated that if a married couple who are related to one another

> can demonstrate to the Danish Immigration Service that the marriage is contracted (or the cohabitation established) according to their own wishes, they will not have their application for spousal reunion rejected on this ground. The aim of the proposal is to help young people in danger of – against their own wishes – being forced or pressured into marriage with a close or otherwise closely related relative.[7]

Here, Haarder claims that spouses who can demonstrate that they married 'according to their own wishes' will be able to obtain a Danish entry visa. Thus the rule of supposition, which initially presumed all marriages between relatives to be forced, actually allows for the initial definition to be reversed, in cases where the plaintiffs can substantiate that they, themselves, wanted the marriage. This possibility of having marriages between relatives reclassified from forced to voluntary marriages makes the bureaucratic procedures for achieving such reclassification relevant to our analysis here. We investigate these procedures in the next section, which shifts to the perspective of three married couples whose lives have been severely affected by the rule of supposition.

The Rule of Supposition and Its Effects on Transnational Couples

The following three cases exemplify the hardships that related couples may encounter as they try to have the Danish authorities reclassify them as living in marriages that were 'not forced'. Such a reclassification could be a prerequisite for obtaining the coveted entry visa into Denmark.

Case 1: Danish-Pakistani Hamid and Pakistani Aisha

In the spring of 2005, Hamid – a Danish citizen, born and raised in Denmark by Pakistani parents and studying to become an engineer – became engaged to Aisha, his maternal first cousin from Pakistan. Their marriage had been planned within the family for years. Hamid knew of the rule of supposition and did therefore not even bother to apply for family reunification in Denmark.

Instead, being a Danish citizen, he was able to exercise his right of free mobility within the EU[8] and move into an apartment in the Swedish city of Malmö. As Malmö is only a forty-five-minute drive from the Danish capital of Copenhagen, Hamid could thus keep studying in Denmark. In the summer of 2005, Aisha and Hamid were married in Pakistan. From his new place of residence, his wife then applied to the Swedish authorities for an entry visa, and in 2006 the couple began their life together in Sweden.[9]

After living in Malmö for almost a year, in December 2006 Hamid applied for permission to return to Denmark with his wife. He had recently qualified as an engineer, a profession included on the 'positive list' that the Danish Government created to ease entry into Denmark for certain groups of highly qualified professionals. In 2007 Hamid found a job in Denmark and started commuting between his home and wife in Sweden and his work and parents in Denmark.

After waiting months for an answer, he called the Danish immigration authorities and learned that his application had been rejected under the rule of supposition, which supersedes the 'positive list'. He learned that because Aisha and he were first cousins, their marriage had been classified as a forced marriage, and their application for a visa to Denmark had been denied. Ironically, had Hamid not been a Danish citizen but instead a Pakistani engineer coming to Denmark with his Pakistani wife to work, they could both legally have entered Denmark on the basis of his professional skills.

Case 2: Danish-Turkish Baha and Turkish Gülser

Baha was born and raised in Denmark of Turkish parents. In 1999, at the age of seventeen, he met Gülser through distant relatives while he was on holiday in Turkey. Over the following years the couple kept in contact by telephone, and during several holiday visits in Turkey their relationship developed to the point where they decided to marry. The wedding took place in Turkey in 2002. When they later applied for family reunification in Denmark, the newly introduced requirement that both partners should be at least twenty-four years of age – a requirement of which they were unaware when they married – led to the rejection of their application.

Consequently, the newly wed Gülser – who had come to Denmark on a tourist visa – had to return to Turkey. Although the separation was difficult, the couple projected that by 2004 they would both be old enough for Gülser to obtain a visa. For the next two years Baha lived in Denmark, continuing his education at a business academy, whilst Gülser commuted between Turkey and Denmark. Using consecutive tourist visas, she could stay with Baha in Denmark for six months at a time, after which, to qualify for a new tourist visa, she had to leave Denmark for a similar period. When they both turned twenty-four, they applied again, only to learn the following:

> [The authorities] gave us a rejection. They said it was a forced marriage. They had some stupid reasons. It was about our grandparents being siblings. I can't understand where they get those crazy ideas. We hadn't known each other before [meeting when Baha was seventeen].

With common great-grandparents, Baha and Gülser were classified as 'closely related' according to the bureaucratic system's use of kinship diagrams (Figure 6.1). Thus their marriage was assumed to be due to force, and their visa application for Gülser was turned down.

Strategies of Reclassification

In both of these examples, each couple found that – regardless of the fact that they considered their marriages to be based on their own free will – the Danish authorities had categorized them as living in forced marriages. However, as stated by then Minister Bertel Haarder, such couples should be able to have their marriages reclassified as 'not forced' if they could prove that the marriage was indeed according to their own wishes.

Naturally, both Hamid and Baha tried to have their marriages reclassified. However, they found the process very difficult. According to Danish jurisdiction, to have their marriage reclassified, couples must be able to demonstrate that they, for example, have 'had a lengthy and detailed acquaintance before the marriage ..., that the couple have planned their wedding themselves, or that the couple has cohabited before marrying' (Danish Immigration Service 2009). Consequently, transnational couples' own direct statements that their marriages are voluntary are given no weight. Instead, the Danish authorities scrutinize the period before the wedding. Hence, couples who do not have an intimate and romantic relationship before the marriage face great difficulties in having their marriages reclassified as 'voluntary marriages', regardless of mutual consent, the desire to live together and the development of a subsequent love relationship. Indeed, a primary avenue of achieving reclassification by the Danish authorities is through documenting premarital cohabitation – a practice that flies in the face of the norms of premarital chastity prevalent in many immigrant groups.

When Hamid learned that his wife's visa application had been rejected, he appealed against the verdict, stating that their marriage had not been forced. To document their relationship, he submitted more than seventy photographs to the authorities: from their wedding in Pakistan, from their apartment in Sweden, and from a family holiday they had taken together, long before their engagement. Regardless of this documentation and the couple's stated wishes to be together, their appeal for reclassification was turned down.

Baha also appealed against the decision in his case, with the same negative result. Subsequently, he did the following:

> I spoke with a lawyer – to learn whether there were alternatives. I had heard a bit about going to Germany or Sweden. But I was totally against it – I did not want to leave, I did not want to quit the fight; this is not the mentality we have here in Denmark. As an ordinary citizen, I also have some rights. In Denmark, it is not illegal to marry your cousin. Yes, some are forced to marry, but that shouldn't affect all of us – us, who have a good life and do well in society.

Baha even contacted local politicians and local media, attempting to have the authorities re-evaluate his case, but to no avail.

By refusing to leave Denmark, the couple had to continue their disrupted family life, with Baha living in Denmark, and Gülser living partly in Turkey and partly in Denmark as a tourist.

Numerous other couples also experienced the authorities' wrongly classifying their marriages as 'forced'. In 2007 a number of couples had their cases adjudicated in the Danish court system, and in several cases the courts overruled the Danish Immigration Service's rejections of family reunification visas. These court cases created a legal precedent for how couples could achieve the coveted reclassification of their marriages as being not forced.[10]

On the advice of his lawyer, at the end of 2007 Baha set out to document his and Gülser's relationship before their 2002 marriage and to document how their wedding had been planned. On a trip to Turkey, he was able to recover phone bills dating back to 1999, proving his and Gülser's extensive contact before the marriage. He also visited the town where they married and found several witnesses who could testify that it was he, rather than his parents, who arranged the wedding ceremony. After receiving this documentation, the authorities finally agreed to reclassify his marriage from forced to voluntary, and in 2008 Gülser obtained her visa and came to Denmark as a marriage migrant.

Hamid and Aisha applied a different strategy for entering Denmark. When Hamid had his first appeal rejected, he simply gave up battling the Danish authorities. Instead, he and Aisha continued to live in Sweden, because at that time, after two years of living in Sweden, Danes could become Swedish citizens.[11] Hamid chose this option. As long as he was a Danish citizen, the strict Danish rules regulating family migration applied to him, if he wanted to return to Denmark with his wife. Given the common rules of mobility within the Nordic region and EU in general, however, as a Swedish citizen he had no problems moving to Denmark with his Pakistani wife and Hamid did so in 2008. As planned from the beginning, the couple settled in the home of Hamid's parents. They have since been blessed with a daughter who has become a Swedish citizen like her father.

These two cases show, first, how Baha managed to have his marriage reclassified by following the rules of the game of the bureaucratic classification system. Second, they show how Hamid – by becoming a Swedish citizen – was able to change which rules were to guide his situation. Following different routes, the two couples in question were thus able to achieve the desired result – the ability to live together in Denmark. Other commonalities are the years of arduous struggles both couples underwent to obtain this result, and the fact that, during the process, the outcome was far from certain.

A third possibility, however, is that of not succeeding in gaining access to Denmark. We illustrate this possibility with a case of a closely related transnational couple who were unable to make the authorities reclassify their marriage as not forced.

Case 3: Failing to Have a Marriage Reclassified

The final case comes from the Ministry of Social Affairs and Integration's database of administrative decisions that 'all are of instructive or principal value, and illustrate present practice'. The anonymized case in question bears the title 'the forced marriage' and exemplifies the interface between applicants and the authorities, where the powers of definition are firmly vested in the latter.

The couple in question belongs to the same ethnic minority group. The couple married in 2000 and their application for family unification was rejected for unstated reasons the same year. They remained married, however, and in 2006 again applied for the wife's entry visa. In 2007, the Ministry (at the time entitled the Ministry of Refugee, Immigration and Integration Affairs) made the following observation in its decision:

> Based on the questionnaire that you and your spouse filled out in 2006, it is evident that you are cousins and have known each other since childhood; that you have had personal and telephone contact both before and after marrying; that you have not cohabited before the marriage; that you, yourselves planned the wedding; that the marriage was contracted due to your own wishes.[12]

Regardless of their premarital contact, their own planning of the wedding, and their testimonies of wanting the marriage (also evident through their staying together, despite their year-long inability to gain family unification), the Ministry rejected the appeal on the following grounds:

> The Ministry places decisive weight on you and your spouse's familial relationship. . . . The fact that you at a personal visit to the ministry declared that the marriage is not a forced marriage, and that you and your spouse love each other, and that evidence shows that your spouse visited Denmark in 2003, 2004 and 2005, and that you visited your spouse in 2005, is not sufficient evidence for the ministry to remove the presumption about forced marriage. (Ibid.)

The Ministry further stated that it lacked documentation for an in-depth and long-term pre-marital personal relationship as anything other than a familial one, and that it saw no proof of the couple's own planning of their wedding. A further argument for the rejection is that both spouses were young when they married.

As the couple was indisputably closely related (probably first cousins), the marriage was thus deemed to be 'too arranged' to overturn the 'forced' classification. We cannot know whether this decision in part stems from the couple's inability to document the details of their relationship before their marriage in 2000, at which time they had no idea that they would later be called upon to substantiate their early contact with one another.

The case shows that the authorities upheld the initial classification of this marriage as forced, despite the couples' personal testimonies and their lengthy struggle to create some semblance of family life through repeated visits to each other's countries. Subsequent to receiving this decision, the wife had immediately to leave Denmark – again.

We do not know what this couple subsequently did – did they separate, did they continue their intermittent family life, or did they both leave Denmark for good? They may even have gone to Sweden, trying to follow the route that the cousins Hamid and Aisha had used successfully to enter Denmark. We do know that, despite a seven-year struggle, this couple was unsuccessful in achieving their aim of beginning a normal family life in Denmark together.

As this example shows, the Danish state's conflation of forced marriages with transnational, arranged marriages between relatives may place ethnic minorities in situations where the bureaucratic system ignores their personal understandings of their marriages and forces them to rescind their future aspirations.

Personal Consequences of the Fight for Reclassification

The very broad Danish definition of forced marriages applied in the rule of supposition has probably prevented some marriages into which young people would otherwise have been pressured or forced against their own wishes.[13] But, as this chapter makes clear, other couples found their desired marriages classified as 'forced', with dire consequences for their personal lives.

As the chapter's three examples illustrate, the state-sanctioned classification system places some transnational couples in a bureaucratic limbo with blurred horizons (Rytter 2012a: 100–101), where they merely wait and hope for a positive outcome of their appeals. This period of uncertainty somewhat resembles the situation of asylum seekers awaiting decisions on applications for residency – a situation that may have serious consequences for their physical and emotional well-being (cf. Vitus 2010; Whyte 2011). As Baha said about his young wife:

> Psychologically, she suffered most. She did not have anything to rely on. It was half a year here and half a year there. That was the only way. When I met her, she had just finished an education in trade and wanted to continue at the police school. But she had to give that up for us to live together. She didn't know when she would come to Denmark. She has been very affected by it. She has really had a tough time.

Both Baha and Hamid expressed frustration and rage. Hamid bitterly regretted his honesty with the authorities: 'Many of my friends do not say that they are marrying within the family, so they do not have any problems, but I do'. Hamid also felt that the long waits for answers to the visa applications were part of an official strategy to cause stress to and weaken applicants through prolonged uncertainty.

On a similar note, Baha – born in Denmark – said that the experience of being denied family life in Denmark had undermined his feeling of national belonging:

> I feel I am unwanted here. But what have I done? I have educated myself. I have no criminal record; I have been diligent and have worked in the labour market. What more can I do? I cannot change my skin colour. I think it is really wrong for the government to decide whether or not my wife and I are suitable for each other.

Thus one consequence of the rule of supposition is that Danish citizens such as Hamid and Baha are locked in a structural position of being 'not-quite-real-Danes' (cf. Rytter 2010), to the detriment of their feelings of belonging in Denmark.

Conclusion

Since 2003, the rule of supposition has generally prevented transnational couples married within the extended family from gaining family unification in Denmark. This rule was not passed primarily because of the potential health risks for children born of related parents. Instead, the rule is part of a larger legislative complex created with a twofold objective: to prevent forced marriages and to reduce especially non-Western marriage migration. If the rule had focused on the genetic risks in consanguineous marriage it would have lost much of its ability to restrict marriage migration, because it would have had to restrict itself mainly to first cousin marriages. Such an argument would also conflict with the present legality of first cousin marriages in Denmark. Instead, it appears obvious that the state policies and immigration regime of 2002–2003 are aimed at stemming the marriage migration of certain categories of individuals. The rules have adversely affected the ability of immigrants, refugees and their descendants to obtain family reunification (regardless of whether or not they are Danish citizens) more than they have limited the majority Danish population from bringing in spouses from abroad (Jørgensen 2012). This objective is especially well met in the rule of supposition: while every young transnational couple in Denmark is potentially affected by the twenty-four-year rule, the rule of supposition exclusively affects marriages in settled ethnic minority communities: majority Danes rarely have family networks or cousins abroad whom they want to marry, and should such a case arise, it is unlikely that the marriage will be 'arranged' in any way.

The rule of supposition has contributed to altering the marital patterns of ethnic minorities in Denmark. As this chapter shows, the rate of consanguineous marriages and marriages within the extended family was substantial among e.g. people of Pakistani and Turkish descent before the legislative changes of 2002–2003. However, as family reunification between closely related spouses has become very difficult to achieve, the proportion of such marriages must have declined significantly. Nonetheless, marriage preferences do not change overnight. Some immigrant groups may still exhibit a preference for marrying within the family network. If so, they have other options: if they already have a network of extended family in Denmark or in other EU countries, they may seek spouses there. They may use the same strategy as Hamid and Aisha and move to Sweden for a while, before settling in Denmark. Or they may seek to conceal their family history and kinship relations from the Danish authorities. Few related spouses are, like Baha and Gülser, successful in having their marriage reclassified from a forced marriage to a voluntary one. And, as the last case in this chapter shows, some couples may marry, only to realize that they may never be able to live together as a couple in Denmark.

Notes

1. The first extended case of Hamid and Aisha is from Mikkel Rytter's fieldwork among Pakistani migrant families in Denmark and Sweden (Rytter 2003, 2006, 2010, 2012a, 2012b). The second case of Baha and Gülser is from Anika Liversage's fieldwork among Turkish families in Denmark and Turkey (Charsley and Liversage 2012; Liversage 2009, 2012a, 2012b; Liversage and Jakobsen 2010). Names in the two cases have been changed to protect the anonymity of the couples.
2. Aliens Act, § 9, stk. 2, no. 7; 31 May 2000.
3. Remarks to Parliament 1999–2000, supplement A, p.5816, on Act no. 424, 31 May 2000.
4. Because of the small sample size, these numbers are not fully reliable (Schmidt and Jakobsen 2004: 127).

5. In the Action Plan (2003), the increased risk of hereditary diseases in consanguineous marriages is mentioned in a fact box, but this genetic risk does not figure within the plan's main body of text.
 6. https://www.retsinformation.dk/Forms/R0710.aspx?id=100336, authors' translation.
 7. https://www.retsinformation.dk/Forms/R0710.aspx?id=100336, authors' translation.
 8. Following the common ambition of creating a Nordic region it has since 1954 been possible for Danish, Swedish, Norwegian and Finnish citizens to move freely within this region.
 9. This strategy of moving to Sweden has been widely used by immigrant couples. Indeed, in 2007, 12 per cent of all twenty-five-year-old Danish-Pakistanis had moved to Sweden (Schmidt et al. 2009: 103). This relatively large proportion is partially attributable to Pakistanis predominantly living in the Danish capital, and thus having only a short move to the other side of the Danish-Swedish bridge. The comparable proportion for Danish-Turks is 5 per cent (ibid).
10. For important court cases, see Danish Immigration Service (2009). Moreover, the 'rule of presumption' was amended slightly in 2005. After the Council of Europe's Commissioner of Human Rights, Alvaro Gil-Robles, criticized the Danish family migration rules, the clause 'including consideration of the unity of the family' was added as a 'special reason' through which leave of entry could be granted to related couples.
11. Today, Danish citizens have to live in Sweden for five years in order to achieve Swedish citizenship.
12. http://www.nyidanmark.dk/NR/rdonlyres/2A811ECA-C947-4DDF-9C37-4A0B14CFE6AF/0/A14_NY_afgorelse.pdf. Accessed 30 May 2012.
13. Some young people from ethnic minorities support the tight rules of family migration, as they believe that these rules support their independence (Schmidt et al. 2009; Schmidt and Jakobsen 2004). Numerically speaking, a prominent consequence of the legislative changes around 2002 has been a marked decrease in non-Western family migration to Denmark (RFF 2009).

References

Action Plan. 2003. The Government's Action Plan for 2003–2005 on Forced, Quasi-forced and Arranged Marriages. The Danish Government, 15 August 2003.

Beck-Gernsheim, E. 2007. 'Transnational lives, transnational marriages: a review of the evidence from migrant communities in Europe', *Global Networks* 7(3): 271–288.

Bladet Forskning [The Research Magazine]. 2004. 'Ingen ekteskapsplaner akkurat' ['No current plans of marriage'], no. 3, June.

Bowker, G.C. and S.L. Star. 2000. *Sorting Things Out – Classification and its Consequences.* Cambridge, MA: MIT Press.

Bredal, A. 1999. *Arrangerte ekteskab og tvangsekteskab i Norden.* [Arranged Marriage and Forced Marriage in the Nordic Countries]. TemaNord 1999: 604, Nordic Council of Ministers, Copenhagen.

———. 2006. *Vi er jo en familie. Arrangerte ekteskap, autonomi og felleskap blant unge norsk-asiater.* Oslo: Unipax.

Celikaksoy Mortensen, E.A. 2006. *Marriage Behaviour and Labour Market Integration: The Case of the Children of Guest Worker Immigrants in Denmark.* Aarhus: Department of Economics, Aarhus School of Business.

Charsley, K. 2006. 'Risk and ritual: the protection of British Pakistani women in transnational marriages', *Jounal of Ethnic and Migration Studies* 32(7): 1169–1187.

Charsley, K. and A. Liversage. 2012. 'Transforming polygamy: migration, transnationalism and multiple marriages among Muslim minorities', *Global Networks* 13(1): 60–78.

Danish Immigration Service. 2009. Brief, available at: http://www.nyidanmark.dk/NR/rdonlyres/C6DCB443-2EAF-4CFA-8478-BE2293D71B87/0/notat_af_16102009_om_praksis_efter_bestemmelsen_i_udlaendingeloens_9_stk_8.pdf. Accessed 30 May 2012.

Fischer, A. 2003. Radio program 'Orientering', Denmark's Radio, 21 October 2003.

Foucault, M. 2002. *Forelesninger om Regjering og Styringskunst.* Oslo: Cappelen Akademisk Forlag.

Gad, U.P. 2011. 'Muslimer som trussel: identitet, sikkerhed og modforanstaltninger', in M. H. Pedersen and M. Rytter (eds), *Islam og Muslimer i Danmark: Religion, identitet og sikkerhed efter 11. september 2001.* Copenhagen: Museum Tusculanum, pp.61–88.

Gullestad, M. 2002. *Det Norske – sett med nye øyne.* Oslo: Universitetsforlaget.

Hervik, P. 2011. *The Annoying Difference. The Emergence of Danish Neonationalism, Neoracism, and Populism in the Post-1989 World.* New York and Oxford: Berghahn Books.

Hervik, P. and M. Rytter. 2004. 'Med ægteskab i fokus', in *Ægtefællesammenføring i Danmark.* Udredning no. 1, Institute for Human Rights, pp.131–160.

Jenkins, R. 2000. 'Categorization: identity, social process and epistemology', *Current Sociology* 48(3): 7–25.

———. 2004. *Social Identity,* 2nd edition. London: Routledge.

Jørgensen, M.B. 2012. 'Danish regulations on marriage migration – policy understandings of transnational marriages', in K. Charsley (ed.), *Transnational Marriage – New Perspectives from Europe and Beyond.* London: Routledge, pp.60–78.

Liversage, A. 2009. 'Life below a "Language Threshold"? Stories of Turkish marriage migrant women in Denmark', *European Journal of Women's Studies* 16(3): 229–248.

---. 2012a. 'Divorce among Turkish immigrants in Denmark', in K. Charsley (ed.), *Transnational Marriage: New Perspectives from Europe and Beyond*. London: Routledge, pp.146–160.

---. 2012b. 'Gender, conflict and subordination within the household – Turkish migrant marriage and divorce in Denmark', *Journal of Ethnic and Migration Studies* 38(7): 1119–1136.

Liversage, A. and V. Jakobsen. 2010. 'Sharing space – gendered patterns of extended household living among young Turkish marriage migrants in Denmark', *Journal of Comparative Family Studies* 41(5): 693–715.

Monday Morning. 2002. Article on cousin marriages, 8 April.

Pedersen, M.H. and M. Rytter (eds). 2011. *Islam og Muslimer i Danmark: Religion, identitet og sikkerhed efter 11. september 2001*. Copenhagen: Museum Tusculanum.

RFF. 2009. Rockwool Fondens Forskningsenhed – newsletter, June.

Rytter, M. 2003. *Lige Gift: En antropologisk undersøgelse af arrangerede ægteskaber blandt pakistanere i Danmark*. Master Thesis no. 261, Department of Anthropology, University of Copenhagen.

---. 2006. 'Ægteskabelig integration. Pakistanske og danske arrangerede ægteskaber', in M.H. Pedersen and M. Rytter (eds), *Den stille integration. Nye fortællinger om at høre til i Danmark*. Copenhagen: C.A. Reitzels Forlag, pp.18–43.

---. 2010. '"The Family of Denmark" and "The Aliens": kinship images in Danish integration politics', *Ethnos* 75(3): 301–322.

---. 2012a. 'The semi-legal family life: Pakistani couples in the borderlands between Denmark and Sweden', *Global Networks* 12(1): 98–117.

---. 2012b. 'Between preferences: marriage and mobility among Danish Pakistani youth', *The Journal of Royal Anthropological Institute* 12(3): 572–590.

Schmidt, G. 2011. 'Law and identity: transnational arranged marriages and the boundaries of Danishness', *Journal of Ethnic and Migration Studies* 37(2): 257–276.

Schmidt, G., B.K. Graversen, V. Jakobsen, T.G. Jensen and A. Liversage. 2009. *Ændrede familiesammenføringsregler – hvad har de nye regler betydet for pardannelsesmønstret blandt etniske minoriteter?* Copenhagen: SFI – The Danish National Centre for Social Research.

Schmidt, G. and V. Jakobsen. 2004. *Pardannelse blandt etniske minoriteter i Danmark*. Copenhagen: SFI – Socialforskingsinstituttet.

Shore, C. and S. Wright. 2011. 'Conceptualising policy. Technologies of governance and the politics of visibility', in C. Shore, S. Wright and D. Pero (eds), *Policy Worlds: Anthropology and the Analysis of Contemporary Power*. New York and Oxford: Berghahn Books, pp.1–26.

Statistics Denmark. 2011. *Indvandrere i Danmark 2011*. Copenhagen: Statistics Denmark.

Storhaug, H. 2003. *Human Visas: A Report from the Front Lines of Europe's Integration Crisis*. Oslo: Human Rights Service.

Suren, P., A. Grjibovski and C. Stoltenberg. 2007. *Inngifte i Norge. Omfang og medisinske konsekvenser.* Oslo: Helseinstituttet.

Vitus, K. 2010. 'Zones of indistinction: family life in Danish asylum centres', *Distinktion: Scandinavian Journal of Social Theory* 12(1): 95–112.

Whyte, Z. 2011. 'Asyl, ish'allah. Tro og mistro i det danske asylsystem', in M.H. Pedersen and M. Rytter (eds), *Islam og muslimer i Danmark. Religion, identitet og sikkerhed efter 11. september 2001.* Copenhagen: Museum Tusculanums Forlag, pp.115–140.

Chapter 7

CHANGING PATTERNS OF PARTNER CHOICE?
COUSIN MARRIAGES AMONG TURKS AND MOROCCANS IN THE NETHERLANDS

Oka Storms and Edien Bartels

> Many problems concerning retarded [immigrant] boys are solved with imported brides. They are brought to the Netherlands as family caregivers/spouses [...] With these marriages, women have life-long sentences, and they often result again in retarded children. Why isn't there a debate in their own community about this problem? [...] I advocate that we stop unrestrained marriage import, family reunion possibilities, and prohibit cousin marriages.
> Amsterdam Council Member Lodewijk Asscher (currently Dutch Minister of Social Affairs) (2009)

In the Netherlands, the majority population regards marriage between cousins as incestuous and inviting the risk of having disabled offspring; the practice is, therefore, taboo. In present-day politics in the Netherlands, cousin marriage is also directly associated with forced marriage (see chapter six on the similar political stance adopted in Denmark). The current government therefore proposes to enact a law prohibiting cousin marriage in cases of forced marriage.[1] Furthermore, consanguineous unions among immigrant groups – specifically Dutch Moroccans and Turks – are also subject to political debate in the context of immigration policy. However, the (recent) political debate on the prohibition of cousin marriages, started in 2009 by the former Amsterdam Alderman Lodewijk Asscher (Labour Party, currently Minister of Social Affairs) quoted above, focuses solely on immigrant groups, especially Moroccans. In this political debate, cousin marriage is directly associated with social issues such as forced marriage, integration and a range of medical problems which are often referred to as retardation. This latter term refers to the increased medical risk that consanguineous couples have of giving birth to a child with an autosomal recessive disorder (up to 3 per cent greater than it is for non-consanguineous couples; Bennett et. al. 2006; Stoltenberg et. al. 1997).

In many other parts of the world, the stance towards consanguineous union is very different. Worldwide, 10.4 per cent of the population have parents who are kin (see chapter one, this volume). In parts of North Africa and the Middle East there are long traditions of preferential cousin marriage, especially parallel first cousin marriage (of a man to his father's brother's daughter). In Western countries, consanguineous marriage has recently received increased attention as a consequence of migration (Bittles 2008; Storms and Bartels 2013).

This conflict of values – taboo and medical risks versus preference – in practising cousin marriage is very evident in a multicultural society such as the Netherlands, where consanguineous marriage is currently referred to as a political 'problem'. By making this reference, a division is created within Dutch society between Us and Them – between Us, the people who have 'normal' marriage patterns, and Them, the people who practise consanguineous marriage.

It is, however, more than just being included and excluded based on marriage preference. Processes of 'Othering' have always existed. In his study *Orientalism* (1978), Edward Said describes the difference between the West and the Orient as it is depicted in oriental literature: Islam as static, unchangeable and repressive to women. In the past, the Other seemed far away. At present, 'the cultural Other has moved into our midst' (Bartels 2008: 2). Asscher (2009), representing this process of Othering, links consanguineous marriage directly to immigrants, retardation, sickness, disability, integration and forced marriage; 'Them' is associated with everything that 'We' do not want and is regarded a threat to Our Dutch identity. This 'cultural other' in our multicultural society is linked to intolerance, terrorist attacks, radicalization, repression of women, honour-related and domestic violence, forced marriage, and S*haria* (Bartels 2008). Most of these processes of inclusion and exclusion provide Us with a justification for feelings of cultural superiority, and for denying that similar problems exist for women in Western societies and also create a cultural boundary that divides both Dutch and European societies.

But cousin marriage is more; it doesn't just create cultural differences, it also makes the cultural Other more or less 'non-human', or in any case an 'immoral' being. We see this reflected in ideas about citizenship. De Koning et al. (2011) state that although the Other often has Dutch citizenship, this no longer indicates a primarily legal status, but rather that citizenship has become an increasingly moral concept. Schinkel (2010), based in part on Vermeulen (2007: 101), shows that an immigrant is not considered a full citizen until he/she is willing to adapt himself/herself to the moral community by accepting certain fundamental standards and values as his/her own. In other words, there are two types of citizenships for immigrants: formal citizenship and moral citizenship. Immigrants, therefore, must first integrate (culturally) properly and abandon harmful and immoral traditional practices, such as consanguineous marriage, before they can be considered to be members of the Dutch moral community (De Koning et al. 2011).

When we look at the political debate on consanguineous unions in the Netherlands we see that a clear focus is placed on risk. First, there is the risk of having a child with a disability. The following question is asked: why is there no debate about the medical risk in the immigrant communities (see the Asscher quotation above as an example)? In other words: it is thought contentious that there has been no shift in the debate to the 'medicalization of partner choice' among Dutch Turks and Moroccans. In this case medicalization basically means not marrying your cousin because of the medical risk. But, at the same time, we do not discuss the prohibition of pregnancy for women of thirty-five and older, who have a similar risk; we only inform them of the risk. Furthermore, consanguineous marriages are associated with immigrant groups but, in the Netherlands, it is not only immigrant groups who practise cousin marriage, it also occurs in closed (religious) communities (e.g. Taussig 2009). Secondly, it is assumed that the risk of forced marriage is increased for consanguineous unions. Prohibiting cousin marriage is presented as a way of reducing the risk of forced marriage. However, the risk of forced marriage in cousin marriage is not at all clear. Remarkably we have no national figures on cousin marriages or on forced marriages and no research has been conducted on the relationship between cousin marriage and force. Thus, what is considered a risk with regard to cousin unions is not as self-evident as it is presented in political debate. Moreover, as we will argue in this chapter, the dissemination and perception of risk is socially mediated and constructed. As Douglas and Wildavsky (1982) argue, there are many risks in life and one cannot take all of them into account. A priority or a choice is made. What is considered a(n) (ultimate) risk by one individual can be perceived quite differently by another. As several scholars have argued (Beck 1992; Giddens 1991; Douglas and Wildavsky 1982; Lupton 2006), in any society, the risks considered most important are politically motivated. So, moral qualifications are made, based on selective risks.

In this chapter we discuss the conflicting ideas held by our Dutch Turkish and Moroccan respondents about the risks related to cousin marriage in the Netherlands and explore their perceptions of medical and social risk. Are the politically dominant risks in Dutch society perceived as such? Are there other perceived risks? This exploration leads to the question: does the politically dominant risk perception influence the patterns of partner choice and if so, how?

First we describe the methodology of our research, then the concept of risk. We continue our analysis of how risk is viewed by examining the different perspectives held by our respondents. Finally we discuss the changing patterns of partner choice in greater detail.

Research Methods

To analyse these marital alliances in the Dutch context, we conducted research among Dutch Moroccan and Turks in three major Dutch cities, where a large proportion of the population has a Moroccan or Turkish background.[2] There are no national figures on the consanguinity rate in the Netherlands. However, research conducted in Rotterdam, the Generation R Study (http://www.generationr.nl), shows that 23.9 per cent and 22.2 per cent of the Turkish and Moroccan pregnant women who were interviewed had a partner who was a consanguineous relative. Among the Turkish respondents, 12.3 per cent were married to a first cousin, 9.8 per cent to a second cousin, and 1.8 per cent had some other family connection. 12 per cent of the Moroccan respondents were married to their first cousin, 7.6 per cent to a second cousin, and there were 2.5 per cent with some other family connection (Waelput and Achterberg 2007).

In seven group discussions, we spoke to eighty-six Dutch Moroccan and Turkish women, first and second generation, some of whom were married to their first or second cousins. Three group discussions were held with Dutch Moroccan women, two with Dutch Turkish women, and there were two mixed group discussions, one of which was with women who all had a child (or children) with a disability. The group discussions were organized by ethnic group-specific welfare organizations that support immigrants who want to gain knowledge of, and integrate in, Dutch society. Eleven in-depth interviews were conducted with women/couples who were consanguineously married and had either (1) a desire for a child, (2) a healthy child/children, and/or (3) a disabled child/children. In addition, we interviewed nine key figures from the immigrant groups and four medical practitioners. In relation to the transnational character of immigrant groups, we also conducted exploratory research on consanguineous marriage and heredity in Morocco in 2009, 2010 and 2011 (Storms and Bartels 2013) and in Turkey in 2012. We also built upon previous research conducted on partner choice, and on arranged and forced marriages among Dutch Moroccans and Turks (De Koning and Bartels 2005; Storms and Bartels 2008).

Cultural Selection: What is 'Risk'?

Risk is a political concept (Beck 1992; Giddens 1991; Douglas and Wildavsky 1982; Lupton 2006) and what is perceived as a risk differs according to context. Caplan (2000: 8) cites the anthropological work of Douglas and Wildavsky who suggest that:

> People fear and this fear has to do with knowledge and the kind of people we are. People see the weight of risks differently, and have to prioritise between them, since plainly no one can worry about all potential risks all the time. But in order to rank dangers there must be some agreement on criteria, which is why acceptability of risk is always a political issue.

Thus, for these scholars there is always a cultural selection of what constitutes danger, and risk perception is determined both by social organization and culture. Inevitably morality is invoked in this use of culture, as Caplan (2000: 9), following Douglas, states: 'Common values lead to common fears, thus the choice of risks and the choice of how to live are linked and each form of life has its own typical risk portfolio'. As Lupton (2006: 15) argues, 'what are perceived to be "risks" in one region or nation may be ignored in another. New risks emerge all the time, often to subside in the public's consciousness or be replaced by others'.

Risk, as cultural and political phenomena related to moral choices, means that people cannot take into account every potential one. So a selection is made. Besides, people might have other priorities, or develop them over time, which can make one risk become more dominant than another. Therefore views on risk, like culture, are dynamic, and change in time and space. These differences are clearly seen in a multicultural society such as the Netherlands.

For the first generation Moroccan and Turkish immigrants, the endogamous kin marriage pattern – practised for centuries in North Africa and the Middle East – is very familiar and still preferred. It is not regarded as risky but as safe: safe for women as they remain in the family after marriage, and safe for children if their parents divorce. Finally, the future of the family is at stake: kin marriage connects members of families, and is a practice that sustains and protects families.

Dutch Turks and Moroccans in the Netherlands are confronted with an array of risks, an array of a different composition than the one facing their families in their country of origin (of their parents). In mainstream Dutch society, on the contrary, the medical and social (i.e. forced marriages) thought on risk in relation to consanguineous marriages is so dominant that any other possible risk factors are excluded from the debate. Living in a multicultural society, Dutch Moroccans and Turks are confronted with 'dominant values which lead to dominant fears', the 'Dutch risk portfolio' in which the preference for marriage with a close relative such as a cousin is perceived not only as risky but as a 'backward' and immoral custom, one which is related to forced marriage as well.

Risk is not always clear, whether this be for groups or individuals. Besides, risks are not perceived equally but are prioritized by the struggles of daily life. As Caplan, referring to Wildavsky and Douglas, comments: 'people see the weight of risks differently' (Caplan 2000: 8), and particular risks will prevail depending on individual situations within certain contexts and times. For example, a single Dutch Moroccan woman in her thirties, who is dependent on her family, may object to cousin marriages because of the medical risk, but if her family receives a marriage proposal from a cousin and/or his family she might prioritize the risk of remaining unmarried, given her age, rather than the medical risk of having a child with an autosomal recessive disorder.

The dominance of the medical concept of risk in the contemporary Western world is also debated. Finkler (2003: 54) gives a clear summary of this in her critique of what she calls 'the medicalization of family and kinship'.

> In brief, the concept of risk forecasts the future based on past occurrences. It shifts human fate from the caprices of the gods to the whims of mathematical probability. Paradoxically, the idea of risk, based as it is on mathematical probabilities, is double faced: on the one hand it recognises that events are random, and on the other it believes that this very randomness can be controlled to attain a degree of command of the future. It therefore permits modern humans to nurture the notion that they can dominate the future by controlling risks.

As Finkler shows, although it is often presented as if it can, secular science cannot offer any control over risks. At the same time, authors such as Beck and Giddens question the process of 'dominating the future by controlling risks', and introduce concepts like 'risk society' and 'securitization'; so in relation to risk, consanguineous marriages can be seen as a norm-setting and a contested concept in a multicultural society like the Netherlands – contested because people disagree with each other about its desirability, and 'norm-setting' because it marks different values for different groups and reveals the different ways that risks are dealt with.

Consanguineous Marriage, Medical Thought and Risk

All our respondents seemed aware of notions of risk relating to genetic defects in close kin marriages. That is, they all knew about the 'discussions' concerning parental consanguinity and the possible risk of having disabled offspring. However, our respondents took various positions on the medical risk. Some of the respondents, especially among the first generation, doubted whether an increased health risk really existed. For example, Meryem, thirty-six years old, born in Morocco, currently living in the Netherlands and married to an unrelated partner, stated:

> My grandfather had six wives. Everybody in the village is family and everybody marries within the village and Masha' Allah [Thank God], everybody is healthy. It is a very healthy family. Then, if I hear about it [parental consanguinity and genetic risk], I doubt. We would have that chance than as well. I believe it, but on the other side, I don't. . .

Because most consanguineously married couples have healthy children, the medical risk is often not perceived as such. 'Because it doesn't happen often, people don't think about it. The link is not made,' explained Mounia, a second generation, twenty-one-year-old, single Dutch Moroccan woman. Also, nearly all our respondents remarked that couples who are non-kin also have children with a disability.

For the majority of the respondents, first and second generation, and those who have children with a disability, the medical risk is not a reason *not* to marry within the family. 'The chance to have a child with a disability? That goes for everyone. The chance is just a bit higher for such marriages [. . .] If those two persons love each other and they enjoy themselves at that moment, you have to bear certain consequences', said a twenty-six-year-old second generation Dutch-Turkish woman, married to her first cousin.

It is clear that these women are aware of the medical risk discourse in one way or another. From this perspective, these medical thoughts are certainly dominant. But that does not mean that medical risk is a priority in their discourses and practices. In short, we found instead that consanguinity in relation to disabled offspring is often considered as just one of the many risks in life.

Our respondents' knowledge about the health risks associated with parental consanguinity varied slightly. With the exception of most of the couples who had children with a disability, none of our respondents had a clear idea about what the risk to health meant, even if they accepted the idea that there was an increased health risk for the offspring of consanguineous marriage. They referred to the obligatory health tests that take place before marriage in their countries of origin where transnational marriages often take place, or to their parents, to determine whether the prospective spouses are healthy and therefore fit to marry each other. In Turkey couples are tested for – among other conditions – thalassaemia, an autosomal recessive disease. But in practice, prospective spouses can marry before the results of these tests are known.

Knowing about a medical discourse does not mean that people agree with it, or that people think in precisely those medical terms. Even if a risk discourse seems dominant, the question is, what does this dominance mean? Is it something to agree with and to follow in practice, or is it something to disagree with, to resist, or, rather, to 'use' to obtain political benefits and create cultural boundaries? Other arguments may also play a role here; religious beliefs, for example, can offer another way of experiencing risk.

Consanguineous Marriage, Islam and Risk

Islam is seen as a 'new' religion in the Netherlands, one that is not (yet) regarded as an integral part of Dutch society but is exclusively related to minority immigrant groups. It is also regarded as a threat to social cohesion (Bartels 2008). Although the preference for kin marriages is not restricted to Muslims, as discussed in the introduction to this volume, and is a known marriage pattern in the Netherlands, it is nowadays often linked to Islam, because the practice is primarily ascribed to Turkish, Moroccan, Pakistani and Afghanistan Dutch, the majority of whom are Muslim.

In the Quran, Surah 'Al Nisa' explicitly states who a Muslim can and cannot marry, and, according to the Quran, cousins are acceptable as spouses. Bartels and Loukili (2012) conducted research into Islamic ethics, consanguineous marriage and preconceptional testing in the Netherlands. The Islamic scholars, imams and medical practitioners whom they interviewed stated that although cousin marriage was an accepted form of marriage within Islam, there have been debates about cousin marriages since the time of the Prophet Mohammed. In the *Hadith* (sayings of the Prophet), arguments both in favour of and against the practice can be found. Yet, our respondents explained their preference for kin marriages primarily in terms of culture rather than religion. Religion, however, plays an important role in how respondents view medical risk in general and in relation to consanguineous marriage in particular.

While some of our respondents who had (a) child(ren) with a disability accepted the medical risk as an explanation, others used a religious discourse as an explanation or combined medical and religious thought. Hajat was a first generation Moroccan Dutch woman in her thirties, who married her first cousin. They had a child with a hereditary disease, and her husband decided to divorce her because of the medical risk of having another child with a similar disease. Hajat accepted the medical condition of her child, but at the same time explained it as follows:

> We are Muslims, we believe in Allah. So, when something happens, we have to thank Allah. [...] We can't make the children with our own hands, but Allah gives us the child. So, when something happens, it happens. It is *Al-Qadr* [fate].

Kaoutar, thirty-nine years old, born and raised in Morocco, takes a similar stance. She studied chemistry in Morocco and fell in love with her cousin who lived in France at the time. She had two severely disabled children.

> I have studied Chemistry, I know about the [medical] risk. [...] But for me that is not an explanation. So I married my cousin. That is why I have ... disabled children, no. [...] For me, I'm Muslim, so I believe in God. I don't know, with us, we have *Al-Qadr*, 'fate' if you translate it. That's it actually.

Hajat and Kaoutar described how God, in the end, decides one's fate. It is clear that, for these respondents, medical and religious thoughts on risk are completely intertwined.

With the remark, 'Allah is the scientist of the scientists', the British Bangladeshi respondents, in a study of genetics, religion and identity, placed the responsibility for genetically related illness and the power to effect cures on Allah (Rozario 2009). Hajat and Kaoutar similarly took the view that Allah gives illness to certain individuals in certain families. As is also noted for British Bangladeshis (Rozario 2009), some of our respondents gained consolation from ascribing this responsibility to Allah. And although there are several studies which describe how having a child with a disability can be perceived negatively, as a punishment from God (e.g. Tonkens et al. 2011), we found there was a positive attitude instead. During a group discussion of Moroccan and Turkish mothers who all had a child with a disability (not all were married to a cousin), the following was stated and agreed explicitly by the other women:

> It is not a punishment, rather the reverse. Especially mothers with a lot of *sabr* [patience] have to fulfil these commitments and mission with their disabled children.

According to this discourse, women who have patience, a highly valued virtue for women, are chosen by God to take care of this special child. In this sense, the religious discourse is empowering. For our informants, medical thinking was important in explaining the health problems of their child(ren) but their religious beliefs brought true acceptance of their child(ren), and enabled them to view their children as being entrusted to them by God: a special commission.

Hatice, a twenty-six-year-old, second generation Turkish woman, married to her maternal first cousin, combined in her response the perception of medical risk with the teaching of Islam, and commented, with regard to the medical risk of having a child with a hereditary disease, that the medical risk was nature and in the end, nature was the work of Allah. Thus, she accepted the medical risk and intertwined this with her religion as a way of explaining the world around her.

Consanguineous Marriage, Social Interaction and Risk

The practice and preference of marrying a member of one's kin is not a static or fixed phenomenon but a social construct that can be transformed by interaction, time and context. We observed a difference in attitudes towards cousin marriage, for example, between the various generations of immigrants. For the first generation women who came to the Netherlands in the 1960s and 1970s to join husbands who had come as guest workers, close kin marriage was a relevant and probably self-evident phenomenon. Most of these first generation women referred to the advantages of marrying a relative such as a first cousin; these included keeping the property within the family, an advantage to which the young generation, brought up in the Netherlands, could not relate. It was clear that the younger generation had different ideas about partner choice and specifically about cousin marriages. A Dutch Moroccan mother of two teenagers, married to her paternal cousin, explained that her son came home from school one day and asked her: 'Mum, may I ask you a question? Aren't you married to your cousin? Isn't that disgusting?', clearly referring to the taboo on cousin marriage in Dutch society.

When discussing the risks associated with marriage within the family, our respondents often mentioned the related social risks. Cousin marriage carries a risk of creating serious rifts in the kinship network if the couple want a divorce, and our respondents often mentioned this as a disadvantage and as a reason for not marrying within the family. 'If there are problems in the marriage, then it is a family affair. If there is a divorce, there is a conflict in the family. When somebody is married outside the family and there is a divorce, it is finished', said Soumia, a forty-four-year-old, Dutch Moroccan woman.

Charsley (2007), however, describes how not marrying in the family can also be a risk. In her study on transnational cousin marriage among British Pakistanis, she describes how a kin marriage is a safe option for women, especially in a migration situation, as the family is likely to treat another family member quite well. Our respondents, particularly women who came to the Netherlands via transnational marriages, also mentioned the importance of being known to the family and accepted by the in-laws. In the political risk discourse, a marriage between cousins (among immigrants) is seen as more likely to be a forced marriage. In the political debate regarding the proposed law on cousin marriage, this is a major objection against the practice. Among our respondents, there were women whose marriages were arranged under pressure, such as twenty-five-year-old Gülcen who was a second generation Dutch Turkish woman. When she was fourteen years old her family decided she should get engaged to her second cousin in Turkey. Gülcen didn't want to get engaged and marry; she wanted to finish high school and then study. 'No' was not accepted and Gülcen was constantly told that this marriage was such a good opportunity for her. In the end, her family, especially her mother, convinced Gülcen. So she got engaged when she was fourteen and married her cousin when she was seventeen years old.

At the same time we found women who had fallen in love with their cousin, without any interference from their family, like twenty-four-year-old Sarah, a second generation Dutch Moroccan woman who had married her first cousin living in Morocco when she was twenty. She never expected to marry a person from Morocco or a cousin: 'I really liked him, but I thought: no, he's my cousin!' But she fell in love with him, a man whom she hadn't known before and had only seen briefly a few times. The two of them decided to get engaged and marry. Sarah's father eventually agreed with the marriage, but tried to convince his daughter to postpone the marriage until she was older.

For the majority of our respondents, cousin marriage was not associated with forced marriage, although we did find that second generation young adults had changing views on partner choice in general, and on cousin marriage in particular. Some young adults appeared to reject cousin marriages: 'For me, it is not the medical reason that is important. For me it is a really weird idea, you grow up together. And then, when you marry, the relationship changes', said Nora, a twenty-one-year-old, second generation Moroccan Dutch woman. It appears that the young adults had internalized the dominant Western view on consanguineous marriage and regard it as incestuous and taboo. For example, Siham, a single twenty-six-year-old, second generation Moroccan Dutch woman, commented:

> I'm not against cousin marriages or arranged marriages. But not for myself. I think it is because I grew up in the Netherlands. You hear:

'it's incest', and I think I unconsciously internalized that. If I lived in Morocco I might think differently about it.

The younger respondents also appeared to accept the medical risk rather more than the (older) first generation. For example, Aysel, a twenty-six-year-old, second generation Turkish woman, married her maternal cousin. When she married in Turkey, they went to the hospital for the obligatory test before marriage and were told about the increased health risk:

> Suppose I get pregnant, the first thing I'll do is go to the hospital. And I'll say 'We're cousins and I want to start a research [. . .]. I think it is very good of Turkey that you have to do a[n obligatory] blood test [before marriage] and that the doctor in the hospital talks to you.

Although we see a trend indicating that cousin marriages might decrease in the future, we also found a 'betwixt and between pattern', which combines the preference for cousin marriages, on the one hand, with a view of cousin marriage as incestuous, on the other. Our respondents subdivided their cousins into those whom they could or could not marry. A cousin with whom you grew up is regarded as a sibling, and siblings cannot marry as that is incest. But, if there is no emotional proximity to the cousin, and this is combined with geographical distance, then a cousin can be an eligible spouse. These respondents often rejected cousin marriage, but interpreted the word 'cousin' differently. Charsley (2007) found the same pattern in her study of transnational cousin marriages among British Pakistanis. In the Netherlands this pattern was illustrated by Özlem, a thirty-eight-year-old woman who married outside the family. She was born in Turkey and raised in the Netherlands from the age of two. With regard to her teenage daughter, she said the following:

> My daughter and her cousin grow up together. They see each other every day. They also go the cinema together, I don't worry about that. [. . .] I'm against cousin marriages and so is my daughter. If the family lives a bit further away, in Turkey, and you see them once or twice a year, that is different. But, not so close.

The following quotation by Nurten, second generation Turkish Dutch, married to her first cousin, also illustrates this stance:

> I played with my second cousins when I was little. And if you grow up together, you regard them as brothers and sisters [. . .] I could not imagine that we would fall in love [. . .] And well, him [husband],

I didn't know, neither did I know his parents. I didn't see him as my cousin. I still don't see him as my cousin.

Not 'being family' but 'feeling like family' appears to be an indicator not to marry. If you don't feel like family, you can still develop a romantic relationship, in which passion and sexuality have a chance. So, this 'betwixt and between' pattern maintains the traditional marriage pattern, but gives ample room for romantic relationships to develop. It seems that partner choice among these groups is developing to a position where romantic love is an important determinant to marry. However, having some emotional distance from a cousin who does not feel like a family member makes them eligible as a spouse, but this has nothing to do with the medical risks.

Changing Patterns of Partner Choice?

What does this mean for partner choice? Can we observe a shift? A proportion of our young, second generation respondents seem to have adopted a 'Western' or 'Dutch' view of cousin marriage, one which views it as a taboo, incestuous practice. However, the common assumption that immigrant groups adjust their views to those of the dominant society is not necessarily justified. While we see some signs of a decline in cousin marriage in the Netherlands, in surrounding countries, such as France and the UK, an increase has been noticed among certain groups. In France, Selby (2010) conducted extensive fieldwork in a Parisian *banlieue*, where almost 90 per cent of her primarily Algerian and Moroccan respondents were first generation women who had married their cousins living in France. In the UK Shaw and Charsley (Shaw 2001; Charsley 2007; Shaw and Charsley 2006) found that second generation or British-born British Pakistanis commonly married nationals, especially cousins, from Pakistan, who then usually migrated to join their spouses in the UK. Shaw (2001) argues that these marriage choices are not determined by cultural rules or preferences alone, 'but must also be understood in terms of the wider political, economic, and social frameworks' (see also chapter five, this volume). For immigrants, the consanguineous marriage form offers the possibility of retaining the ideals of their own culture and religion. Similarly, Selby (2010: 11) argues that in the French 'social context where North African values and mores are sometimes understood as threatened, "traditional" women in particular have become the symbolic bearers of the diasporic community's identity'.

We did not observe a 'medicalization of partner choice' among our respondents. Whether medical risk will constitute a reason for choosing an unrelated spouse in the future is questionable. The medical risk is primarily experienced when a couple has a child with a genetically related illness. The couple may have known about the medical risk and thought 'it will not happen to us', or may have attributed the birth of an affected child to a higher power, Allah (fate). Some of the respondents who married a cousin and became parents of a child with a disability caused by genetic disease said that they would not marry a cousin again, but others said they would, despite the medical risk.

Rather than describing risk as medical or social, Dutch Moroccans and Turks feel that the risk of consanguineous marriage is primarily social as divorce can threaten the stability of the whole family. Any risk in relation to religion is non-existent. If Allah determines your fate, risk plays no role. A disabled child can even be seen as a gift from Allah to prove one's faith. At least some of the second generation seem to have adopted the 'Western' view of consanguineous marriages as incestuous and therefore as incest. And as noted, we can also identify a 'betwixt and between pattern'.

This raises the question about the relationship between cousin marriage and arranged marriage. In their research, Shaw (2001) and Charsley (2006) describe cousin marriages as being predominantly arranged marriages. Although we can see this too, mostly for our first generation respondents, we also found 'love marriages' between cousins, especially among the young adults. We can see a trend developing in which cousin marriage, as a 'preferred' marriage form in terms of family continuity, is, to a certain extent, changing. For our respondents who entered a 'love marriage', cousins are part of the 'marriage market', and among the available eligible spouses, even though in the Netherlands cousins are not generally regarded as being eligible spouses. The respondents who entered a love marriage with a cousin are very much aware of this, expressing this, for example, by referring to their initial personal resistance to their feelings of romantic love for their cousin (as in Nurten's case, above).

There are other developments that support and sustain the trends described. Research done by De Koning and Bartels (2005) and Storms and Bartels (2008), on partner choice among Turkish and Moroccan people in the Netherlands, indicates that first and especially second generation immigrants disapprove of arranged marriage and forced marriage. The latter research shows that individual partner choice is increasing, whereas the ideal of marrying a partner from one's country of origin is weakening. Both trends presume a decline in cousin marriage.

It has become increasingly self-evident that second generation Dutch Turks and Moroccans are choosing their own marriage partners. The meaning of 'free choice' for these young adults differs, however, from what in the dominant 'Dutch view' is regarded as a free choice. 'Free choice', for them, can also include asking their parents to look for a partner, whilst reserving the right to accept or refuse the person found. Some of them want to choose a partner themselves, but they also want to stick to certain 'rules', not only because these 'rules' are customary within their family, but also because they themselves support them. Forced marriage is disapproved of, but the large grey area between forced marriage and free choice is defined in a variety of ways and largely remains open to question (Storms and Bartels 2008).

Highly educated Moroccan and Turkish young people, in particular, are most likely to feel 'different' from the inhabitants of their, or their parents', ancestral country of origin and this affects their choice of a particular marriage partner. We observed a trend whereby some of these young people consider an 'immigrant marriage' as a marriage with a partner 'from another culture'. They prefer to marry a Dutch Moroccan or Turkish partner. Also, the boundary of ethnicity is becoming less important as a marker for partner choice, while religion, Islam in this case, is becoming more important (Storms and Bartels 2008). This is consistent with the observation that since the 1990s, religious identity has increased in significance for Moroccan and Turkish immigrants and their descendants in the Netherlands (De Koning 2008).

To conclude, looking at these changing patterns of partner choice, it appears that cousin marriages among Dutch Turks and Moroccans are likely to diminish in the future. And for those members of the second generation who do choose a cousin as a spouse, it seems to be more and more often a 'love marriage', based on individual choice.

Note

1. According to this proposed law, spouses who want to disprove the allegation that their marriage has been forced will have to state specifically that they have not been forced to marry. Otherwise, they will be unable

to marry. This 'draft' law has been accepted in the Second Chamber [the Lower House] and proposed to the First Chamber [Upper House], which awaits a response to their questions (June 2014).
2. The research is funded by the Centre for Society and the Life Sciences in the Netherlands, CSG.

References

Asscher, L. 2009. 'Amsterdam is nog niet eerlijk' [Amsterdam is not fair yet], *Volkskrant* (daily newspaper): 11–4. http://www.volkskrant.nl/vk/nl/2664/Nieuws/archief/article/detail/329048/2009/04/21/Amsterdam-is-nog-niet-eerlijk.dhtml

Bartels, A.C. and G. Loukili. 2012. '"Testing isn't the problem". Views of Muslim theologians, spiritual counselors, Imams and physicians on pre-conceptional testing', *Medische Antropologie. Tijdschrift over gezondheid en cultuur* [Medical Anthropology. Journal of Health and Culture] 24(2): 321–333. http://tma.socsci.uva.nl/24_2/bartels_loukili.pdf.

Bartels, E. 2008. *Antropologische dilemmas en onderzoek naar Islam*. Talmalezing. [Anthropological dilemmas and research into Islam]. Amsterdam: VU University. http://www.fsw.vu.nl/nl/Images/Talmalezing%202008%20Bartels_tcm30-56361.pdf

Beck, U. 1992. *Risk Society. Towards a New Modernity*. London: Sage Publications.

Bennett, R.L., A.G. Motulsky, A. Bittles, L. Hudgins, S. Uhrich and D. Lochner Doyle. 2006. 'Genetic counselling and screening of consanguineous couples and their offspring, Recommendations of the National Society of Genetic Counselors', *Journal of Genetic Counseling* 11: 97–119.

Bittles, A.H. 2008. 'A community genetics perspective on consanguineous marriage', *Community Genetics* 11(6): 324–330.

Caplan, P. (ed.). 2000. *Risk Revisited*. London: Pluto Press.

Charsley, K. 2007. 'Risk, trust, gender and transnational cousin marriage among British Pakistanis', *Ethnic and Racial Studies* 30(6): 1117–1131.

Douglas, M. and A. Wildavsky 1982. *Risk and Culture. An Essay on the Selection of Technological and Environmental Dangers*. Berkeley: University of California Press.

Finkler, K. 2003. 'Illusions of controlling the future: risk and genetic inheritance', *Anthropology and Medicine* 10(1): 51–70.

Giddens, A. 1992. *Modernity and Self-Identity. Self and Society in the Late Modern Age*. Cambridge: Polity Press.

de Koning, M. 2008. *Zoeken naar een 'zuivere' islam. Geloofsbeleving en identiteitsvorming onder jonge Marokkaans-Nederlandse moslims* [Searching for a 'pure' Islam. Faith experience and identity formation among Moroccan-Dutch Muslims]. Amsterdam: Bert Bakker.

de Koning, M., and E. Bartels. 2005. *Over het huwelijk gesproken. Partnerkeuze en gedwongen huwelijken onder Marokkaanse, Turkse en Hindostaanse Nederlanders* [Speaking about marriage. Partner choice and forced marriages in Moroccan, Turks and Hindustani Dutch people]. The Hague: Adviescommissie Vreemdelingenzaken, http://www.acvz.org/publicaties/VS-ACVZ-NR9-2005.pdf

de Koning, M., E. Bartels and O. Storms. 2011. 'Schadelijke traditionele praktijken en cultureel burgerschap. Integratie, seksualiteit en gender' [Harmful traditional practices and cultural citizenship. Integration, sexuality and gender], *Tijdschrift voor Genderstudies* 14(1): 35–52.

Lupton, D. 2006. 'Sociology and risk', in G. Mythen and S. Walklate (eds), *Beyond the Risk Society. Critical Reflections on Risk and Human Security.* Berkshire: Open University Press McGraw-Hill Education, pp.1–25.

Rozario, S. 2009. '"Allah is the scientist of the scientists": modern medicine and religious healing among British Bangladeshis', *Culture and Religion: An Interdisciplinary Journal* 10(2): 177–199.

Said, E.W. 1978. *Orientalism.* New York: Vintage Books.

Schinkel, W. 2010. 'The virtualization of citizenship', *Critical Sociology* 36(2): 265–283.

Selby, J. 2010. 'Marriage-partner preference among Muslims in France: reproducing tradition in the Maghrebian diaspora', *Journal of the Society for the Anthropology of Europe* 9(2): 4–16.

Shaw, A. 2001. 'Kinship, cultural preference and immigration: consanguineous marriage among British Pakistanis', *Journal of the Royal Anthropological Institute* 7(2): 315–334.

Shaw, A. and K. Charsley. 2006. 'Rishtas: adding emotion to strategy in understanding British Pakistani transnational marriages', *Global Networks* 6(4): 405–421.

Stoltenberg, C., P. Magnus, R.T. Lie, A.K. Daltveit and L.M. Irgens. 1997. 'Birth defects and parental consanguinity in Norway', *American Journal of Epidemiology* 145(5): 439–448.

Storms, O. and E. Bartels. 2008. *De keuze van een huwelijkspartner. Een studie naar partnerkeuze onder groepen Amsterdammers* [The choice of a marriage partner. A research project into partner choice among Amsterdam immigrant groups]. Amsterdam: Vrije Universiteit. http://www.fsw.vu.nl/nl/Images/huwelijkenamsterdam%20Spdf_tcm30-60514.pdf

———. 2013. '"Notre huile est dans notre farine". An exploration into the meaning of consanguinity in Northern Morocco against the backdrop of the medical risk of disabled offspring', in H. Vroom, P. Verdonk, M.A. Abdellah and M. Cornel (eds), *Looking Beneath the Surface: Medical Ethics from Islamic and Western Perspectives.* Amsterdam and New York: Rodopi, pp.85–101.

Taussig, K.S. 2009. 'Calvinism and chromosomes: religion, the geographical imaginary, and medical genetics in the Netherlands', *Science as Culture* 6(4): 495–524. W

Tonkens, E., L. Verplanke and L. de Vries. 2011. *Alleen slechte vrouwen klagen. Problemen en behoeften van geïsoleerde allochtone spilzorgers in Nederland* [Only bad women complain. Problems and needs of isolated allochtonous caregivers in the Netherlands]. Amsterdam: Universiteit van Amsterdam, MOVISIE.

Vermeulen, B.P. 2007. *Vrijheid, gelijkheid, burgerschap. Over verschuivende fundamenten van het Nederlandse minderhedenrecht en -beleid: immigratie, integratie, onderwijs en religie* [Liberty, equality, citizenship. On shifting foundations of the Dutch Minority Law and policy: immigration, integration, education and religion]. The Hague: Sdu Uitgevers.

Waelput, A.J.M. and P.W. Achterberg. 2007. *Kinderwens van consanguine ouders: risico's en erfelijkheidsvoorlichting*. Bilthoven: RIVM.

PART III

CONSANGUINITY AND MANAGING GENETIC RISK

Chapter 8

USING COMMUNITY GENETICS FOR HEALTHY CONSANGUINITY

Joël Zlotogora

Since the establishment of the State of Israel in 1948, the Israeli population has witnessed many changes and a very significant health improvement was achieved. For instance, the infant mortality rates declined more than tenfold from 37.3 in 1955 to 3.6 per 1,000 live births in 2011. However, across this time period, a significant gap has remained between infant mortality rates in the Israel's Jewish population (2.7 per 1,000 live births in 2011) and among Israel's non-Jews (6.6 per 1,000 live births in 2011) (Statistical abstracts of Israel 2013). These differences have been explained by the higher rates of congenital malformations and genetic diseases among Arab and Druze live-borns than among Jews, which are paralleled in differences between these populations in their consanguinity rates. In a study comparing the infant mortality rates among Jews on one side and Arabs and Druzes on the other, conducted over a four-year period (1996–1999), the infant mortality was twice as high among non-Jews than among Jews (9 versus 4.4 per 1,000 live births) (Zlotogora et al. 2003). While the rate of children with malformations/genetic syndromes was 3.1 times higher among non-Jews than among Jews (3.94 vs. 1.25 per 1,000 live births), a higher infant mortality among non-Jews was also observed in each of the etiologic categories analysed (Zlotogora et al. 2003). Poor compliance with prenatal care and low rates of termination of pregnancy are among the significant other factors responsible for these differences. The emphasis placed on the high rates of malformations/genetic syndromes led to public health interventions by means of health education to prevent consanguineous marriages (Strulov 2005). In addition, local programmes were investigated, such as a programme inspired by 'Dor Yeshorim' among the ultra-Orthodox Jews that was instituted in one of the Bedouin tribes in the Negev (Raz 2005). The aim of the pilot programme was to allow for the use of information about carriers of genetic diseases (starting with deafness, which was frequent in the tribe) in decisions about marriage. These different interventions were not successful, one of the main reasons being that they overlooked the social importance of consanguineous marriage (Modell and Darr 2002).

In the last decade, efforts have been made to change the 'public health approach' by developing and offering a programme that does not interfere with the choices of the individuals, but delivers genetic counselling to the Muslim Arabs and Druze communities in Israel. This chapter describes the 'community genetics' approach that is being developed in Israel to deliver targeted genetics services to particular subsections of the Israeli population that have been identified, from epidemiological data, as being particularly at risk of serious genetic disease. The programme is described from the perspective of a practitioner who developed this programme and has been delivering genetics services accordingly. The chapter is based on the author's clinical experience and research as a clinical geneticist employed in the community genetics department of the Ministry of Health, and represents the author's views and not necessarily those of the Ministry. It first provides some background details of the heterogeneity of the Israeli population and the structure of its health service, and then discusses the rationale and mode of operation of the programme for genetic counselling in the community.

Background

The Israeli Population

In 2012 the Israeli population included 7,910,500 citizens of whom 6,282,000 were Jews (79.4 per cent) and 1,370,600 Muslim Arabs (17.3 per cent) (Statistical abstracts 2013). The other groups include mainly Christian Arabs (157,100) and Druze (130,500), each representing less than 2 per cent of the population.

The Jewish population is residentially concentrated in the cities while the Arabs and Druze usually live in villages/tribes that were founded by a few individuals approximately ten generations ago. The localities in which the non-Jewish population lives are very different, including relatively large towns as well as very small villages, some of which are far away from all services. There is also a large amount of variation in the daily way of life and access to health services within the various Israeli Arab and Druze communities. In most of the Israeli localities the population derives from a single religious community; however some of the localities are mixed, and include either all the different religious communities or only some of them. Consanguineous marriage was frequent among Jews in their various communities in the Diaspora but has declined significantly since their immigration to Israel (Cohen et al. 2004). Among Israeli Arabs and Druze, similarly to the Arab population in the region, consanguineous marriages remain frequent. In more than 25 per cent of Muslim Arab and Druze marriages the spouses are first cousins, with an additional 20 per cent related in other ways (Vardi-Saliternik et al. 2002). Consanguinity is less frequent among Christian Arabs (21 per cent of marriages are to first cousins and 11 per cent more distantly related) but more frequent among the Bedouins (35 per cent of marriages are to first cousins and 34 per cent more distantly related). Genetic diseases have been reported to be frequent in each of the different Jewish communities as well as among Arabs and Druzes, mainly as the result of their respective isolation.

Health Care Infrastructure

Since 1995, with the adoption of a new Health law, the entire population is covered by health insurance. Health services are mainly provided through four health funds and the Ministry of Health. Primary health care in Israel is delivered via local family clinics across most of the country. Genetics services are provided almost exclusively in hospitals.

A national programme for the detection and prevention of birth defects was established in 1980, operated by the Ministry of Health. This public health programme was provided free of charge, and included newborn screening, prenatal diagnosis to women at risk of a genetic disease, and population carrier screening. The population carrier screening was at first only for Tay Sachs and thalassaemia but additional screening tests are now recommended following the characterization of the molecular basis of many other diseases relatively prevalent in the Israeli population. Because of financial difficulties, the expansion of the programme has been incremental. The first step, in 2002, included screening for severe genetic diseases with a frequency higher than 1/1,000 live births (carrier frequency of 1:16 for autosomal recessive diseases) within specific localities/tribes in the Arab and Druze population (Zlotogora, Carmi, and Shalev 2009). A later expansion in 2008 saw the inclusion of cystic fibrosis carrier screening for the whole population. In January 2013 the final step was achieved and the screening programme now includes carrier screening for all severe diseases within communities in which the carrier frequency is 1:60 or higher (Zlotogora 2014).

Genetics Clinics 'in the Community'

Traditionally, genetic counselling is given in genetics clinics within large hospitals. The establishment of genetics clinics in the community has been proposed as a better way of delivering genetic counselling, in particular for inbred populations (Morton et al. 2003). One obvious advantage of setting up genetics clinics in rural communities located far from major hospitals is the reduction of travel for the patients. Indeed, improving access to genetics services has been demonstrated to be very useful for the diagnosis and treatment of genetic diseases (Lowry and Bowen 1990; Morton et al. 2003). Even when the distances to the genetic unit are small, the presence of local and accessible clinics is important in communities in which, customarily, women do not travel alone and husbands are working.

However, the main advantage of the presence of genetics clinics in the community is the close contact between the geneticists and the family physicians (Zlotogora et al. 2006). For instance, in the Israeli Arab population, the family physician is a central figure in the life of the locality, and is consulted on all health related subjects as well as about many other family problems. Most of the families ask the advice of their family physician when making difficult decisions, such as those that result from genetic counselling. In addition, individuals planning to marry, or their parents, often consult the family physician before the marriage, in particular if it is a consanguineous marriage. Therefore the close contact between the family physician and the geneticist as a result of the next-door-room consultations is key for improved communication and genetic counselling to the family. This close contact is also important for the integration of genetics into family medicine. Having a geneticist within the regional family medical clinical team enables easier referrals from family physicians and nurses, and facilitates self-referral.

With the improvement in general health and the reduction of environmental causes of illnesses in Israel, many of the health problems in the Arab population are now related to heredity. However, while in populations where consanguinity is uncommon it is held that 'the rarer the occurrence of a disorder, the more frequently the parents are found to be consanguineous' (http://www.britannica.com), this is not true in populations where consanguinity is frequent. Since the relationship between consanguinity and rare disorders is regularly emphasized, this often leads the medical personnel to link consanguinity and diseases, giving the patient the impression that he or she is to be blamed for their choice of marriage partner. A 'routine' use of genetic counselling may also help to reduce the stigmatization associated with genetic problems.

A Model for Genetic Counselling in Inbred Populations

Genetic counselling in inbred populations presents several challenges. Since families are large, often with multiple loops of consanguinity, a significant amount of time is needed in order to draw a pedigree; however, individuals are prone to give inaccurate data about relationships in previous generations (Zlotogora et al. 1998). In addition, since medical details concerning relatives are mostly kept confidential, they are often unknown to the consultants. When clinical information is given it is often vague, limited to 'retardation' or death of the individual, and is often explained as being secondary to external events. On the other hand, the family history remains the major tool for determining the risks to the couple and the tests that should be performed.

It has been our experience that the way to reconcile these contradictions is to accumulate information about genetic diseases present in the locality in the form of a database to be used during the genetic consultations (Zlotogora et al. 2006). This personal experience has been built up from operating two local genetics clinics aimed exclusively at the Arab population, serving the town of Nazareth and eight surrounding localities, comprising in total approximately 75,000 inhabitants. The first step before opening the clinics was to collect the relevant medical and genetic information on the population from the files of the hospital genetic unit serving this population. The data were entered onto a laptop computer using commercially available family-pedigree software (Reunion, Leister Productions). This software was chosen because it allows for the rapid introduction of the information about each individual and their relatives and allows the data to be retrieved in a pedigree format as well as a list. The medical records, including the family relationships and identifying data, were entered in the programme as a separate database for each locality/town according to the origin of the family. It should be emphasized that these databases are mainly an extension of the medical files and are used and kept as such. One of these localities has been the focus of a research project for which complete medical data, as well as data on relationships, for almost all the inhabitants and their ancestors were gathered, representing therefore an ideal illustration of the potential of such a venture (Zlotogora et al. 2007). The data are continuously updated with new individuals, new diagnoses and expansion of family data during the counselling sessions.

The locality for which data are almost complete is a Muslim village which, in 2012, had 11,800 inhabitants, most of whom were related to the founders of the village approximately 250 years ago (Statistical abstracts of Israel 2013). In all the cases where individuals from this locality came for genetic counselling, the completeness of the database allowed us to verify the data given by the probands (the individuals being reported on or given counselling) and to complete these data if needed. The database includes information on 25 distinct autosomal recessive disorders diagnosed in 115 families from the village (see Table 8.1).

As the table shows, the most frequent disorders diagnosed were deafness (43 families) and retinitis pigmentosa (27 families). As expected, there were also a few families with autosomal dominant or X linked inheritance, most caused by new mutations. In 11 of the recessive diseases the molecular basis was characterized. Some of the mutations, such as those causing thalassaemia, FMF and one of the mutations causing deafness, are frequent among Arabs in the region and therefore most of them have probably been introduced at least once into the village through marriage with a carrier from outside. However, most of the mutations are unique; probably the result of new mutations that occurred in the village, the information stored in the database has enabled their distributions and origins to be determined (Zlotogora et al. 2007). For instance

TABLE 8.1 Autosomal Recessive Diseases Diagnosed in a Single Village among Descendants of the Founders

1	Deafness connexin related*	43 families
2	Retinitis pigmentosa*	27 families
3	Thalassaemia*	5 families
4	Sickle-cell anaemia*	4 families
5	Glutaric aciduria type II*	4 families
6	Syndrome with arthrogryposis	3 families
7	Gaucher disease*	3 families
8	Syndrome with mental retardation*	3 families
9	Adrenal lipoid hyperplasia	2 families
10	Familial Mediterranean Fever*	2 families
11	Syndrome with hemochromatosis	2 families
12	Ichthyosis*	2 families
13	Syndrome with mental retardation	2 families
14	Usher syndrome	2 families
15	Aplastic anaemia	1 family
16	Syndrome with cholestasis	1 family
17	Heart cardiomyopathy	1 family
18	Congenital hypothyroidism	1 family
19	Hyperphenylalaninemia*	1 family
20	Metachromatic leukodystrophy*	1 family
21	Pyruvate carboxylase deficiency	1 family
22	Syndrome with renal dysfunction	1 family
23	Syndrome unknown (1)	1 family
24	Syndrome unknown (2)	1 family
25	Syndrome unknown (3)	1 family

*the mutation(s) has been characterized

Gaucher disease was diagnosed in three families in the village and the mutation N370S in the GBA gene, unknown in the surrounding Arab localities but well known in other populations, was characterized in all the families. This mutation appeared in the village nine generations ago and is found in 7.1 per cent of the descendants of the founder couple while it is absent in other inhabitants of the village (Figure 8.1).

Another disease, metachromatic leukodystrophy, was diagnosed in a single family of the village due to homozygosity for a novel mutation in the ARSA gene. This mutation was found only among the descendants of the grandparents of the affected children. The information on the origin of the mutations and their distribution among families of the village allows clinicians to determine to whom to offer genetic screening or testing. For mutations that were

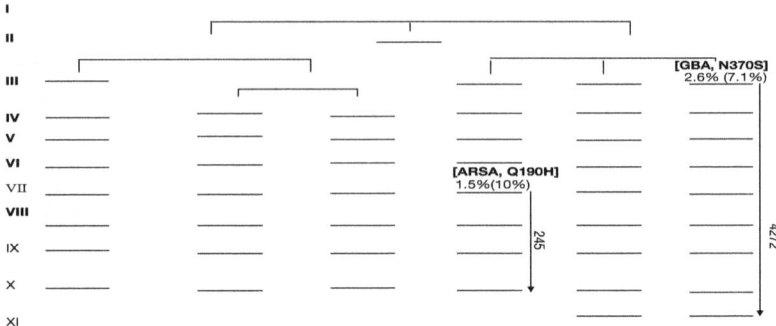

FIGURE 8.1 Origin of Two of the Mutations in a Single Village

The figure represents a simplified pedigree of the founding couple and the three founding brothers. Roman numbers on the left of the pedigree give generations. Couples are represented by a horizontal line. Each mutation appears at the place of the first ancestor couple, the percentage is the carrier rate in the random sample. In parenthesis appears carrier rate among the descendants of the couple. The arrows on the right of each couple represent their descendants and their numbers in the computer file. GBA is the gene in which the mutation N370S is responsible for Gaucher disease in the village. ARSA is the gene in which the mutation Q190H is responsible for metachromatic leukodystrophy in the village.

present among the founders of the village, genetic screening is relevant to the whole village, while for mutations that appeared later in time, testing may be offered only according to the calculated risk for the couple.

As an expansion of these local records, a database including the entire Israeli population was built (the Israeli national genetic database is available at http://server.goldenhelix.org/israeli/). The database enables online consulting of all the existing knowledge about the genetic disorders in the Israeli population according to ethnicity and religion (Zlotogora et al. 2009). The database includes all the available data about genetic diseases among Jews according to their communities of origin and among Arabs and Druze according to the localities where they are living. In order to protect the privacy of the patients and ensure anonymity, access to data on diseases according to locality is provided only to Israeli geneticists on the basis of a username and password. This feature allows a list to be obtained of the disorders and their frequencies in each locality. This part of the database includes all the monogenic disorders among Arabs and Druze as known by the curator in each locality, as well as molecular data if available. In January 2014 there were 1053 entries reported in 122 different localities, representing only a part of the diseases existing in this population since the completeness depends directly upon the cooperation of the clinicians working in the localities. In 18 of those localities there were data on 15 or more different diseases.

While the use of ethnicity and religion in genetic databases and screening programmes may be subject to debate, in Israel both have been well accepted. This may be related to the fact that the Israeli population is not homogeneous and distinctions even between Jews, between Ashkenazi and others according to their country of origin, are made in everyday life. In the medical context, these distinctions are reinforced by observed differences between communities in the frequency of genetic conditions.

Population screening for Tay Sachs disease among Ashkenazi Jews was the first community oriented screening. Thereafter, the community of origin has been routinely used in medical genetics either for Jews, Arabs or Druzes without generating any debate either within the medical community or the general public. The availability of these data is very important for genetic counselling since it enables clinicians to offer patients more accurate and accessible information and genetic testing as needed.

Conclusion

Genetic counselling for consanguinity, as for any other purpose, must aim to allow counselees to reach their best decision in connection with their principles and ways of life. There are advantages in consanguineous marriages and their medical aspects represent only one facet of the many other factors involved in the decisions. The genetic counsellor should aim to offer ways of reducing the medical risks while leaving the final choice to the counselees. Such an approach may enable the medical impact of consanguinity to be reduced without interfering with the ancestral traditions and the wishes of the counselees. From our experience, the best way to apply these principles is to implement genetics clinics within the community. A public health programme based on the model described here is in its first steps of development in Israel. The aim is to operate community genetics clinics in all the localities where Arabs and Druze are living.

References

Cohen T., R. Vardi-Saliternik and Y. Friedlander. 2004. 'Consanguinity, intracommunity and intercommunity marriages in a population sample of Israeli Jews', *Annals of Human Biology* 31: 38–48.

Lowry, R.B. and P. Bowen. 1990. 'The Alberta Hereditary Diseases Programme: a regional model for delivery of genetic services', *CMAJ* 142: 228–232.

Modell, B. and A. Darr. 2002. 'Science and society: genetic counselling and customary consanguineous marriage', *Nature Reviews Genetics* 3: 225–229.

Morton, D.H., C.S. Morton, K.A. Strauss, D.L. Robinson, E.G. Puffenberger, C. Hendrickson and R.I. Kelley. 2003. 'Pediatric medicine and the genetic disorders of the Amish and Mennonite people of Pennsylvania', *American Journal of Medical Genetics Part C* 121C: 5–17.

Raz, A. 2005. *The Gene and the Genie: Tradition, Medicalization, and Genetic Counselling in a Bedouin Community.* Durham, NC: Carolina Academic Press, Ethnographic Studies in Medical Anthropology Series.

Statistical abstracts of Israel. 2013. Central bureau of statistics, Jerusalem, Israel.

Strulov, A. 2005. 'The Western Galilee experience: reducing infant mortality in the Arab population', *Israel Medical Association Journal* 7: 483–486.

Vardi-Saliternik R., Y. Friedlander and T. Cohen. 2002. 'Consanguinity in a population sample of Israeli Muslim Arabs, Christian Arabs and Druze', *Annals of Human Biology* 29: 422–431.

Zlotogora, J. 2014. 'Genetic and genomic medicine in Israel', *Molecular Genetics & Genomic Medicine* 2: 85–94.

Zlotogora J., S. Barges, B. Bisharat and S.A. Shalev. 2006. 'Genetic disorders among Palestinian Arabs. 4: Genetic clinics in the community', *American Journal of Medical Genetics A* 140: 1644–1646.

Zlotogora, J., B. Bishara and S. Barges. 1998. 'Can we rely on family history?' *American Journal of Medical Genetics* 77: 79–80.

Zlotogora, J., R. Carmi, B. Lev and S.A. Shalev. 2009. 'A targeted population carrier screening programme for severe and frequent genetic diseases in Israel', *European Journal of Human Genetics* 17: 591–597.

Zlotogora J., Y. Hujerat, S. Barges, S.A. Shalev and A. Chakravarti. 2007. 'The fate of 12 recessive mutations in a single village', *Annals of Human Genetics* 71: 202–208.

Zlotogora, J., A. Leventhal and Y. Amitai. 2003. 'The impact of congenital malformations and Mendelian diseases on infant mortality in Israel', *Israel Medical Association Journal* 5: 416–418.

Zlotogora, J., S. van Baal and G.P. Patrinos. 2009. 'The Israeli National Genetic Database', *Israel Medical Association Journal* 11: 373–375.

Chapter 9

PREMARITAL CARRIER TESTING AND MATCHING IN JEWISH COMMUNITIES

Aviad E. Raz

This chapter focuses on the use of carrier screening for premarital matching, as it has developed in Jewish communities characterized by endogamy (and sometimes consanguinity), high prevalence of severe recessive diseases, arranged marriages, and a religious ban on abortion. When administered by the state, such programmes for 'healthy endogamy' (see chapter eight, this volume) may result in criticism for their medicalization of spouse selection, marriage and family planning. Although the Jewish programme, which was developed by the community and for the community, has often received justified praise, this chapter will also consider some of its downsides, including the stigmatization of (presumed) carriers as well as social pressure and the compromising of autonomy.

The chapter begins with an overview of the cultural context, history and practice of the carrier screening programme called Dor Yesharim ('upright generations') in the *Haredi* (ultra-orthodox Jewish) community. To explore the local patterns of utilization and interpretation, I consider the contents of the instructions provided by Dor Yesharim representatives and analyse interviews conducted with ultra-orthodox Jewish women, including matchmakers. The chapter concludes by discussing the reactions to Dor Yesharim among modern-religious Jews and how they shed light on the complexity of lay negotiations with communal discourses of genetic risk associated with consanguinity and endogamy.

Dor Yesharim and Healthy Endogamy

Dor Yesharim is perhaps the most widely known example of successful community-based premarital carrier screening and matching. The programme was developed by a Rabbi and implemented by ultra-orthodox Jewish communities in the USA, Europe and Israel (Eckstein and Katzenstein 2001; Merz 1987; Abeliovich et al. 1996; Broide et al. 1993). Because of the Jewish objection to abortion, ultra-orthodox women – in stark contrast to secular Israeli women – do not use prenatal testing; for example, less than one per cent of ultra-orthodox women older than thirty-five undergo amniocentesis and other invasive tests, compared to 94 per cent of Israeli secular women (Sher et al. 2003). Jewish law (*halacha*) forbids abortion (unless the woman's life is endangered) thus making prenatal genetic testing irrelevant. Many of the marriages in this population are arranged. First and second degree consanguinity rate is relatively low (between 3 and 7 per cent), but there is a high rate (~25 per cent) of intra-community marriages, namely endogamy (Cohen et al. 2004). Orthodox Judaism contains opposing approaches to consanguinity: while Rabbi Judah the Pious prohibited marriages between first cousins and between uncles and nieces, in the Bible such marriages abound among the founding fathers – Isaac was married to Rebecca, his first cousin once removed. Also, Rachel and Leah were both cousins of Isaac's son Jacob, their husband. Marriage to a sister's daughter is encouraged in the Talmud (Yevamot 62b and again Sanhedrin 76b).

Dor Yesharim extends the traditional norm of pre-arranged endogamous matchmaking to include carrier matching for genetic diseases that are prevalent in the Ashkenazi Jewish population, such as Tay-Sachs (the system is detailed below). The uptake is over 95 per cent and in recent years hardly any children affected with Tay-Sachs have been born in this community to couples who married during the last decade (Eckstein and Katzenstein 2001; Sagi 1998). Rabbi Josef Eckstein, an ultra-orthodox Jew from Brooklyn, New York, founded Dor Yesharim (Hebrew for 'generation of the righteous' or 'upright generation'; 'yeshorim' is the Ashkenazi pronunciation of the Hebrew word 'yesharim') in 1983, after losing four of his own children to Tay-Sachs disease. Its representatives visit ultra-orthodox high schools and draw blood samples from students, who are then issued a number. The blood samples are screened for several genetic diseases and the results stored in Dor Yesharim's offices.

When young men and women reach a marriageable age, and receive a recommendation from a *shadchan* (matchmaker) about a potential mate, they or their parents are supposed to make a phone call to a representative of Dor Yesharim, who retrieves the assigned numbers for each member of the potential couple and checks to see if they are carriers of the same genetic disease. If they are, they are told that a union is 'not advisable'. The only result that the tested individuals receive is either 'advisable' or 'non-advisable' for marriage. They do not receive their specific carrier status, neither at the time of the examination or at the time of the check. In this way, most carriers would never find out what gene they carry and thereby are supposed to avoid being anxious about that information as well as being seen as defective. The match is considered to be compatible if both parties are not carriers of the same recessive trait. Each member of the couple may be a carrier for a different disorder, but that information is not revealed, as it does not affect their compatibility as a couple. If marriage is deemed inadvisable, genetic 'counselling'[1] (by phone only) is available to these individuals. Consulting the Dor Yesharim database is meant to take place very early in the matchmaking. If individuals have received testing anywhere other than Dor Yesharim, or are already engaged or married, they will not be able to use the Dor Yesharim system.

Dor Yesharim tests for several genetic disorders – Tay-Sachs disease, cystic fibrosis, Gaucher disease type I, Canavan disease, familial dysautonomia, Bloom syndrome, Fanconi anemia, glycogen storage disease type 1a, mucolipidosis type IV, and Niemann-Pick disease type A – most of which have significantly higher frequencies among Ashkenazi Jews (Zlotogora and Leventhal 2000). It has been endorsed by religious community leaders and has become a standard prerequisite in ultra-orthodox matchmaking. Since its inception, over 220,000 individuals have been tested, over 500 incompatible couples identified, and virtually no afflicted children were born (Eckstein and Katzenstein 2001). Recently Dor Yesharim has aimed at increasing its activities, reaching out to other religious communities within Jewish society, such as the 'modern orthodox'.

In the ultra-orthodox (*Haredi*) community in Israel, which comprises about 800,000 people (out of 5.4 million Jews living in Israel, a country of about 8 million), average fertility rates reach 7–7.5 births per woman (Remennick 2006), compared to a fertility rate of 2.8 children per woman in the general Israeli population (Landau

2003). The ultra-orthodox community, although usually seen from the outside as a homogenous enclave, is actually comprised of many sub-groups, struggling at times bitterly over material resources and religious hegemony (Grilek 2002). Social differentiation is mainly along ethnic lines (e.g., Ashkenazi, mainly of European origin, vs. Sephardi/Mizrahi, originating in North Africa, the Mediterranean and Asia), and along different spiritual movements going back to the eighteenth and nineteenth centuries (e.g., Hassidim vs. Lithuanians). Ashkenazi groups in particular are still quite diversified in relation to these movements.

Israeli geneticists and health professionals working with Dor Yesharim usually acknowledge that its confidential testing compromises autonomy, but they justify it by claiming that (a) carrier matching was selected by this community, (b) the programme decreases the potential of stigmatization, and (c) above all, it is 'the only way the orthodox community can avoid the agony caused by the birth of babies affected by very devastating diseases' (Sagi 1998: 427). Still, many Israeli geneticists support Dor Yesharim while being critical of its self-government:

> Consider for example the situation of someone who left Judaism and finds himself in my clinic. We don't want to spend all this money on all the genetic tests which he already did as part of Dor Yesharim. But Dor Yesharim would not give away this information. There was one time I needed to know the results of a certain person who gave his permission, but Dor Yesharim refused. They see themselves as owning the genetic information which actually belongs to the individual. (Prof. Moshe Friedman, medical geneticist, Shiba hospital, cited in Bart 2003: 18)

Similar criticism has also been voiced by modern orthodox rabbis in the USA, for example by Yeshiva University's Rabbi Moshe Dovid Tendler:

> The idea that Dor Yeshorim has genetic information and refuses to share it with the person it belongs to is unfair, irrational and almost anti-American. If you submit blood, you should be able to have the results. (Cited in Gessen 2008: 183)

Dor Yesharim should be praised for introducing genetic screening to a population that might not have otherwise considered participating in such an effort. However, beyond official statements and statistics of uptake and mortality, we know very little about its actual reception in the community.

The Hidden Aspects of Community Assimilation

In what follows I draw on my previous ethnographic studies to portray the assimilation of premarital carrier testing and matching in ultra-orthodox and modern-religious Jewish communities in Israel and the USA (Raz and Vizner 2008; Raz 2009). For all the respondents, utilization of Dor Yesharim was a consensual matter that crossed group affiliation, age and socio-economic status. As one community member aptly summarized it, 'The success of Dor Yeshorim – for us this is very simple, because in our community there aren't many choices. God forbid, if there is a baby like that, you cannot abort, so you must do what you can to prevent it. I did the test when I was 17. Everyone in my class did it, it's a routine' (twenty-seven, ultra-orthodox Jewish female, married with children, Lithuanian).

While premarital carrier matching in the form offered by Dor Yesharim has become a taken-for-granted part of life in the *Haredi* community, this high compliance did not represent genetic literacy, nor did it follow the original rationale of the programme. The rationale is meant to be conveyed to young community members through school instructions. These instructions, delivered by a Dor Yesharim representative, have a common format. They begin with a description of the life story of Rabbi Eckstein, the founder of Dor Yesharim, and his four children who died of Tay-Sachs. The instructor, usually a married *Haredi* woman, stresses the difficult characteristics of the disease, and provides basic explanations concerning genetics and heredity of recessive traits. This presentation is not meant to be educational but rather to lead the audience to the conclusion that too much genetic information is bad and that premarital genetic matching, as endorsed by the Rabbis, is the best solution for the community. The following illustrative quotations are taken from a typical instruction observed by Raz and Vizner (2008). Stressing the fact that people are accustomed to marry their kind, the instructor said that '25 per cent risk is very high and those who are wise would not enter such risk to begin with'. Commenting that secular people do a DNA test and receive an individual answer concerning their carrier status, the instructor stressed that 'this system is wrong because in this way people are stigmatized. We don't want the people of Israel to be divided into categories of carriers and non-carriers, thus putting a blemish on a large part of the public. The leaders of Israel have forbidden it. This is how the system of Dor Yeshorim came into existence'.

The instruction illustrates the public message separating the occasion of the DNA test from the actual answer, meant to be provided only with regard to the compatibility of two people and only before engagement. The instruction also highlights the directive and preventive aspects of the programme with its blunt emphasis on the negative aspects of life with a genetic disease, as well as of life as a presumed carrier, namely someone with genetic diseases in the family. The latter message is arguably two-pronged. The instruction repeatedly stresses the stigma of presumed carriers and its aim to help them find a compatible match. This is done by stressing the importance of using Dor Yesharim as part of the process of matchmaking. The emphasis appears to be on doing rather than on understanding. The stigma of presumed carriers is in itself not questioned or countered, but rather ascertained and even reinforced through bleak statements. While well-intended, the instruction could be interpreted by its audience in a manner that reproduces stigmatization. The views of community members, examined in the following section, support this conjecture.

Misunderstandings Regarding the Genetic Basis of Carrier Matching

A growing debate over the (mis)representation of genetic knowledge in the media and among the public has emphasized the need to counter genetic determinism and prevent the use of genetics to reinforce discriminatory messages (Condit 2007; Lock and Gordon 1998; Nelkin and Lindee 1995). Indeed, what does a 'gene for' or 'carrier' mean to lay people? This question becomes particularly pertinent in the context of traditional communities. Community members explained (Raz and Vizner 2008) that a reply from Dor Yesharim regarding 'incompatibility' meant that the match had to be broken, and that each person needed to look for another partner. However, when asked what the basis for genetic incompatibility was, many simply said that they did not really understand it. The message of Dor Yesharim regarding the benefit of 'not knowing' one's carrier status was so strong that it spilled over to the interpretation of carrier matching:

> I don't know exactly the source for this so-called genetic incompatibility. One of the couple has a problem, but they don't tell you who it is. (Forty-nine, female, married with children, Lithuanian)

> The meaning of the genetic test is to see if the blood is compatible. (Twenty, female, married, Hassidic)

> Don't have to get to the bottom of this. I was told by the Rabbi, and also read in the [community] newspapers, that compatibility means there is no problem with the match. I don't understand the meaning behind it, and who the carrier is exactly. (Thirty-five, female, married with children, Hassidic)

Such misunderstandings were probably also expressed in the emerging patterns of utilization that are incongruent with the original rationale of the programme, as the following section demonstrates.

Carrier Matching and the Matchmaking Process

In ultra-orthodox Jewish circles, dating is limited to the search for a marriage partner. Both sides (usually the parents, close relatives or friends of the persons involved) make inquiries about the prospective partner, e.g. on his/her character, intelligence, level of learning, financial status, family and health status, appearance and level of religious observance. A *shidduch* (match) often begins with a recommendation from family members, friends, a professional matchmaker or others who see matchmaking as a *mitzvah* (good deed). Matchmaking guidebooks for the *Haredi* community warn that the matchmaking process is often in favour of the 'wealthy and healthy' and against all others (Jacobs and Marks 2006). Perceived negative aspects of the candidate include, for example, medical or psychiatric issues of the candidate or in their family, financial issues, broken homes, orphans, or converts. Often the disadvantaged end up being matched with people with other disadvantages.

The practical assimilation of Dor Yesharim by community members hinges on the timing of and the precedence given to this check within the matchmaking process. In other words, the question is when exactly the phone call to Dor Yesharim takes place in the matchmaking. The following interview excerpt illustrates a typical matchmaking 'checklist' and the place of carrier matching within it:

> My expectations from my match were that he would be *tzadik*, very Hassidic, that's the most important thing. Then I wanted to know about his family – what is their style, are they suitable for us or not. After that – how he looks like, I didn't want him to be too fat.

Q: How then was the matchmaking process conducted?

A: We listened to the suggestions of the matchmaker. We found out about the candidates. We called people and asked about the candidate. Then, if he proved to be a good match, we met. Then we called Dor Yeshorim. (Twenty, female, married, Hassidic)

The matchmaking process, as we have found from community members, proceeded according to the traditional criteria. Finding out about genetic compatibility was done only after everything else had been agreed on. Most people already discontinued the process once they learned about the existence of genetic diseases in the candidate's family, and therefore did not get to the point of asking Dor Yesharim about the genetic compatibility of the prospective candidates. The following quotations illustrate this finding.

> Only after we examine social and family compatibility, and a meeting is being planned, then we also check for genetic compatibility. Sometimes we call Dor Yeshorim before the two young people meet; sometimes we do it before the parents meet. I know of stories in which the answer from Dor Yeshorim was that there is no compatibility, and the match was broken. There isn't much heartbreak since it is not about love. However, genetic considerations are not part of the matchmaking; we do it only after the process has proceeded. Chances are that the genetic check won't make a difference. (Fifty, female, married with children, some of them already married too, Hassidic)

> First we hear about the candidate, from a matchmaker or someone else we know. They give us the basic details, like who is the family, religiosity, personality, background. We see if there's a basis to continue. After two meetings, if we see that we want to continue, we call Dor Yeshorim. (Thirty-four, female, married with children, Lithuanian)

Similar answers were also given by younger respondents. The following are typical examples from both Lithuanians and Hassidic:

> My parents checked everything they could on the guy. I then met him, and thought about it. We met again, after which I decided that I want to continue. Then, after that second meeting, we called Dor Yeshorim. In this way, if you have to make a stop, you stop before there is an emotional connection. (Twenty, female, married, Lithuanian)

> The matchmaker called our house and told my parents about the candidate. They also asked other people who knew the family. After all this checking, we called Dor Yeshorim, before we met. I think my parents called Dor Yeshorim after they met with his parents and

reached an agreement about how to proceed in terms of who is giving how much money. (Twenty, female, married, Hassidic)

When respondents were asked why the genetic criterion is not the first to be examined, their answers were ambiguous. A few acknowledged that 'maybe it's a mistake not to do it in the very beginning. But usually the answer is okay' (thirty-one, female, married with children, Hassidic). We heard again and again, in different variations, statements like: 'genetic compatibility comes first. No compatibility – no match' (twenty-seven, married with children, Lithuanian). However, it clearly transpired that checking for genetic compatibility actually did not come first in the matching process. This was also confirmed by the matchmakers we interviewed. Dor Yesharim was therefore selectively incorporated into the traditional matchmaking scheme.

The Misunderstood Rationale of Dor Yeshorim and the Power of Presumed Carrier Stigma in the *Haredi* Community

The vast majority of community members expressed the view that a genetic disease in the family was a stigma that greatly reduced the prospects for matching. As one of the respondents (nineteen, female, married, Lithuanian) said:

> This is well-known. You do Dor Yeshorim so that the genetics will be good. So that you don't have children who suffer. I have in my class a friend with three brothers who are sick with CF and she tells everyone: Do the test!
> Q: Is your friend married?
> A: No and it is difficult for her to find a match. Since both of her parents have the defected gene, it is very difficult for her. People do not understand this. She will have to compromise.
> Q: How about you, would you consider a match with such a family?
> A: No, I wouldn't. I know it is a stigma. But – I wouldn't go for it because it is frightening.

Respondents spoke about the concept of 'marriage value' in a normative and taken-for-granted, sometimes even business-like, manner:

> You see, genetic diseases reduce the value of candidates for matching. People will not listen. Those who are aware would be prepared

to listen if it's not hereditary, but those who don't want, would not listen. Many in the public are unaware. (Thirty-four, female, married with children, matchmaker, Hassidic)

Would I marry my son to a girl from a family with genetic diseases? To begin with, no. Let's say, hypothetically, the family is really good, but still if it's genetic . . . you know in many cases unfortunately it turns out that they need to give more money, I don't know how to tell you . . . Maybe if they give more money [as dowry] it might be a consideration. Look, it's only talking, God help us, for this we have the community leaders. (Twenty-seven, female, married with children, Lithuanian)

The following quotation, told by a Hassidic matchmaker and based on her personal as well as professional experience, captures the misunderstood rationale of Dor Yesharim and the power of presumed carrier stigma in traditional matchmaking:

It was very important for me to do Dor Yeshorim. Genetics is Dor Yeshorim. Dor Yeshorim is the final indication. I will not go beyond that. I felt this was the maximal attempt I could do for the match. My parents also tried to find out everything possible in terms of health. If there is someone unhealthy in the family, even cousins, they will not continue to ask about the candidate. First thing we need to check is health. If there is a genetic problem, don't proceed to matching. (Twenty-six, married with children, Hassidic, matchmaker)

Were those with a genetic disease in the family more likely to consider the possibility of a match with a similar person? The majority of the respondents who had genetic disease in their family expressed a negative view concerning this possibility. It appears that living with the burden of stigma did not make these women more critical of stigmatization. Rather, their attitudes reflected and reinforced the very stigma with which they were labelled. In fact, some of them expressed a more extreme position regarding the need to 'bring better genes to the match' (in the words of one of the respondents). Despite being aware of the stigma, none of the respondents expressed overt criticism towards the community responsible for that hierarchy of matching, or towards Dor Yesharim. This lack of criticism arguably hinged not only on collective socialization but also on the misunderstanding concerning genetic testing and the rationale behind carrier matching, which – if used according to the original plan – could have eliminated the very stigma of being a presumed carrier of 'bad genes'.

The Two-Fold View of Disability: Testing and Supporting

Yet another theme that emanated from interviews with community members concerned perceptions of disability in the community. All of the respondents spoke, on the one hand, about the increased acceptance of and support for people with disabilities in the ultra-orthodox community, and on the importance of premarital genetic testing on the other hand. Most of them acknowledged this gap between testing (before marriage) and supporting (a child born with a disability) by stressing the suffering imposed by the disability on the child as well as on the family:

> Children and people with disabilities are well accepted in the *Haredi* community; maybe their acceptance is even better than in secular society. It is different than before, when there was shame and denial and people were afraid to go out with their disabled child. Today there is much more openness and acceptance. I am talking for example about Down's. But concerning genetic diseases that run in the family – this will no doubt affect matching prospects. People don't take a chance. (Fifty, female, married with children, Lithuanian)

The matchmakers also related to this issue from a professional point of view. As one of the matchmakers (twenty-six, female, married with children, Hassidic) said:

> Today there is much more awareness. Once there was much more fear. A family with Down's syndrome – that was something I was afraid of handling. Today there is much more awareness, Down's children are admitted into normal classes, there is special education. Of course, the value for marriage decreases. The families know about it very well. I once had a family where the candidate had a brother with mental retardation. They carried with them papers confirming that they have done all the tests to prove it was not genetic. In each meeting they would pull out the documents and show them ... In the case of retardation, this is half the trouble. But in the case of genetic disease, people would be afraid of entering a match.

An overarching narrative was evident in most accounts concerning the growing recognition of disability within the *Haredi* community as well as the importance of premarital testing. The typical explanation was the misery suffered by the child and the caregiver. Similar accounts of preventing disability through prenatal testing were found to characterize secular Israeli women (Remennik 2006), who also perceived this as an indispensable part of good motherhood, an expression of responsibility towards one's own future, existing children and other family members, as well as society at large. The *Haredi* respondents, however, also made a distinction, unique to them, between disability in general and disability inherited through genetic diseases – stressing the latter's negative effect on matchmaking.

To sum up, the actual meaning and practice of carrier matching as experienced by community members hinge on misunderstandings regarding the genetic basis of carrier matching, and differ from the original design and public messages of the programme. Carrier matching is not done at the earliest stage of the matchmaking (as recommended by Dor Yesharim) but rather late in the process and only after the traditional examination of other criteria had already been completed. This means that the existence of genetic diseases in the family can disqualify a candidate well before the occurrence of carrier matching, which in such cases does not take place because the match has already been discontinued.

Dor Yesharim is a well-intended and sophisticated scheme. Its establishment and global institutionalization reflect the efforts and concerns of many people. Furthermore, this programme has a true potential to reduce stigmatization. However, the actual ways in which it is being utilized differ from the original intentions of its designers. Dor Yesharim arguably carries at least some of the responsibility for this situation. By building itself on the dictum of 'not knowing one's genetic identity' – expressed in the nondisclosure of each individual's carrier status – Dor Yesharim also inadvertently reinforces the message that being a carrier is something which one is better off without knowing, and hence, ultimately, that being a carrier is bad. This message was interpreted by community members through the explicit stigma traditionally associated with genetic diseases. Dor Yesharim reinforces stigmatization in its practical message that it is bad to be a carrier and therefore better not to know one's status.

Dor Yesharim declined to discuss these findings, but issued a statement that strongly refuted the contention that its programme fuels stigma. 'With regard to carrier status, Dor Yeshorim does not and would not explicitly or implicitly convey the notion that being a carrier is a shameful condition', the statement said. Dor Yesharim added that the communities it serves 'embrace it wholeheartedly as the best way to eliminate the incidences of Jewish genetic recessive diseases. The program is recognized as the only completely successful program of its type anywhere in the world and in any community. Its success and overwhelming participation rate, in the communities it serves, speaks for itself' (Levenson 2010: ix).

Even if Dor Yesharim has not positioned itself as an educational but also as a screening programme, its community instructions have a significant educational function and its messages need to be taken into account. The aim of the programme has not been to change the ultra-orthodox society but to find a solution that is compatible with community values. It is true that stigmatization for any 'abnormality' has existed long before in the community and is still an important component of the matching process. But even if Dor Yesharim was not created as an educational programme, it has a *de-facto* educational function. Hence, if Dor Yesharim would add a robust education component to their programme, it could go a long way to normalizing the perception of genetic risk in this community. While Dor Yesharim was not briefed to solve this problem, but to reduce the suffering caused by these genetic diseases without further stigmatization, can its proponents ignore its unintended consequences? And if they do so, can genetic counsellors and health professionals ignore it and continue to wholeheartedly praise the programme from afar?

Dor Yesharim and the Modern-Religious Jewish Community

Dor Yesharim was created by and operates in an insular community guided by a particular moral sense regarding the individual's religious obligations, deference to parents and elders in choosing a spouse through arranged endogamous marriage, and opposition to abortion. However, it still addresses principal issues that are pertinent to everybody who is engaged with carrier testing, issues such as stigma, anxiety, the right not to know, and autonomy. Despite its obvious success, Dor Yesharim has received ample criticism from liberal-secular Jews. Jewish journalist Masha Gessen (2008: 171) argued that 'the convoluted design of the program follows an unfailing paternalistic logic'. Slifka (2007: 272) mentioned in this context Linus Pauling's suggestion, in 1968, that carriers of sickle cell and other genetic traits should be tattooed as children, in order to prevent them from falling in love and having children together; 'as appalling as this suggestion may seem', she argues, 'it is not all that different from the Dor Yeshorim concept embraced by those at risk for Tay-Sachs'.

While liberal and secular criticism is important, its premises are not the standard view embraced by many lay people, especially in traditional and religious communities. The applicability of the

Dor Yesharim system thus requires an empirical test. The development of culturally-sensitive carrier screening is after all an ongoing issue in religiously/ethnically diverse populations. Other instances where less 'open' carrier testing have been implemented, or at least debated as possibilities with ethnic/religious communities at elevated risk for genetic conditions, include Arab-Israelis (chapter eight, this volume), Arab-Bedouins in Israel (Raz 2004), and Pakistani communities in the UK (Shaw 2011; see chapter five, this volume). In Cyprus, carrier screening for thalassaemia has been carried out since the 1970s, first with the State and the Church actively discouraging marriages between carriers (Hoedemaeker and ten Have 1998) followed by the introduction of prenatal and later pre-implantation genetic diagnosis which allowed this restriction to be lifted (Bornik and Dowlatabadia 2008; Cowan 2008). In the Netherlands, initiatives of pre-conceptional carrier screening for Cystic Fibrosis and haemoglobinopathies are being promoted but usually without directly targeting particular ethnic communities (such as immigrants from Surinam and the Netherlands Antilles, or from Turkey and Morocco), even though members of such ethnic communities have a higher risk of being carriers (see chapter ten, this volume).

Recently, Dor Yesharim has been reaching out to the modern-religious Jewish community. In Israel, the USA and major cities in Europe, a young modern-religious Jew can receive testing from either Dor Yesharim or a medical centre. This is 'The Most Important Test You'll Ever Take' according to the title of a flyer prepared for students at New York's Yeshiva University, where students choose between confidential testing with Dor Yesharim and open testing at the New York University medical centre (Eisenberg 2003).

Among modern-religious Jews in Israel who were approached by Dor Yesharim, mixed utilization was found (Frumkin, Raz et al. 2011), such as couples who marry 'inadvisably', or had received the test through Dor Yesharim with the decision to proceed to marriage and to receive genetic counselling in case both partners/spouses are found to be carriers. The vast majority of modern-religious respondents agreed that the partners should decide whether to marry or not, even if Dor Yesharim informs them that they are not advisable for marriage. Nevertheless, considerations of social pressure, cost-benefit and reduced stigma and anxiety led some respondents to be in favour of starting with confidential carrier matching and continuing with genetic counselling. Modern-religious community members argued in favour of confidential carrier testing as reducing the anxiety that may come with too much information. Carrier status might indeed be a personal burden. With Dor Yesharim, you just pick up the phone and that is it; you don't get as much information as in the medical centre. The downside is evidently the compromising of romantic love and individual autonomy. As one modern-religious community member summed it up:

> Dor Yesharim is not appropriate for our [modern-religious] community in which people first decide with whom they want to marry, and check their genetics only after that. It may be easier to reproduce artificially than to find another husband. So I think the best way is to have the test in an open and individual manner after engaging or even after the marriage. Moreover, Dor Yesharim is annoying: they hide information. If I take the test, I want to know what's wrong. (Female, thirty, married with children)

More generally, the comparison of anonymous/confidential carrier matching (in Dor Yesharim) and open individual carrier testing (in the medical clinic) is underpinned by the ethical debate between communitarian and liberal approaches to bioethics (Strike 2000). Anonymous carrier matching provides an alternative model to the liberal-secular ethics of individual autonomy and informed consent. It replaces the informative counselling procedure with minimum information that may reduce anxiety and stigmatization and is congruent with a communal view of carrier screening as a social, rather than medical, service (Prainsack and Sigal 2006). However, as we saw the attitudes in the modern-religious Jewish community presented more criticism than trust regarding anonymous carrier matching. Anonymous carrier matching is therefore not expected to gain the same success and monopoly among modern-religious consumers as it did in *Haredi* communities. Contrary to their stereotype as opposing repro-genetic technologies, many members of these communities need and use repro-genetic technologies and require the services and counselling those technologies entail. All those involved in community-based genetic testing should be alert to these questions and to the delicate balance of advocacy and control they invoke.

Note

1. The word 'counselling' appears within quotation marks since in the standard professional view of genetic counsellors, counselling should not be done via the telephone but requires a personal meeting.

References

Abeliovich, D., A. Quint, N. Weinberg, G. Verchezon, I. Lerer, J. Eckstein and E. Rubinstein. 1996. 'Cystic Fibrosis Heterozygote screening in the orthodox community of Ashkenazi Jews: the Dor Yesharim approach and heterozygote frequency', *European Journal of Human Genetics* 4: 77–82.

Bart, D. 2003. 'Two is not always together', *Makor Rishon* 25 July (in Hebrew), pp.17–20.

Bornik, Z.B. and H. Dowlatabadia. 2008. 'Genomics in Cyprus: challenging the social norms', *Technology in Society* 30(1): 84–93.

Broide, E., M. Zeigler, J. Eckstein and G. Bach. 1993. 'Screening for carriers of Tay-Sachs disease in the ultraorthodox Ashkenazi Jewish community in Israel', *American Journal of Medical Genetics* 47: 21–35.

Cohen, T, R. Vardi-Saliternik and Y. Friedlander. 2004. 'Consanguinity, intracommunity and intercommunity marriages in a population sample of Israeli Jews', *Annals of Human Biology* 31(1): 38–48.

Condit, C. 2007. 'Science and society: how geneticists can help reporters to get their story right', *Nature Reviews Genetics* 8: 815–820.

Cowan, R. 2008. *Heredity and Hope: The Case for Genetic Screening.* Cambridge, MA: Harvard University Press.

Eckstein, J., and H. Katzenstein. 2001. 'The Dor Yeshorim story: community-based carrier screening for Tay-Sachs disease', *Advances in Genetics* 44: 297–310.

Eisenberg, N. 2003. 'Science and the ethics of genetic screening', *Yeshiva University Review* Summer: 9–15.

Frumkin, A., A. Raz et al. 2011. '"The most important test you'll Ever Take"? Attitudes towards confidential carrier matching and open individual testing among modern-religious Jews', *Social Science and Medicine* 73(12): 1741–1747.

Frumkin, A. and J. Zlotogora. 2007. 'Genetic screening for reproductive purposes at school: is it a good strategy?' *American Journal of Medical Genetics* 146A, 2: 264–269.

Gessen, M. 2008. *Blood Matters: From Inherited Illness to Designer Babies, How the World and I Found Ourselves in the Future of the Gene.* New York: Harcourt.

Grilek, M. 2002. *The Haredim: Who Are We Really?* Jerusalem: Keter (in Hebrew).

Hoedemaeker, R. and H. ten Have. 1998. 'Geneticization: the Cyprus Case', *Journal of Medicine and Philosophy* 23(3): 274–287.

Lock, M. and D. Gordon (eds). 1988. *Biomedicine Examined.* Boston, MA: Kluwer Academic.

Merz, B. 1987. 'Matchmaking scheme solves Tay-Sachs problem', *Journal of American Medical Association* 258: 263–269.

Nelkin, D. and L. Andrews. 1999. 'DNA identification and surveillance creep', *Sociology of Health and Illness* 21(5): 689–706.

Nelkin, D. and M. Lindee. 1995. *The DNA Mystique: The Gene as a Cultural Icon*. New York: Freeman and Company.

Prainsack, B. and G. Sigal. 2006. 'The rise of genetic couplehood: a comparative view of pre-marital genetic screening', *Biosocieties* 1: 17–36.

Raz, A. 2004. *The Gene and the Genie: Tradition, Medicalization, and Genetic Counseling in a Bedouin Community*. Durham, NC: Carolina Academic Press, Ethnographic Studies in Medical Anthropology Series.

———. 2009. *Community Genetics and Genetic Alliances: Eugenics, Carrier Testing, and Networks of Risk*. London: Routledge.

Raz, A. and Y. Vizner. 2008. 'Carrier matching and collective socialization in community genetics: Dor Yesharim and the reinforcement of stigma', *Social Science & Medicine* 67(9): 1361–1369.

Remennick, L. 2006. 'The quest after the perfect baby: why do Israeli women seek prenatal genetic testing?' *Sociology of Health and Illness* 28(1): 21–53.

Sagi, M. 1998. 'Genetic screening in Israel', *Science in Context* 11(3–4): 419–431.

Shaw, A. 2011. 'Risk and reproductive decisions: British Pakistani couples' responses to genetic counseling', *Social Science and Medicine* 73: 111–120.

Sher, C., O. Romano-Zelekha, M. Green and T. Shohat. 2003. 'Factors affecting performance of prenatal genetic testing by Israeli Jewish women', *American Journal of Medical Genetics* 30(120A): 418–422.

Slifka, L.S. 2007. 'Review essay: the troubled dream of genetic medicine', *Pediatric Nursing* 33(3): 271–274.

Strike, K. 2000. 'Liberalism, communitarianism, and the space between', *Journal of Moral Education* 29(2): 133–147.

Zlotogora, J. and A. Leventhal. 2000. 'Screening for genetic disorders among Jews: how should the Tay-Sachs screening program be continued?', *Israel Medical Association Journal* 2(9): 665–667.

Chapter 10

PRECONCEPTION CARE FOR CONSANGUINEOUS COUPLES IN THE NETHERLANDS

Marieke E. Teeuw, Pascal Borry and Leo P. ten Kate

Current counselling and screening recommendations for consanguineous couples before a pregnancy (also referred to as the preconception phase) focus on taking a thorough medical history and informing couples about their increased risk, but no additional screening is advised based on consanguinity alone (Bennett et al. 2002; Modell and Darr 2002). If the couple has a 'positive' family history for a genetic disorder (if there is a known family history of a genetic condition), genetic counsellors can predict the percentage of additional risk for a child with this specific disorder and can offer, if available, carrier and prenatal testing to the couple. The absence of a family history of a genetic condition, however, still leaves the couple with an average increased risk of 2 per cent of having affected offspring, which is the mean result of couples with a 25 per cent increased risk (or more) and couples without increased risk (see also chapter two, this volume). Because of rapid developments in genetic technology it is conceivable that in the near future new diagnostic facilities will be available which will improve preconceptional risk assessment (Bell et al. 2011; Teeuw et al. 2010). Consanguineous couples, with their increased risk for monogenetic disorders, are likely to benefit from these new technologies.

The Netherlands is one of the countries in Western Europe with a high percentage of consanguineous marriages among its migrant population and with an ongoing public debate focusing on the controversial status of consanguineous marriage. This chapter outlines the public debate and health care policy with regard to consanguineous marriages in the Netherlands. It also describes how advances in genetic technology can improve genetic counselling facilities for consanguineous couples and – given the complex societal context – identifies issues that will have to be addressed before the implementation of a new technology focused on consanguineous couples.

Migration and Increased Prevalence of Consanguineous Marriages

The Netherlands, like many other Western countries, originally had a low percentage of consanguineous marriage, although several small communities where consanguineous marriage and endogamy is a common tradition can be identified (McCullough and O'Rourke 1986). With the migration of groups from countries where consanguineous marriage is preferred, these types of marriages are now more common. From the 1950s onwards, immigrants from Morocco and Turkey have settled in the Netherlands. In the absence of a registration system that tracks the percentage of related spouses among all marriages, the number of consanguineous couples in the Netherlands is based on estimations. A cohort study in one of the major cities in the Netherlands, in which a large percentage of the newborns were included, has shown that 22.2 per cent of Moroccan, 23.9 per cent of Turkish and 0.1 per cent of the Dutch mothers were married to a second cousin or closer related spouse (Waelput and Achterberg 2007). A comparable survey was done in Belgium, which showed a percentage of 28 per cent Moroccan and 22 per cent Turkish consanguineous marriages (Reniers 2010).

Prejudices and Misunderstandings about Cousin Marriages

A common misunderstanding among the Dutch population is that first cousin marriages (between third degree relatives) were forbidden in the past in the Netherlands (Asscher 2010). However, the law that was enacted in 1838, and withdrawn in 1970, applied to uncle-niece marriages (second degree relatives) and to marriages between a brother and sister-in-law (no genetic relation) (Article 88 of the Old Netherlands Civil Code). Over the last decade alone cousin marriage has been discussed in public debates on several occasions. In 2001 and 2002, for example, the debate flared up as research showed that the perinatal mortality rate in the Netherlands was high in comparison with that of surrounding countries. One of the risk factors held accountable was the high consanguinity rate among migrant couples in the Netherlands (Schulpen et al. 2001). The emphasized relationship between parental consanguinity, congenital disorders and the Moroccan and Turkish migrant population has led to public discussions and to questions from politicians about the desirability of a ban on cousin marriage. The Minister of Health responsible instructed The National Institute for Public Health and the Environment (RIVM) to perform a literature study on the risks of parents' consanguinity for the health of their offspring (Waelput and Achterberg 2007) (see the discussion of this report below). In 2008, after the release of the report, parliamentarians again posed questions about the consequences for children of cousin marriage and possible preventive measures.

Although the previous government had taken a position in which it lets values like autonomy and non-directiveness prevail, the current Dutch government coalition that was formed in October 2010 intended to prohibit cousin marriage. The ban on cousin marriages was ranked among measures intended to limit immigration, which included a prohibition of forced marriage. No mention was made of the increased medical risks. The new element in the discussion on banning cousin marriages, namely the alleged connection with forced marriages, has caused a blurring of the debate. Now, there seem to be two arguments that are used interchangeably, neither of them supported by evidence that a ban on cousin marriage would be proportional and effective in resolving the issues raised.

National Recommendations about the Care for Consanguineous Couples: Reports of the National Institute for Public Health and the Environment and the Health Council

In the above mentioned report of the National Institute for Public Health (RIVM) (Waelput and Achterberg 2007), parental consanguinity is described as one of a number of risk factors that are involved in congenital disorders in children. The reproductive risk associated with parental consanguinity is comparable to, for example, the increased risk caused by advanced maternal age, drug use during pregnancy or a history of genetic disorders in the family. The fact is stressed that the increase in risk concerns rare diseases, which are part of the total number of congenital disorders. The percentage of infant deaths within the first year of life that can be attributed to their parents' consanguinity is very low. However, the rare autosomal recessive disorders seen in the progeny of consanguineous couples are often severe diseases that have an enormous impact on the child, the parents and the rest of the family. The RIVM describes the increased awareness of the need for genetic counselling – preferably before a pregnancy is effectuated – and possible genetic screening. This applies especially to consanguineous couples, but also to other couples who are at increased risk. Moreover, they state that ideally all future parents should have access to counselling for risks that involve their future children and to possible reproductive options, like prenatal diagnosis (PND), pre-implantation genetic diagnosis (PGD), sperm or egg donation, the decision not to have children, adoption, or to accept the fact that the (unborn) child is affected.

In 2007 a report was published by the Health Council: 'Preconception care, for a good beginning' (Health Council of the Netherlands 2007), which advises a systematic approach to public and individual preconception care. This advice was later ratified by the Steering Committee on Pregnancy and Childbirth (Stuurgroep Zwangerschap en Geboorte 2009). Preconception care was defined as 'the entire raft of measures to promote the health of the mother-to-be and her child' (Health Council of the Netherlands 2007). This report also focuses on genetic factors that influence reproduction and recommends a systematic examination of family history, ethnicity and parental consanguinity in the preconception phase. This report stresses the importance of giving comprehensive information to parents-to-be, with a referral for genetic counselling if needed. Until now, however, the government has not taken action to start implementing this advice and policy-makers have not implemented a national programme for preconception care.

Present Organization of Preconception Care for Consanguineous Couples

Although there seems to be consensus about the need for supplying information about parental consanguinity as a reproductive risk that may require genetic counselling, a national infrastructure is still lacking. Primary care, as a place for accessible continuous care, with a focus on informing the patient, providing preventive medicine and, if necessary, referring for secondary or tertiary care (Rawaf et al. 2008), seems the most appropriate context for the provision of preconception care. In the Netherlands, two professionals provide primary care for pregnant women or women who wish to become pregnant: the midwife and the general practitioner. Both the general practitioner and the midwife could thus be charged with the task of informing would-be-parents about their risks and lifestyle measures before conceiving a baby. Part of this consultation could address the risks associated with consanguinity and mapping the medical (genetic) family history. The primary care professional should have the time and skills to enable him or her to identify people at risk and those who would benefit from a visit to a genetics clinic. In order to make this scenario work, solid agreements between the various caregivers and good professional guidelines are essential.

Existing recommendations for professionals in Dutch primary care are not uniform in the way they approach parental consanguinity. In an opinion paper of the Royal Dutch Organization of Midwives (KNOV), the professionals are advised to note any consanguinity and genetic family history of a couple in the preconception or prenatal phase (De Jong 2005). Midwives are notified of the possibility of carrier screening and referral to a clinical geneticist. Recently a guideline was published by The Dutch College of General Practitioners (NHG) about preconception care, where the focus is on referral for genetic testing in cases where there is a positive family history (De Jong-Potjer et al. 2011). Special attention is given to carrier testing for haemoglobinopathies. However, no special policy on how general practitioners can address consanguinity in their practice has been formulated.

The fragmented availability of guidelines and information about risks of parental consanguinity has led to a situation where the question of if and how the subject is addressed, and if the couple is referred to a clinical genetic centre when needed, depends greatly on the individual health care professional. Taking a thorough genetic family history and drawing a pedigree also requires special skills (Bennett et al. 2002). The knowledge and skills of non-genetic health care professionals regarding genetics have been shown to be sometimes inadequate. Knowledge levels show deficiencies and improvements are needed in education to prepare professionals for the impact of ongoing rapid advances in genetic technology (Baars et al. 2005; Houwink et al. 2011).

The number of referrals to clinical genetics centres for consanguinity counselling at this time is very low, but there is ambiguity regarding the criteria for referrals. Consanguinity is coded only if the couple is referred on the basis of their kinship alone; parental consanguinity is often not recorded if the referral is made on the basis of a positive family history. In 2006, fifty couples nationwide were referred on the basis of their consanguinity alone. In that year there were over 22,000 referrals in total to a clinical genetics centre (information VKGN [Vereniging Klinische Genetica Nederland]). Although these cases are indicated as a legitimate reason for referral and therefore also reimbursed by the health care insurance, no consensus exists between the individual genetics centres in the Netherlands as to what is best practice in preconception counselling for consanguineous couples. Some of the eight clinical genetics centres that exist in the Netherlands offer extensive genetic counselling with a focus on medical family history, pedigree analysis and estimation of the inbreeding coefficient. In addition, ancestry-based carrier testing can be offered. Others only briefly address a possible positive family history by telephone consultation and, in the absence of any genetic family history, quote the average risk figure. One of the factors that might play an important role in the reluctance of health care professionals to refer consanguineous couples for genetic counselling or to offer extensive genetic counselling is the lack of consensus and the perceived limited genetic testing options for consanguineous couples. It is clear that preconception care for consanguineous couples in the Netherlands is not uniformly organized and is not systematically reaching those couples who might benefit from it. The available information about the risks, the identification of a couple at risk and referral for genetic counselling are all dependent on the individual qualities of caregivers and/or the active request of a couple.

The Nature of the Risk and Implications for Current and Future Genetic Counselling and Testing Options

Only a minority of consanguineous couples have an increased risk of a congenital disorder in their children. The majority of first cousin couples have no excess risk at all. However, apart from the medical family history, present techniques do not provide a way of identifying consanguineous couples at increased risk, nor can they identify the disease for which the consanguineous parents are carriers (if this disease has not occurred in the family before).

Still, in the present situation of limited options, taking a thorough family history remains very important for good genetic counselling, because it can provide the only link to an appropriate genetic carrier test for the couple.

With the rapid development of genetic technology, it is conceivable that reproductive options for consanguineous couples will increase. In the past decade a large number of new genes, causative for many different diseases, have been discovered. One of the most successful strategies in finding recessive genes has been the use of consanguineous families (Alkuraya 2010). On a clinical level, apart from the fact that a child's disease has been diagnosed, this molecular information can also be used for other purposes such as making carrier testing available for others in the family. It is expected that possibilities for genetic testing in the preconception phase will also increase (Bell et al. 2011). The great advantage of preconception tests compared to prenatal testing and diagnosis is that the former expands the number of reproductive choices available and removes the time pressure for the decision-making.

New genetic techniques might also increase the possibility of predicting the risk for a consanguineous couple with more precision than is hitherto possible. One approach that would make this possible is to focus on the proportion of DNA that originates from the common ancestor(s) which could predict the risk for future parents with more precision (Carr et al. 2011; Teeuw et al. 2010).

Next generation sequencing is a relatively new technique that is said to have fundamentally changed the nature of genetic experimentation and that will allow us to understand more about the nature of human beings (Mardis 2011). In a relatively simple way one is able to determine most of the coding information in the DNA of the genome and thus obtain information about possible pathological recessive mutations. This technique could in theory be applied to would-be-parents in order to determine whether they are carriers of the same mutation. This makes the technique very attractive for consanguineous couples, because these couples are at higher risk of being carriers for an autosomal recessive disorder. Current obstacles, however, are the costs of these experiments and the fact that there may be problems of interpretation and problems with regard to the results. In the next couple of years, however, databases will be filled with information about thousands of genomes and this will make it easier to interpret variants in DNA. Also, the costs of these experiments will probably decrease to a point where they become more attractive for clinical care.

Preconception Care from the Perspective of the Target Population

The views of the Dutch Turks and Moroccans towards parental consanguinity and genetic risk, preconception testing and reproduction options were the focus of qualitative multidisciplinary research (see chapter seven, this volume). The research included both focus group discussions and interviews with Dutch Turkish and Dutch Moroccan people from the first and second generation of migrants. Findings showed that the respondents primarily value consanguineous marriage in the context of its social advantages and disadvantages. All the respondents were familiar with the debate about the possible medical risks for the offspring, but many respondents did not consider the risk as applying to them personally and had little understanding of the concept of heredity. Also, various respondents mentioned that the care for a child with a congenital disorder should be regarded as a special task given to them by God. Taking responsibility for that care is seen as an important virtue in their perspective.

The possibility of preconception testing is, however, valued positively by almost all respondents, because they feel that information on the topic is useful and can help parents to prepare themselves for a child with a disorder. The question arose as to whether you should test before or after the wedding: on one hand they felt that once they are married it is not possible, for example, to refrain from having children; but on the other hand they considered genetic testing a very difficult subject to address before getting married. The respondents also had hesitations regarding the relationship between test results and individual reproductive choices. Most of the respondents renounce the option of abortion as a possible outcome of preconception and consequently prenatal testing, because they feel that their religion forbids it (see chapter seven, this volume). This latter point was also found in an interview study among Islamic scholars in the Netherlands. Theologians, Muslim spiritual counsellors, and imams were interviewed about their views on preconception care and testing for consanguineous couples (Bartels and Loukili 2012). They almost all considered preconception testing a positive development from an Islamic point of view, and gave several reasons for this. Among these were the fact that Islam encourages people to pursue a good health status (both for themselves and their children), that scientific information coming from physicians deserves respect, and that expansion of knowledge must be pursued. In concordance with the results from the interviews with Dutch Turks and Moroccans, the scholars also foresaw ethical problems with regard to the reproductive options offered to couples found to have a high risk. Refraining from having children, the use of donor gametes, prenatal diagnosis with possible termination of pregnancy, pre-implantation genetic diagnosis (PGD) and adoption, which are among these reproductive options, are questioned or prohibited from an Islamic perspective (Bartels and Loukili 2012).

These issues are the focus of debates by Islamic scholars in other countries as well. Several discussions concerning, for example, the reproductive options of artificial insemination with donor gametes or adoption in relation to adultery and kinship ties in Islamic law can be identified. Sunni and Shiite scholars have different opinions; nevertheless some Islamic scholars accept and promote new reproductive technology (Inhorn 2006; Serour 2008). Although both the target population and Dutch Islamic scholars react positively towards preconception testing, they view this technological possibility primarily as a means of increasing knowledge about the risk of having a child with a hereditary disease, but they foresee problems when it comes to the consequences of a 'positive' test. The couple will be confronted with choices that are difficult for any couple, but may be even more complicated in the light of their religious beliefs. It should also be recognized, however, that people of a particular religious identity may make health-related decisions with reference to non-religious considerations (Ahmed et al. 2006, 2008; Hewison et al. 2007). One factor complicating the discussion of these issues in the Netherlands is that the Turks and Moroccans comprise minorities following different Islamic schools of law with different interpretations on such issues as preconception testing and the reproductive options associated with new reproductive technologies (Bartels and Loukili 2012).

Towards the Implementation of a Consanguinity Risk Tool

It is not hard to imagine that somewhere within the near future a valid and useful 'risk tool' will become available for consanguineous couples that will allow genetic preconception counselling to be more focused and will enable couples to be better informed about their risk status and to have sufficient time to make more informed decisions. Nonetheless, while imagining this, it is also easy to foresee that a number of complex issues will arise when this has taken effect. In the present setting of low-uptake with regard to genetic counselling for consanguineous couples, as well as the controversial status of consanguineous marriage in the Netherlands, the vulnerable position of the target population and the lack of consensus about preconception care, it is surely of great importance to address several of these issues when offering such a new risk tool. The introduction of any new technologies in society entails a process of mutual shaping which can be described as co-evolution, earlier described for preconception carrier testing for cystic fibrosis and haemoglobinopathies (Achterbergh et al. 2007). Agreement needs to be reached between the different actors who are involved in the implementation of the new technology.

Pragmatic challenges also emerge with the implementation of these technologies. Will such preconception testing be offered to all couples, and especially all consanguineous couples? Will couples be actively invited by their general practitioners or casually asked during another consultation? Will midwives play a role with special consultations for couples planning a pregnancy? Or will couples be called or invited for consultation through public health advertisements? Such practical considerations cannot be answered without ethical discussions about the desirability of such an offer.

Firstly, such an offer might provide challenges to some core values that are prominent in genetic counselling (Biesecker 1998; Mahowald et al. 1998). In the tradition of clinical genetic counselling, respect for the autonomy of the person has been developed as a main principle. An individual has a fundamental right to freedom of choice, including control over his or her own life. This includes the right not to know and non-directive counselling. The notion of the 'right not to know' is increasingly accepted internationally. Article 5 of the Unesco Declaration on the Human Genome and Human Rights (Unesco 1997) states that each individual has the right 'to decide whether or not to be informed of the results of genetic examination' and that the resulting consequences of this decision should be respected. This has also been recognized in the European Convention for the Protection of Human Rights and Dignity of the Human Being with regard to the Application of Biology and Medicine which states (in article 10 (2)) that 'Everyone is entitled to know any information collected about his or her health. However, the wishes of individuals not to be so informed shall be observed.' It has been stressed that genetic counselling should aim to provide accurate, full and unbiased information to individuals and families. Non-directive counselling does not mean just presenting information and letting people make their own decision without any help or support. The counselling sessions should be oriented to empower individuals and families to make their own decisions: it should guide and help people to work more conclusively towards their own reproductive decisions (Biesecker 1998). It is clear that the counsellor is not completely unbiased, but the counsellor should be aware of his or her personal values and should not attempt to impose them on individuals or families (Elwyn et al. 2000; Oduncu 2002). However, the discussion of the respect for autonomy of a patient in the context of a clinical encounter between a patient and a doctor may differ greatly from a discussion in the context of a public health programme where a preconception test would be offered to all couples or to all consanguineous couples wishing to become pregnant. In this latter case, special care should be taken to avoid applying societal pressure to perform a test and to preserve the voluntary character of testing. Currently, at the request of the Minister of Health, research is being done on ways to organize preconception and perinatal care, especially focusing on high-risk groups. It remains to be seen, however, how this will apply to consanguineous marriages and preconception genetic testing.

Secondly, the potential preconception test that would be offered to (consanguineous) couples raises more fundamental questions relating to lexicalization and geneticization. The concept of geneticization is central to some sociological approaches to genetics and genomics. Coined by Abby Lippmann, this term describes 'the ever growing tendency to distinguish people one from another on the basis of genetics; to define most disorders, behaviours, and psychological variations as wholly or in part genetic in origin' (Lippman 1991). Geneticization represents not only 'a way of thinking' about human differences but also 'a way of doing', as genetic technologies are 'applied to diagnose, treat, and categorize conditions previously identified in other ways' (Lippman 1991). Lippman claims that the roots of geneticization lie in the older critical term 'medicalization' which was developed in the 1970s by authors such as Irving Kenneth Zola and Ivan Illich. Like its precursor, geneticization is an inherently critical concept, offering a negative view of genetic technologies and their effect on human society. Geneticization is described as a 'process of colonization' and is explicitly linked to 'corporate interests and eugenic idea(l)s' (Lippman 1991, 2003). Furthermore, some authors have argued that the concept of geneticization does not work in the exploration of the ethical and social impact of genetic technologies: 'Since geneticization is inherently negative towards genetic technologies, using it to assess the ethics of genetic technologies results in the rather predictable conclusion that such technologies have unwelcome, unethical effects' (Hedgecoe 2002: 8). The implementation of any consanguinity risk tool will inevitably be confronted with questions regarding the underlying values and norms motivating the implementation. It will raise issues regarding the medicalization of normal life processes such as marriage and family planning. Similar to the ethical issue regarding the respect for autonomy, outlined above, in this discussion much also depends on the way in which the tool is presented and used in practice. Studies and recommendations that focus on the systematic offer of preconception genetic testing (De Wert et al. 2012; Human Genetics Commission 2011; Lakeman et al. 2008) can be helpful in identifying pitfalls and organizing safeguard measures when implementing the consanguinity risk tool in practice.

Thirdly, the test offer will have to be acceptable to the target population and not have negative consequences for them. The target population is already vulnerable because its traditional marriage practice is seen as controversial in the Netherlands, and because of their ethnicity and religion; therefore there exists a risk of additional stigmatization (Fost 1992; Markel 1992). If one considers – because of possible stigmatization – adopting a less active strategy by only offering the test to people who find their own way to primary care and genetic centres with a request for counselling and testing, other rights are at stake. How is it possible to guarantee equity of access to such a resource when those who might most benefit from it do not know about the risk or the possible testing options? Because this is all taking place in a society where the political and public climate is prejudiced against these types of marriages, the great challenge here is to balance these different rights and to aim for – first of all – an autonomous and informed decision of the couple to go or not go for genetic counselling. Moreover, after undergoing a test, whether the result is positive or negative, the couple should be able to make an autonomous and informed decision based on the various reproductive options in a safe and non-directive atmosphere.

In order to be prepared for these challenges, it is important to investigate the needs and wishes of the intended users of the future consanguinity risk tool. These factors need to be addressed as attitudes and understanding can be greatly influenced by culture and ethnic background (Shaw and Hurst 2008). The meaning of genetic risk is strongly influenced by community norms and cultural preconceptions. Therefore particular attention needs to be paid to communication with the target population (Condit 2010; Raz and Vizner 2008). The participation of the target population in this research can help in identifying the key issues and in obtaining support for the development of the test. The recent empirical research from anthropological and ethical perspectives has contributed to the knowledge of the target populations' attitudes towards and understanding of genetic risk, risk information and reproductive options. It is essential that the ethical issues raised when a couple is identified as having a high risk and presented with their reproductive options are taken into account.

Conclusion

In the Netherlands, as in many other Western countries, prejudices and misunderstandings about parental consanguinity in public debates, with politicians even considering a ban on cousin marriage, coincide with a strong tradition of consanguineous marriage among its migrant populations. In the meantime, in health care, a general consensus exists that consanguineous couples should be aware of their elevated reproductive risk. There is no consensus, however, on how this can be achieved. Advances in genetic technology are likely to change the available preconception genetic counselling options, but their implementation requires a paradigm shift. Simultaneously, with the development of a new risk tool, it is necessary to achieve consensus between the different actors involved and, above all, the target population. If primary care professionals play an active role and/or the tool is offered on a large scale, current infrastructure, skills and facilities will need adaptation. Depending on the way in which the genetic counselling and risk tool is offered, it may be important to address the knowledge and skills of health care professionals regarding genetics and parental consanguinity in particular. Decisions will need to be made about how primary health care professionals will be empowered with the necessary knowledge and skills to allow them to refer consanguineous couples. Moreover, the ethical issues raised in the context of developing and offering a consanguinity risk tool aimed at a minority group will also need to be identified and elaborated, especially as they concern a minority marriage tradition that is considered controversial.

References

Achterbergh, R., P. Lakeman, D. Stemerding, E.H. Moors and M.C. Cornel. 2007. 'Implementation of preconceptional carrier screening for cystic fibrosis and haemoglobinopathies: a sociotechnical analysis', *Health Policy* 83(2–3): 277–286; available from: PM:17368860.
Ahmed, S., Atkin, K., Hewison, J. and Green, J. 2006. 'The influence of faith and religion and the role of religious and community leaders in prenatal decisions for sickle cell disorders and thalassaemia major', *Prenatal Diagnosis* 26(9): 801–809; available from: PM:16927359.
Ahmed, S., J. Hewison, J.M. Green, H.S. Cukcle, J. Hirst and J.G. Thornton. 2008. 'Decisons about testing and termination of pregnancy for different fetal conditions: a qualitative study of European White and Pakistani mothers of affected children', *Journal of Genetic Counseling* 17: 560–572.
Alkuraya, F.S. 2010. 'Autozygome decoded', *Genetics in Medicine* 12(12): 765–771; available from: PM:21189493.
Asscher, L. 2010. *De ontsluierde stad*. Amsterdam: Bert Bakker.
Baars, M.J., L. Henneman and L.P. ten Kate. 2005. 'Deficiency of knowledge of genetics and genetic tests among general practitioners, gynecologists, and pediatricians: a global problem', *Genetics in Medicine* 7(9): 605–610; available from: PM:16301861.
Bartels, A., Loukili G. 2012. '"Testing isn't the problem". Views of Muslim theologians, spiritual counsellors, Imams and physicians on preconceptional testing', *Medische Antropologie* 24(2): 321–332.
Bell, C.J., D.L. Dinwiddie, N.A. Miller, S.L. Hateley, E.E. Ganusova, et al. 2011. 'Carrier testing for severe childhood recessive diseases by next-generation sequencing', *Science Translational Medicine* 3(65): 65ra4; available from: PM:21228398.
Bennett, R.L., A.G. Motulsky, A. Bittles, L. Hudgins, S. Uhrich, et al. 2002. 'Genetic counseling and screening of consanguineous couples and their offspring: recommendations of the National Society of Genetic Counselors', *Journal of Genetic Counseling* 11(2): 97–119.
Biesecker, B.B. 1998. 'Future directions in genetic counseling: practical and ethical considerations', *Kennedy Institute of Ethics Journal* 8(2): 145–160; available from: PM:11657426.
Carr, I.M., S.A. Markham and S.D. Pena. 2011. 'Estimating the degree of identity by descent in consanguineous couples', *Human Mutatation* 32(12): 1350–1358; available from: PM:21901788.
Condit, C.M. 2010. 'Public attitudes and beliefs about genetics', *Annual Review of Genomics and Human Genetics* 11: 339–359; available from: PM:20690816.
De Jonge, A. 2005. *KNOV-standpunt preconceptiezorg [Royal Dutch Organisation of Midwives standpoint preconception care]*. Bilthoven: KNOV.
De Jong-Potjer, L.C., M. Beentjes, M. Bogchelman, A.H.J. Jaspar and K.M. Van Asselt. 2011. 'NHG-standaard preconceptiezorg [The Dutch College

of General Practitioners guideline preconception care]', *Huisarts en Wetenschap* 54(6): 310–312.
De Wert, G., W. Dondorp and B. Knoppers. 2012. 'Preconception care and genetic risk: ethical issues', *Journal of Community Genetics* 3(3): 221–228.
Elwyn, G., J. Gray and A. Clarke. 2000. 'Shared decision making and non-directiveness in genetic counselling', *Journal of Medical Genetics* 37(2):135–138; available from: http://jmg.bmjjournals.com.
Fost, N. 1992. 'Ethical implications of screening asymptomatic individuals', *Faseb Journal* 6(10): 2813–2817; available from: ISI:A1992JD95400008/.
Health Council of the Netherlands. 2007. *Preconception Care: For a Good Beginning*. The Hague: Gezondheidsraad.
Hedgecoe, A. 2002. 'Reinventing diabetes: classification, division and the geneticization of disease', *New Genetics & Society* 21(1): 7–27.
Hewison, J., J.M. Green, S. Ahmed, H. Cuckle, J. Hirst, Cl. Hucknall and J.G. Thornton. 2007. 'Attitudes to prenatal testing and termination of pregnancy for fetal abnormality: a comparison of white and Pakistani women in the UK', *Prenatal Diagnosis* 27: 419–430.
Houwink, E.J., S.J. van Luijk, L. Henneman, C. van der Vleuten, G.J. Dinant and M.C. Cornel. 2011. 'Genetic educational needs and the role of genetics in primary care: a focus group study with multiple perspectives', *BMC Family Practice* 12(5); available from: PM:21329524.
Human Genetics Commission. 2011. *Increasing Options, Informing Choice: A Report on Preconception Genetic Testing and Screening*. London: Human Genetics Commission.
Inhorn, M.C. 2006. 'Making Muslim babies: IVF and gamete donation in Sunni versus Shi'a Islam', *Culture, Medicine and Psychiatry* 30(4): 427–450; available from: PM:17051430.
Lakeman, P., A.M. Plass, L. Henneman, P.D. Bezemer, M.C. Cornel and L.P. ten Kate. 2008. 'Three-month follow-up of Western and non-Western participants in a study on preconceptional ancestry-based carrier couple screening for cystic fibrosis and hemoglobinopathies in the Netherlands', *Genetics in Medicine* 10(11): 820–830; available from: PM:18941425.
Lippman, A. 1991. 'Prenatal genetic testing and screening: constructing needs and reinforcing inequities', *American Journal of Law & Medicine* 17(1–2): 15–50; available from: PM:1877608.
———. 2003. 'Eugenics and public health', *American Journal of Public Health* 93(1): 11; available from: PM:12511371.
Mahowald, M.B., M.S. Verp and R.R. Anderson. 1998. 'Genetic counseling: clinical and ethical challenges', *Annual Review of Genetics* 32: 547–559.
Mardis, E.R. 2011. 'A decade's perspective on DNA sequencing technology', *Nature* 470(7333): 198–203; available from: PM:21307932.
Markel, H. 1992. 'The stigma of disease: implications of genetic screening', *American Journal of Medicine* 93(2): 209–215; available from: PM:1497018.
McCullough, J.M. and D.H. O'Rourke. 1986. 'Geographic distribution of consanguinity in Europe', *Annals of Human Biology* 13(4): 359–367.

Modell, B. and A. Darr. 2002. 'Science and society: genetic counselling and customary consanguineous marriage', *Nature Reviews Genetics* 3(3): 225–229; available from: PM:11972160.

Oduncu, F.S. 2002. 'The role of non-directiveness in genetic counseling', *Medicine Health Care and Philosophy* 5(1): 53–63.

Rawaf, S., M.J. De and B. Starfield. 2008. 'From Alma-Ata to Almaty: a new start for primary health care', *Lancet* 372(9647): 1365–1367; available from: PM:18922572.

Raz, A.E. and Y. Vizner. 2008. 'Carrier matching and collective socialization in community genetics: Dor Yeshorim and the reinforcement of stigma', *Social Science & Medicine* 67(9): 1361–1369; available from: PM:18701203.

Reniers, G. 2010. *Post-immigration Survival of Traditional Marriage Patterns: Consanguineous Marriage among Turkish and Moroccan Immigrants in Belgium.* Ghent: Department of Population Studies, University of Ghent.

Schulpen, T.W., J.E. van Steenbergen and H.F. van Driel. 2001. 'Influences of ethnicity on perinatal and child mortality in the Netherlands', *Archives of Disease in Childhood* 84(3): 222–226; available from: PM:11207169.

Serour, G.I. 2008. 'Islamic perspectives in human reproduction', *Reproductive BioMedicine Online* 17 (suppl. 3): 34–38; available from: PM:18983735.

Shaw, A. and J.A. Hurst. 2008. '"What is this genetics, anyway?" Understandings of genetics, illness causality and inheritance among British Pakistani users of genetic services', *Journal of Genetic Counseling* 17(4): 373–383; available from: PM:18607703.

Stuurgroep Zwangerschap en Geboorte. 2009. *Een goed begin. Veilige zorg rond zwangerschap en geboorte.*

Teeuw, M.E., L. Henneman, Z. Bochdanovits, P. Heutink, D.J. Kuik, M.C. Cornel and L.P. ten Kate. 2010. 'Do consanguineous parents of a child affected by an autosomal recessive disease have more DNA identical-by-descent than similarly-related parents with healthy offspring? Design of a case-control study', *BMC Medical Genetics* 11: 113; available from: PM:20637082.

Unesco. 1997. *The Universal Declaration on the Human Genome and Human Rights.* www.unesco.org.

Waelput, A.J.M. and P.W. Achterberg. 2007. *Desire to have Children in Consanguineous Parents: Risks and Genetic Counseling.* Bilthoven: RIVM, National Institute for Public Health and Environment.

Afterword
The Marriage of Cousins in Victorian England

Adam Kuper

Charles Darwin married his cousin Emma Wedgwood in January 1839, a few weeks before his thirtieth birthday. Emma was not only his first cousin. She was also his sister-in-law. Her oldest brother, 'young Jos', had married Charles's sister, Caroline, in 1837 (Figure 11.1).

Cousin marriage was eminently respectable. In 1840, a year after Charles Darwin's wedding, Queen Victoria married Prince Albert of Saxe-Coburg and Gotha, who was her mother's brother's son. The Prime Minister, Melbourne, did suggest that their close relationship might be a problem, but the press was more concerned that Albert had no money and might be a fortune-hunter, and that he was younger than the queen, who surely required mature guidance (Matthew and Reynolds n.d.).

To be sure, family intimacies could cause complications. In 1852, Edward White Benson came down from the university and moved in with his mother's brother's daughter, Mary Sidgwick, with whom his younger sister was also living. He almost immediately began to woo Mary's daughter, also Mary, but known as Minnie, although she was only twelve years old:

> Let me try to recall each circumstance: the arm-chair in which I sat, how she sat as usual on my knee, a little fair girl of twelve with her earnest look, and how I said that I wanted to speak to her of

Afterword: The Marriage of Cousins in Victorian England

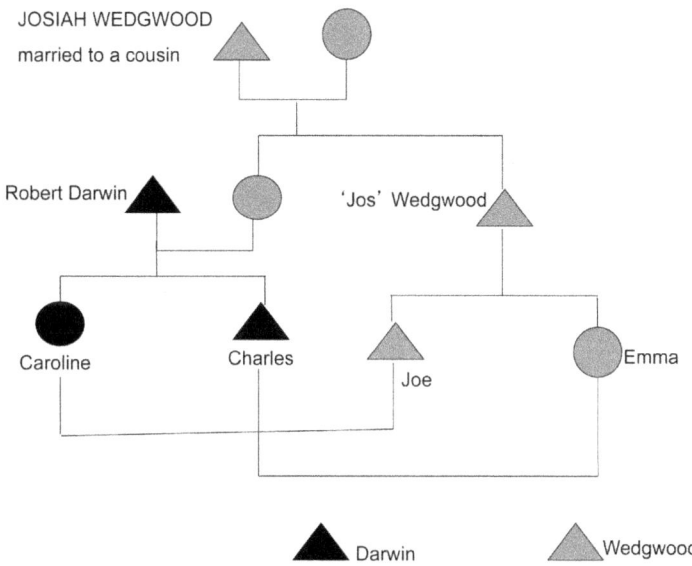

FIGURE 11.1 Darwin's Marriage
○ = female, □ = male, ▲ = Darwin, ▲ = Wedgwood

something serious, and then got quietly to the thing, and asked her if she thought it would ever come to pass that we should be married. Instantly, without a word, a rush of tears fell down her cheeks ... She made no attempt to promise, and said nothing silly or childish, but affected me very much by quietly laying the ends of my handkerchief together and tying them in a knot, and quietly putting them into my hand. (Tosh 1991: 54)

This jars with contemporary susceptibilities, but for the Victorians the development from girlish adoration to adult love was acceptable, certainly between cousins.

Benson continued to live alongside Minnie and her mother for the next five years. His sister died in 1850 and John Tosh suggests that Minnie 'probably became his surrogate sister too' (Tosh 1991: 57). Their engagement was announced when Minnie was seventeen, and they married in 1859, when she was eighteen.

Benson went on to become Archbishop of Canterbury. Reading his letters to his wife, Tosh judges the marriage to have been sexually fulfilled (Tosh 1991: 57–59), but Mary Benson later confessed that she was bullied by her husband and never lost her fear of him (Chapman n.d.). Their son, the novelist A.C. Benson, 'wondered if they ever *really* loved. Certainly I never remember them seeking each other's company or wanting to be alone together' (Chapman n.d.). And after the death of her husband, Minnie had a passionate affair with Lucy Tait, the daughter of Benson's predecessor as Archbishop of Canterbury. For whatever reason – their father's inability to show them love, their mother's homosexuality, or, surely less plausibly, because their parents were cousins – none of the six Benson children married (Sanders 2002: 13, 25).

But there were some doubts about cousin marriage, even in these educated circles. Parliament had legalized first cousin marriage in England in 1540, with the endorsement of the Church of England. Nevertheless, some people had religious doubts. Was cousin marriage perhaps incestuous?

In 1826 a brilliant young lawyer, Henry Nelson Coleridge, travelled to the West Indies, ostensibly for health reasons, but actually because his parents hoped that a foreign adventure would distract him from his infatuation with a cousin (Durrant n.d.). It did not work out that way. On his return Henry published, anonymously, *Six Months in the West Indies*, and he slipped in a defiant declaration: 'I love a cousin; she is such an exquisite relation, just standing between me and the stranger to my name, drawing upon so many sources of love and tieing them all up with every cord of human affection – almost my sister ere my wife!'

Henry's uncle, Samuel Taylor Coleridge, read this passage uneasily. He was then thoroughly dismayed to discover that Henry's beloved was his own daughter, Sara, and that they were secretly engaged to be married:

> How much truth is there in this plea, Henry himself has let out, unawares, in the words 'my Sister ere my Wife' – words which have given offence, I find, to three or four persons of our acquaintance and I own shocked my feelings ... Surely, the best interests of Society render it expedient, that there should be some Outworks between the Citadel, that contains the very Palladium of the Human Race, and the Open Country. (Coleridge 1956–1971: 590, n.1)

In the end he gave way. 'If the matter were quite open, I should incline to disapprove the marriage of first cousins; but the church has decided otherwise on the authority of Augustine, and that seems enough upon such a point' (Coleridge 1835: 55, entry for 10 June 1842). Henry's parents were also opposed to the marriage, but for purely secular reasons: they thought that Samuel Taylor was mad (Jones 1998: 240–411). But Henry married Sara, in 1829, with her father's blessing though in the face of his own family's continued disapproval. Henry was, Sara declared, her 'cousin-husband, certainly nearer and dearer to me for being cousin, as well as husband' (Anderson 1986: 289). The couple settled in Hampstead, near Sara's father's base in Highgate. After his death they devoted themselves to editing his manuscripts. When Henry died, Sara buried him in the same vault as her father, in Highgate cemetery (Durrant n.d.).

In the second half of the nineteenth century, any lingering religious scruples about cousin marriage were overtaken by a growing concern in scientific circles about the health consequences of close-kin unions. 'I'm not quite sure that it's a good thing for cousins to marry', remarks Dr Crofts in Trollope's *The Small House of Allington*, published in 1863. 'They do, you know, very often', he is reminded, 'and it suits some family arrangements' (Trollope 1863). To be sure, the doctor had a personal interest in the matter. A young woman he hoped to marry had just become engaged to her cousin. However, Dr Crofts was talking as a responsible medical man. The British medical press was raising questions about the risks to offspring of cousin marriages (e.g. Gardner 1861; Child 1862) and a bright young doctor would have been familiar with the professional debates. (And in the end he gets his girl.)

Charles Darwin had picked up on these concerns very early. He was worried about heredity and also about the consequences of cousin marriage. Shortly before his own marriage to his first cousin, Emma Wedgwood, he had consulted a new book, Alexander Walker's *Intermarriage: Or the Mode in Which, and the Causes Why, Beauty, Health, and Intellect Result from Certain Unions, and Deformity, Disease and Insanity from Others* (1838). It touched a sensitive nerve. His Darwin grandmother, the wife of Erasmus Darwin, was addicted to gin and suffered from bouts of madness. Charles Darwin's own mother, unwell throughout his childhood, had died from an agonizing stomach ailment, probably peritonitis, at the age of fifty-two. Charles was eight years old when she died, and as an adult he was obsessively concerned with his own ill health, particularly the recurrent stomach complaints that recalled his mother's fatal illness. Both his mother and Emma were Wedgwoods, and the Wedgwoods were notorious for their ill health (Browne 1995). Whenever one of his children fell ill, Charles was inclined to see the same symptoms in himself, and to worry that it exposed a family propensity.

Or were the frequent illnesses of his children, and the health problems of the Wedgwoods, perhaps the consequence of cousin marriages? (Browne 2002: 277, 279, 282). This was a growing concern in scientific circles in Britain in the 1860s. 'In many families, marriages between cousins are discouraged and checked', Francis Galton noted in 1865 (Galton 1865). Charles Darwin's son George published a paper recommending that cousin marriage should be avoided (Darwin, G. 1873).

The first thorough study of the subject in the United Kingdom was published in 1865, by Arthur Mitchell, Deputy Commissioner in Lunacy for Scotland. Scotland was an obvious choice. It was widely believed that marriage between close relatives was rampant in remote Scottish regions, particularly in the Highlands and Islands. Mitchell noted that popular opinion in Scotland condemned 'blood-alliances' as 'productive of evil' (Mitchell 1865: 718). And indeed national statistics showed that nearly 14 per cent of 'idiots' in Scotland were children of kin. In 44 per cent of families with more than one mentally handicapped child, the parents were blood relatives; 6 per cent of the parents of deaf mutes were close relatives.

Nonetheless, Mitchell was not convinced that this was the whole story. Fewer than 2 per cent of marriages in Scotland were between first or second cousins. The rate was indeed higher in some isolated regions, but the evidence for bad effects was uncertain. In one small town on the northeast coast of Scotland, 9 per cent of marriages were with first cousins and 13 per cent with second cousins. Mitchell acknowledged that the children of these cousin marriages were often unprepossessing, but then many fishing families in the region were 'below par in intellect' (Mitchell 1865: 1075). A more telling case was Berneray-Lewis (now Great Bernera, off the Isle of Lewis). Here 11 per cent of marriages were with first and second cousins, yet Mitchell remarked that 'instead of finding the island [Berneray-Lewis] peopled with idiots, madmen, cripples, and mutes, not one such person is said to exist in it' (Mitchell 1865: 907).

Perhaps environmental factors – 'occupation, social habits, etc'. – influenced the outcome. One 'shrewd old woman' remarked to him: 'But I'll tell ye what, Doctor, bairns that's hungert i' their youth aye gang wrang. That's far waur nor sib marriages' (Mitchell 1865: 913). Mitchell concluded that close-kin marriage tended to reinforce 'evil influences'.

Darwin was fascinated. Between 1868 and 1877 he published three monographs on cross-fertilization in animals and plants (Darwin 1868, 1876, 1877). In the first of these books, *The Variation of Animals and Plants under Domestication*, he proposed that 'the existence of a great law of nature is almost proved; namely, that the crossing of animals and plants which are not closely related to each other is highly beneficial or even necessary, and that interbreeding [i.e., inbreeding] prolonged during many generations is highly injurious' (Darwin 1896: 14).

Darwin thought this was probably true of human beings, although he was reluctant at first to press the issue. ('Before turning on to Birds, I ought to refer to man, though I am unwilling to enter on this subject, as it is surrounded by natural prejudices') (Darwin 1896: 122). However, he was bound to consider the implications for his own family. His scientific project and his personal concerns could hardly be separated. 'The philosophical difficulties and practical consequences of cousin marriages troubled him for years afterwards', Janet Browne observes. 'There was no other theme in Darwin's science that more clearly reflected the personal origins of his intellectual achievement. He could scarcely have arrived at pangenesis without this attention to his marriage, his children's ill health, and his own sickness' (Browne 2002: 282).

He began to canvass his correspondents. William Farr, the senior statistician in the Registrar General's office, suggested to him that the 1871 census should include a question on cousin marriage (Farr 1868). Darwin began to lobby for it. His neighbour and ally, John Lubbock, had just been elected to parliament. In the summer of 1870 Darwin asked him to put Farr's proposal to the House. He even drafted arguments for Lubbock to use.

> In England and many parts of Europe the marriages of cousins are objected to from their supposed injurious consequences; but this belief rests on no direct evidence. It is therefore manifestly desirable that the belief should either be proved false, or should be confirmed, so that in this latter case the marriages of cousins might be discouraged. If the census recorded cousin marriages it could be established whether they were less fertile than the average. Later it might also be possible to find out whether or not consanguineous marriages lead to deafness, and dumbness, blindness, &c. (Darwin 1870)

Lubbock put it to the House that 'consanguineous marriages were injurious throughout the whole vegetable and animal kingdoms'. It was obviously 'desirable to ascertain whether that was . . . the case with the whole human race' (Hansard 1870: 817). The response was unenthusiastic. One member remarked that Parliament was already busy every year debating the legality of marriage with the deceased wife's sister: 'if there were to be legislation about the marriage of first cousins also, the whole time of the House would be taken up in deciding who was to be allowed to marry anybody else'

(Hansard 1870: 1009). According to George Darwin, the proposition was rejected, 'amidst the scornful laughter of the House, on the ground that the idle curiosity of philosophers was not to be satisfied' (Darwin, G. 1875a: 153). Yet forty-five members voted for Lubbock's motion in committee; ninety-two voted against, but Lubbock remarked in his summing up that virtually everyone who spoke shared his concern (Hansard 1870: 1006–1010).

Farr now proposed to Darwin that an 'inquiry might be undertaken through private channels' (Farr 1870). Darwin agreed. He entrusted the study to his eldest son, George. George Darwin was not only an amateur genealogist but also an accomplished mathematician. And, influenced by the eugenic theories of his cousin Francis Galton, he had advocated controls on marriage between unsuitable partners. He recommended that the mentally ill should be kept from marrying, and suggested that there might be good scientific reasons to prevent the marriage of first cousins (Darwin, G. 1873: 424). Clearly he was primed for his father's commission.

Charles Darwin laid out the research design. George was to compare the incidence of close-kin marriage in the general population with that among the parents of patients in asylums. If it turned out that marriages between close relatives produced a disproportionate number of 'diseased' children, this would 'settle the question as to the injuriousness of such marriages' (Darwin, G. 1875a: 153).

The first step was to find out how common it was in England for first cousins to marry. Apparently nobody knew the answer. George Darwin was given estimates that ranged from 10 per cent to one in a thousand. 'Every observer', he concluded, 'is biased by the frequency or rarity of such marriages amongst his immediate surroundings' (Darwin, G. 1875a: 178). He would have to discover the facts for himself. Expert in the new statistical techniques that were being developed by Farr and Francis Galton, George decided to attempt a scientific survey – one of the very first statistical studies of a social problem in the UK. After making ingenious use of public records and mail questionnaires he concluded that about 4.5 per cent of marriages in the aristocracy were with first cousins; 3.5 per cent in the landed gentry and the upper-middle classes; about 2.25 per cent in the rural population; and among all classes in London, about 1.15 per cent.

The next step was to gather statistics from mental asylums. Charles Darwin wrote on George's behalf to the heads of the leading institutions. Several provided detailed responses. These indicated that only 3 to 4 per cent of patients were the offspring of marriages between first cousins. 'For Heavens sake', Charles urged his son, 'put a sentence in some conspicuous place that your results seem to indicate that consanguineous marriage, as far as insanity is concerned, cannot be injurious in any very high degree' (Darwin 1874). George complied. 'It will be seen [he concluded] that the percentage of offspring of first-cousin marriages [in mental asylums] is so nearly that of such marriages in the general population, that one can only draw the negative conclusion that, as far as insanity and idiocy go, no evil has been shown to accrue from consanguineous marriages' (Darwin, G. 1875a: 168).

Other studies suggested that the offspring of cousin marriages were more likely to suffer from blindness, deafness, or infertility. George accepted that these conditions were highly hereditary, but saw no convincing evidence that they were caused by cousin marriage. In fact, first cousin marriages were, if anything, more fertile than others. Presumably a man was more likely to marry a cousin if he had many to choose from. First cousin marriage would therefore be more common among people who came from large – and so presumably fertile – families (Darwin, G. 1875a: 168–172).

Only one small piece of evidence gave George pause. Among men who had rowed for Oxford or Cambridge, men who were obviously the fittest of the fit, sons of first cousin parents appeared slightly less frequently than might have been expected (2.4 per cent as opposed to 3–3.5 per cent among their peers) (Darwin, G. 1875b: 178).

George Darwin was well aware that his conclusions flew in the face of a common and ancient prejudice. He conceded that marriages between cousins might be quite all right for the rich but bad for the poor:

> I may mention that Dr Arthur Mitchell, of Edinburgh, conducted an extensive inquiry, and came to the conclusion that, under favourable conditions of life, the apparent ill-effects were frequently almost nil, whilst if the children were ill fed, badly housed and clothed, the evil might become very marked. This is in striking accordance with some unpublished experiments of my father, Mr Charles Darwin, on the in-and inbreeding of plants; for he has found that in-bred plants, when allowed enough space and good soil, frequently show little or no deterioration, whilst when placed in competition with another plant, they frequently perish or are much stunted. (Darwin, G. 1875a [1896]: 178)

In short, cousin marriage caused no harm in the best families. Charles Darwin endorsed these conclusions (Darwin 1876: 460–461; 1896: 104). In later editions of *Variation* he modified his original rule, weakening the claim: 'it is a great law of nature, that all organic beings profit from an *occasional* cross with individuals not closely related to them in blood'(Darwin 1896: 94) [emphasis added.] On the other hand, the experience of animal breeders indicated that 'the advantage of close interbreeding [i.e., inbreeding], as far as the retention of character is concerned, is indisputable, and often outweighs the evil of a slight loss of constitutional vigour' (Darwin 1896: 94).

Francis Galton wrote enthusiastically to George Darwin that he had 'exploded most effectually a popular scare'. He added that his cousin could make a fortune from his discovery:

> Thus: there are, say, 200,000 annual marriages in the kingdom, of which 2,000 and more are between first cousins. You have only to print in proportion, and in various appropriate scales of cheapness or luxury: WORDS of Scientific COMFORT and ENCOURAGEMENT To COUSINS who are LOVERS then each lover and each of the two sets of parents would be sure to buy a copy; i.e. an annual sale of 8,000 copies!! (Cousins who fall in love and don't marry would also buy copies, as well as those who think that they might fall in love.).
> (Pearson 1914–1930: 188)

Galton's protégé, Karl Pearson, made a follow-up study in 1908. He was less systematic than George Darwin, relying on correspondence from readers of the *British Medical Journal*. These select respondents reported a very high incidence of first cousin marriages in their families. A smaller proportion of marriages were with more distant cousins, but Pearson remarked that second and third cousins in these families were also often related in more than one line. He lumped them all together and concluded that 'consanguineous marriages in the professional classes probably occur in less that 8 per cent and more than 5 per cent of cases'. Yet only 1.3 per cent of patients in the Great Ormond Street Hospital for Children were the children of cousins. Pearson concluded that 'the diseases of children are not largely due to any consanguinity between their parents' (Pearson 1908: 1395).

Endorsed by the Darwinian establishment, George Darwin's conclusions reassured many people whose family trees featured marriages between cousins. Englishmen could also rest more easily when they considered that Queen Victoria was married to a first cousin, and that several of her descendants had also married cousins. And Darwin's conclusions seemed only common sense to landowners in the House of Lords, who knew that the inbreeding of good stock was sound policy.

References

Anderson, N.F. 1986. 'Cousin marriage in Victorian England', *Journal of Family History* 11(3): 289.

Browne, J. 1995. *Charles Darwin: Voyaging.* London: Jonathan Cape.

———. 2002. *Charles Darwin: The Power of Place.* London: Jonathan Cape.

Chapman, M.D., n.d. 'Benson, Edward White', *Oxford Dictionary of National Biography.*

Child, G. 1862. 'On marriages of consanguinity', *British and Foreign Medico-Chirurgical Review* 29: 461–471.

Coleridge, S.T. 1835. *Specimens of the Table Talk of the Late Samuel Taylor Coleridge,* ed. H.N.C. [Henry Nelson Coleridge], 2 vols, vol. 6. London: John Murray.

———. 1956–1971. An autograph note, published in *Collected Letters of Samuel Taylor Coleridge,* ed. Earl Leslie Griggs, 6 vols, vol. 1. Oxford: Oxford University Press.

Darwin, C. 1868. *The Variation of Animals and Plants under Domestication.* London: Murray.

———. 1876. *The Effects of Cross and Self Fertilisation in the Vegetable Kingdom.* London: Murray.

———. 1877. *The Various Contrivances by which Orchids are Fertilised by Insects.* London: Murray.

———. 1896. *The Variation of Animals and Plants under Domestication* [Revised edition, 1875 *The Variation of Animals and Plants under Domestication*]. 2 vols. London: Murray.

Darwin, C. to G.H. Darwin. 1874. *Darwin Correspondence.* Cambridge Papers, Cambridge University Library

Darwin, C. to J. Lubbock. 1870. *Darwin Correspondence*: Cambridge Papers, Cambridge University Library. Reproduced in *The Life and Letters of Charles Darwin,* ed. F. Darwin. London: John Murray, 1887.

Darwin, G.H. 1873. 'On the beneficial restrictions to liberty of marriage', *Contemporary Review* 22: 412–426.

———. 1875a. 'Marriages between first cousins in England and their effects', *Journal of the Statistical Society of London* 38(2): 153–182.

———. 1875b. 'Note on the marriages of first cousins', *Journal of the Statistical Society* 344–348.

Durrant, C., n.d. 'Coleridge, Henry Nelson', *Oxford Dictionary of National Biography.*

Farr, W. to C. Darwin. 1868. *The Darwin Correspondence.* Cambridge Papers, Cambridge University Library.

———. 1870. *The Darwin Correspondence.* Cambridge Papers, Cambridge University Library.

Galton, F. 1865. 'Hereditary talent and character', *Macmillan's Magazine* 12: 319.

Gardner, J. 1861. 'On the intermarriage of relations as the cause of degeneracy of offspring', *British Medical Journal* 1: 290.
Hansard 44, 1870. 3rd series.
Jones, K. 1998. *A Passionate Sisterhood: The Sisters, Wives and Daughters of the Lake Poets*. London: Virago Press.
Matthew, H.C.G. and K.D. Reynolds, n.d. 'Victoria', *Oxford Dictionary of National Biography*.
Mitchell, A.1865. 'On the influence which consanguinity in the parentage exercises upon the offspring', 3 parts, *Edinburgh Medical Journal* 10(1): 781.
Pearson, K. 1908. 'Cousin marriages', *The British Medical Journal* 1: 1395.
––––––. 1914–1930. *The Life, Letters and Labours of Francis Galton*, 3 vols, vol. 2. London: Cambridge University Press.
Sanders, V. 2002. *The Brother-Sister Culture in Nineteenth-Century Literature*. Basingstoke: Palgrave Macmillan.
Tosh, J. 1991. 'Domesticity and manliness in the Victorian middle class: the family of Edward White Benson', in M. Roper and J. Tosh (eds), *Manful Assertions*. London: Routledge, pp.44–73.
Trollope, A. 1864. *The Small House of Allington*. London: Smith, Elder.

Notes on Contributors

Edien Bartels is Senior Researcher at the Department of Social and Cultural Anthropology, VU University, Amsterdam. She has conducted fieldwork in North Africa, Morocco and Tunisia, and with Moroccan migrants in the Netherlands. Her PhD thesis, 'One daughter is better than a thousand sons' (1993), examined Arab women, symbols and power relationships between the sexes. Her projects include: Moroccan migrants and the development of Islam in Morocco and the Netherlands; migrant women and children who have been forcibly returned to their countries of origin; female circumcision in the Netherlands; migrant partner choice; and social innovation in the Netherlands. Her current interdisciplinary research concerns consanguineous marriages among Turkish and Moroccan Dutch people. She has published numerous articles and reports on these themes, and on intercultural social care and psychiatry.

Claire Beaudevin is a social anthropologist, and a Research Scientist at the National Centre for Scientific Research (CNRS), France. She works in Paris in the Cermes3, a research unit dedicated to social science studies of medicine, sciences and health. Her current research focuses on genomics and clinical genetics: in Arabia where she studies genetics and genomics within research and public health; and in France, on research/clinical oncogenetic platforms. Her recent publications include 'Old diseases and contemporary crisis. Inherited blood disorders in Oman' (*Anthropology and Medicine*, 2013) and 'Of red cells, translocality and origins' (in S. Wippel, ed., *Regionalizing Oman*, Springer, 2013).

Alan Bittles is Adjunct Professor and Research Leader in the Centre for Comparative Genomics, Murdoch University and Adjunct Professor of Community Genetics in Edith Cowan University, both in Perth, Australia. He has conducted extensive population- and laboratory-based research into the prevalence, types and health outcomes of consanguineous marriage in South, Southeast and East Asia, the Middle East, North Africa, Western Europe and Australasia. He has published over 200 refereed papers, books and book chapters, a large number of which focus on various aspects of consanguinity. His most recent book is *Consanguinity in Context*, published by Cambridge University Press in 2012.

Pascal Borry is Assistant Professor of Bioethics at the Department of Public Health and Primary Care, University of Leuven, Belgium. His research focuses on the ethical, legal and social implications of genetic and genomics. He has published over seventy articles on topics that include direct-to-consumer genetic testing, public health genomics, bio-banking, research on human tissue, genetic testing, preconception screening and neonatal screening; in 2006 he received the 'Professor Roger Borghgraef' triennial prize for his work in biomedical ethics. He has been a visiting scholar at the Case Western Reserve University, the Université de Montréal and McGill University, and the VU Medical Center, Amsterdam. He is the programme coordinator of the Erasmus Mundus Master of Bioethics. He is a board member of the European Society of Human Genetics and a member of its Professional and Public Policy Committee.

Martina Cornel is Professor of Community Genetics and Public Health Genomics at the VU University Medical Center, Amsterdam. A physician and epidemiologist, she has since 2000 mainly worked on the responsible implementation of genetic testing and screening. She is chair of the Public and Professional Policy Committee of the European Society of Human Genetics, which has developed recommendations on topics that include: genetic testing in minors; principles for good practice in paediatric biobanks; and whole genome sequencing in health care. She is a member of the Netherlands Health Councils' standing Committees on Population Screening and Genetics, and chairs the Netherlands Program Committee Neonatal Heelprick Screening.

Lidewij Henneman is Associated Professor in the Department of Clinical Genetics, section of Community Genetics, EMGO Institute for Health and Care Research, VU University Medical Center Amsterdam, the Netherlands. She is a health scientist. Her research focuses on the implementation and psychosocial/behavioural impact of (new) genetic applications, including the attitudes, prior knowledge and expectations of potential users such as health care professionals, patients and wider society. Her particular interests are preconception carrier screening and (non-invasive) prenatal testing. She has published over 65 international articles, and is chair of the Netherlands Association of Community Genetics and Public Health Genomics (NACGG).

Adam Kuper is a Centennial Professor at the London School of Economics and Visiting Professor at Boston University. His most recent books are *Incest and Influence: The Private Life of Bourgeois England* (Cambridge, MA: Harvard University Press, 2009), *The Reinvention of Primitive Society* (London: Routledge, 2005), and *'Culture': The Anthropologists' Account* (Cambridge, MA: Harvard University Press, 1999).

Anika Liversage is a senior researcher and program director at SFI – the Danish National Centre for Social Research. Her research interests are immigrant family relations, with a particular focus on issues of gender and power. She speaks Turkish, having lived in the country for four years, and much of her work concerns changes in Turkish immigrant families in Denmark. Recent publications are 'Gender, conflict and subordination within the household – Turkish migrant marriage and divorce in Denmark' (*Journal of Ethnic and Migration Studies*, 2012) and – with Katharine Charsley – 'Transforming polygamy: migration, transnationalism and multiple marriages among Muslim minorities' (*Global Networks*, 2013).

Laila Prager is Junior Professor of Social Anthropology at the University of Hamburg. She was previously a researcher and senior lecturer at the University of Münster and a researcher at the Institute of Ethnology at the University of Leipzig (2007–2013). She has done extensive fieldwork among Bedouins in Syria, Jordan and the UAE, Arab-speaking Alawis in Southeastern Turkey, and Alawi migrant communities in Germany. Her publications include a monograph on Alawi transnational migrants, articles on Alawi *ziyara* traditions and their inter-religious dimensions (*The Muslim World*, 2013), and entries on 'Customary Marriage', 'Honor Killing', and 'Matrifocal Families' (in S. Loue and M. Sajatovic, eds, *Encyclopedia of Immigrant Health*, New York, 2012).

Aviad E. Raz is Professor in the Department of Sociology and Anthropology, Ben-Gurion University, Israel. From 2012 to 2014 he was an AICE Visiting Professor at the Department of Sociology, University of California, San Diego. His research focuses on religious/ethnic groups and identities in contemporary Israeli society, especially in the context of health and family studies. He studies the social and bioethical aspects of new reproductive technologies, genetics and patient organizations. He also conducts research on organizational culture and entrepreneurship. Raz has written seven books and over forty-five articles and chapters on topics in organizational and medical sociology, anthropology, culture and science.

Mikkel Rytter is Associate Professor in the Department of Culture and Society at Aarhus University, where he is part of the research programme on 'Contemporary Ethnography'. His recent publications include *Family Upheaval. Generation, Mobility and Relatedness among Pakistani Migrants in Denmark* (Berghahn, 2013), *Migration, Family and the Welfare State: Integrating Migrants and Refugees in Scandinavia* (co-edited with K.F. Olwig and B.R. Larsen, Routledge, 2012), and *Mobile Bodies, Mobile Souls. Family, Religion and Migration in a Global World* (co-edited with K.F. Olwig, Aarhus University Press, 2011). Mikkel Rytter is head of CESAU – Centre of Sociological Studies, Aarhus University.

Alison Shaw is Professor of Social Anthropology in the School of Anthropology and Museum Ethnography, University of Oxford, and Adjunct Professor at the University of California, Los Angeles. Her research focuses on ethnicity and health; social aspects of genetics; and kinship, gender and transnational marriages. She has conducted anthropological fieldwork in Pakistan and with British Pakistanis on Pakistani migration and settlement in Britain, and more recently with British Pakistani families referred for genetic counselling. Her publications include *Kinship and Continuity: Pakistani Families in Britain* (2000) and *Negotiating Risk: British Pakistani Experiences of Genetics* (2009).

Oka Storms is a PhD student in the Department of Social and Cultural Anthropology at the Faculty of Social Sciences, VU University, Amsterdam. She has conducted anthropological fieldwork in Morocco on the reforms of the *Mudawwana*, consanguinity and Dutch-Moroccan abandoned children. In the Netherlands her research focuses on partner choice and consanguinity among Dutch Moroccans and Turks. A recent publication (with Edien Bartels) is 'Notre huile est dans notre farine: an exploration into the meaning of consanguinity in Northern Morocco against the backdrop of the medical risk of disabled offspring' (in H.M. Vroom, P. Verdonk, M.A. Abdellah and M.C. Cornel, eds, *Looking Beneath the Surface*, 2013).

Marieke Teeuw is a medical doctor in the Department of Clinical Genetics at the VU University Medical Center, Amsterdam. Her research is focused on improving genetic counselling in cases of consanguinity. She has conducted genetic studies as well as research among health care providers and the target population. Her publications include: 'Do consanguineous parents of a child affected by an autosomal recessive disease have more DNA identical-by-descent than similarly related parents with healthy offspring? Design of a case-control study' (2010) and 'Consanguineous marriage and reproductive risk: attitudes and understanding of ethnic groups practicing consanguinity in Western society' (2013).

Leo P. ten Kate is Emeritus Professor of Clinical Genetics and Former Head of the Department of Clinical Genetics at the VU University Medical Center, Amsterdam. His research focuses on the potential benefit of disease-related genetics and genomics knowledge and technologies in human populations and communities. He is chair of the editorial board of the Journal of Community Genetics, and coordinator of the international multidisciplinary Community Genetics Network (over 1,100 members). He is one of the teachers of the course on genetic risk calculation for Dutch trainees in Clinical Genetics. His more than 190 publications include *Community Genetics: Its Definition* (2010) and *Consanguinity and Endogamy in the Netherlands: Demographic and Medical Genetic Aspects* (2014).

Joel Zlotogora is Adjunct Professor in Human Genetics at the Hebrew University of Jerusalem, Israel. He works in the Ministry of Health and is responsible for the neonatal and preconception screening programs in Israel. His research interests include clinical genetics, medical consequences of consanguinity and the prevention of genetic diseases. He has published over 200 articles on these topics.

INDEX

Adana, 89, 90, 92, 95–96, 103
al-aqārib/ al-qarāba (the close ones), 66, 69–71
Alawi religion, 91, 99
amniocentesis, 76, 83, 186
Antakya, 89–90, 92, 95
Antalya, 89, 90
arranged marriages, 26, 120–21, 124, 127, 131, 135–37, 140, 147, 150, 165, 168, 185
autosome, 47, 59
autosomal recessive diseases/conditions, *see* recessive conditions/diseases

Bahrain, 65, 74
Benson, Edward White, marriage to a cousin, 218–20
birādarī/biraderi, 8, 40, 115–17, 123
biomedical knowledge,
  local adaptations of, 90, 99, 103–4
Bradford, 14, 36, 42, 115, 116, 117, 118, 121
Browne, Janet, 223
British Pakistanis
  birādarī structures of, 115–16
  consanguineous marriage among, 12, 20, 113, 114, 116, 117, 164, 166, 167
  marriage practices of, 120–21, 124–25, 126
  diversity of, 21
  number and distribution of, 115
  media stereotypes of, 20, 114
  views of genetic risk among, 20, 122–23, 125–26

carrier frequency, 18, 49, 50– 51, 62, 178
carrier screening, *see* screening
carrier status
  and risk-taking, 82–83

carriers
  of inherited blood disorders, *see* inherited blood disorders
  as a social category, 77–78, 80–82; *see also* stigma; stigmatization
Centre for Arab Genomics Studies (CAGS), 73
chorionic villus sampling, 76
clinical genetics services/ genetic counselling
  in Israel, 176, 178, 179, 183
  in the Netherlands, 207
  in Oman, 65
  in the United Kingdom, 20, 88, 114
coefficient of inbreeding, 34, 52
Coleridge, Henry Nelson, marriage to a cousin, 220–21
Coleridge, Samuel Taylor, on cousin marriage, 220
compound heterozygosity, 54, 60
consanguineous marriage/consanguinity
  as 'causing' inherited blood disorders, 26, 80; *see also* inherited blood disorders
  civil legislation on, 18, 38
  definition of, 1, 5, 33–34
  difference from cousin marriage, 5
  Dutch views of, *see* Netherlands
  as forced marriage, *see* forced marriage
  health risk to offspring of, 39–42
  'healthy consanguinity', 22, 26–27
  genetic risk in, 1–2, 5, 13–18, 25–26, 39–42, 46, 47–49, 50–59, 113–14, 117–18, 120, 207; *see also* recessive disease; carrier frequency; endogamy
  global prevalence of, 2, 18, 34, 36, 40–42; *see also* endogamy
  global trends, 10–13, 18, 38–39
  lay discourses of genetic risk in, 9, 96–104, 105n3
  media reporting on, 14, 20, 25, 118–20
  medical discourse of risk in, 88–90, 93

consanguineous marriage/consanguinity (*cont.*)
  public health debate on, 15–17, 88, 203–4
  as public health target, 14, 68, 70, 92, 113–14
  religious attitudes towards, 1, 8, 33, 36–38, 162
  stigmatization of, 16–18, 21–22, 27–28
  translation in Arabic, 69–70
Copenhagen, 142
cousin marriages
  Anthony Trollope on, 221
  Arthur Mitchell on, 222
  Charles Darwin on, 221–26
  definition of, 1, 34–35
  difference from consanguineous marriages, 5
  first, *see* first cousin marriage in England
  and genetic risk, *see* consanguinity and genetic risk
  George Darwin on, 224–26
  Karl Pearson on, 226
  Samuel Taylor Coleridge on, 220
  traditional socio-cultural perspectives on, 1, 5–12
  transnational, 12, 161, 166; *see also* transnational marriages
Çukurova, 90, 91, 95
Cyprus, management of beta-thalassaemia in, 19, 73–74, 84, 198

Danish People's Party, 132, 135
Darwin, Charles, 10, 24, 219
  on consanguineous marriage, 221–26
  on cross-fertilisation, 222–23
  on heritability, 221–22
  marriage to a cousin, 218
Darwin, George, cousin marriage study, 224–26
Denmark,
  couples' negotiations/experiences of the rule of supposition, 144–49
  Pakistanis in, 21, 130, 131–32, 137–38, 141–42, 145, 149, 149n1, 150n9
  rule of supposition of forced marriage, 130, 132–24, 137–43; *see also* forced marriages
  Turks in, 130, 131–32, 137, 142–44, 149n1
  twenty-four-year rule, 132, 142, 149
discourse of humanism, 134–35
discourse of nationalism, 134–35
Dor Yesharim,
  and Israeli geneticists, 188
  and the modern-religious community, 198–99

  as a programme for 'healthy endogamy', 23, 186–89
  and stigma, 196

endogamy, 40–41, 99–100, 104–5, 115
ethnicity, 23
  in genetic databases, 182, 183
  see also inherited blood disorders
Eti-Turk, 91, 95

Farr, William, 223, 224
first cousin marriage in England,
  legalized in 1540, 220
  parliamentary debate on, 223–24
forced marriages, 15, 27
  in Denmark, 119, 130–31, 134–40, 143, 147–48
  'human visas', 135
  in the Netherlands, 168–69, 203, 204
  in the United Kingdom, 120–21, 126

Galton, Francis, 222, 224, 226
gene frequency, 49
Generation R Study, 157
genetic counselling, 58, 59, 42, 72
  in inbred populations, 179, 180, 181
  in Oman, 74, 75
  targeted, 68
  in Turkey, 95–96, 102
genetic databases,
  computerized family pedigree, 180
  Israeli national database, 23, 182, 183
genetic knowledge,
  lay understandings, 9, 96, 66, 90, 99, 104n1, 190–91, 103–4
genetic risk,
  in consanguineous marriage, *see* consanguineous marriage
  expert views of, 66
  expressed in numbers, 78–79
  lay perceptions of, 66, 77–79, 81, 82, 83
  as social risk, *see* stigma, stigmatization
geneticization, 3–5, 212–13
genetics services, *see* clinical genetics
Germany,
  Alavi in, 91
  debate about consanguineous marriage in, 88
governmentality (Foucault), 93, 133

Haarder, Bertel, 139–41, 143
haemoglobinopathies, *see under* inherited blood disorders
Hatay, 90–92, 95–96, 99–104, 104n2
health, as government business, 89, 92–96

heterozygosity, 60
homozygosity, 41, 60

Ibn Khaldun, 69
identical by descent, 52, 60, 62
identical by state, 54, 60
inbreeding coefficient, *see* coefficient of inbreeding
incest, 154, 166, 167, 168
inheritance
  lay views of autosomal recessive, 78–79
  Mendelian, 123
  patrilineal blood ties, 9, 122–23, 127
inherited blood disorders, 19, 20, 65, 66, 69, 71, 73, 74, 75 , 76, 77, 79, 80, 81, 82, 83, 84, 92, 94–95, 101–3, 106–7
  carrier prevalence, in Oman, 84, 60
  carriers of, 66, 69, 75, 77–78, 80, 81, 82, 83, 84
  Mediterranean Anemia (Turkish: *Akdeniz Anemisi*) 89, 94, 96, 102–3
  sickle-cell anaemia, 19, 66, 67, 72, 81, 94, 105–7
  thalassaemia, 19, 66, 73, 74, 78, 80, 81, 82, 83, 94–96, 105–7
Iran, 73
Islam
  and consanguineous marriage, 1, 8, 16, 36, 37, 73, 162, 167, 168
  and disability, 162–64
  as marker for partner choice, 81, 124, 126, 169
  as Muslims as 'other', 135, 155, 162
  and preconception testing, 162, 209–10
  and termination of pregnancy, 209
  and use of new reproductive technologies, 16, 82, 162, 163, 164, 209–10
Israel
  community genetics clinics, 178, 179
  consanguinity rates, 176
  health care infrastructure, 177
  infant mortality, 175
  population, 176

Judaism,
  and abortion, 186
  and cousin marriage, 186
  and disability, 195–97
  and fertility, 187
  Haredi community, 196–98
  modern-religious community, 198–99
  and *shidduch*, 191–92

kafā'a,
  see under marriage

law of integration, Denmark, 136
Lebanon, 91, 105
Liberal-Conservative government, in Denmark, 132, 137
Liberal Party, in Denmark, 139
love marriages, 161, 165, 167, 168, 169
Lubbock, John, 223

Malmö, Sweden, 142
marriage, 67, 68, 69, 71, 72, 74, 75, 76, 79–81, 83
  with (first) cousin, 67, 68, 69, 71, 72, 83
  kafā'a in, 76
  with non-Omanis, 74
  in Omani law, 74, 76
  organization process of, 75, 79–81
  watta satta, 9
  see also love marriages, arranged marriages
medical genetics, *see* clinical genetics
medical termination of pregnancy, 73, 74, 77, 83, 84, 175, 209, 210
medicalization, 3–5, 22, 25, 66, 73–77, 84, 127, 156, 160, 168, 185, 212–14
Mersin 90–92, 95–96, 109
Mitchell, Arthur, study of cousin marriage in Scotland, 222, 225
moral panic, 14–17, 135
multicultural society, 155, 159, 160

nationalism, 134–35
neonatal screening, 49, 73, 75
Netherlands,
  Alawi in, 91
  Moroccans in, 36, 154, 157–58, 159, 161, 164, 165–66, 169, 210
  National Institute for Public Health and Environment, 204
  prevalence of consanguineous marriage in, 203
  recording ethnicity data in, 23
  Turks in, 21, 36, 154, 157–58, 159, 164, 165, 166–67, 169, 198, 203, 210
  views of consanguineous marriage in, 20, 21, 24, 155–57, 165, 168, 203, 204, 211, 213, 214; *see also* preconception care; preconception screening
next generation sequencing, 208
  see also preconception testing
Norway,
  Pakistanis in, 21, 34, 116, 117, 135, 138, 138, 140, 150n8
  Turks in, 138

Oman, Sultanate of,
  genetic disorders in, 69
  healthcare system, 65, 66, 73, 77, 83
  lay views of consanguineous marriage in, 70–72
  medical views of consanguineous marriage in, 67–70
  medicalization in, 66, 73–77, 84
  prevalence of consanguineous marriage in, 67, 68
  tribal database in, 69–70, 75
  tribal system in, 69–70

Pakistan,
  consanguinity rates in, 37, 39, 40, 116
  regions of, 115
Pearson, Karl, on cousin marriage, 226
preconception care
  counselling recommendations, 203
  and Islam, 162, 209–10
  in Netherlands, 205–7
preconception screening, 22, 23–24, 162, 198
preconception testing, 208
  ethical issues, 211–14
  lay views of, 209–19
  pragmatic issues, 211
preimplantation genetic diagnosis (PGD), 76, 77
premarital screening, 23, 26, 73–76, 79, 84, 89, 92, 94–96, 101–3, 113, 176
  health examinations, 92
prenatal
  diagnosis/testing 19, 20, 76, 88, 89, 95, 96, 99, 101–2, 122, 125–26, 177–78, 186, 195, 198, 202, 205, 210
  screening, 19, 20, 88, 99, 113

Qatar, 65, 73, 74

recessive gene, definition, 60
recessive risk
  carrier couples' responses to, 125–26, 127; *see also* risk
  where both parents are carriers, 47–49
recessive conditions/diseases
  association with parental consanguinity, *see* consanguineous marriage
  definition, 1–2, 46–49, 60
  inheritance of, 10, 34, 47–49
  patterns and prevalence, 13, 18, 22, 40–42, 181
  risk estimates for, 50–59

risk, 77, 79, 80, 81, 82, 83, 156–57, 158–60
  expressed in numbers, 79
  genetic risk, 59, 77, 82
  lay perceptions of, 77, 79, 82, 83, 160–67
  and patrilineality, 9, 123, 127
  taking, 125

Saudi Arabia, 65, 67, 72, 73, 74, 76, 82
September 11th 2001, 132, 135
sickle-cell anaemia
  See under inherited blood disorders
Social Democrats (The Social Democratic Party) in Denmark, 136
Social Liberal (Party), in Denmark, 136
stigma
  of carriers, 77–78, 80–82, 189–90, 193–95
  of cousin marriage, 16–17
  and *Dor Yesharim*, 196
  see also stigmatization
stigmatization, 2, 16, 23, 26, 77, 80, 81, 83, 102, 179, 185, 188, 190, 194, 196, 197, 199, 213; *see also* stigma
Syria, 91, 107

taboo, 17, 28, 154, 155, 164, 165, 167
thalassaemia, *see under* inherited blood disorders
Tosh, John, 219
transnational marriages, 12, 116, 121–26, 132, 134, 161, 164–65
Trollope, Anthony, 221
Turkey
  Alawi population of, 90–92, 95
  campaign against cousin marriage in, 19, 20, 22, 89, 92–96
  haemoglobinopathy prevention in, 92–96, 161
  Ministry of Health, 89, 93–94
  premarital examinations in, 92–93
  prevalence of consanguineous marriage in, 89

United Arab Emirates,
  genetics services in, 65, 73
  increase in consanguineous marriage, 39

Victoria, Queen of England, marriage of, 218, 226

Wedgwood, Emma, marriage of, 218

www.ingramcontent.com/pod-product-compliance
Lightning Source LLC
Chambersburg PA
CBHW070920030426
42336CB00014BA/2472